Discourse and Social Psychology

D0060867

DISCOURSE AND SOCIAL PSYCHOLOGY

Beyond Attitudes and Behaviour

Jonathan Potter and Margaret Wetherell

Ⓢ Sage Publications
London. Newbury Park. Beverly Hills. New Delhi

SAGE Publications Ltd
28 Banner Street
London EC1Y 8QE

SAGE Publications Inc
275 South Beverly Drive
Beverly Hills, California 90212
and
SAGE Publications Inc
2111 West Hillcrest Drive
Newbury Park, California 91320

SAGE Publications India Pvt Ltd
C-236 Defence Colony
New Delhi 110 024

British Library Cataloguing in Publication Data

Potter, Jonathan
    Discourse and social psychology : beyond
    attitudes and behaviour.
    1. Oral communication — Social aspects
    I. Title II. Wetherell, Margaret
    302.2′24   P95

Library of Congress Catalogue Card Number 87-060198

ISBN 0-8039-8055-8
ISBN 0-8039-8056-6 Pbk

Phototypeset by System 4 Associates, Gerrards Cross, Buckinghamshire
Printed in Great Britain by J. W. Arrowsmith Ltd., Bristol

Contents

Introduction 1
Three illustrative examples 2
Definitions of discourse analysis 6

1. Foundations of discourse analysis 9
Chomsky and psychology 9
Words as deeds: speech act theory 14
'Doing' talking: ethnomethodology 18
Signs of structure: semiology 24
Social study of language 28
Problems and limitations 29

2. Unfolding discourse analysis 32
Some major components of discourse analysis 32
Variable discourse and traditional social psychology 36
The suppression of account variability 39
Attitudes in discourse 43
Beyond attitudes 53

3. Making rules work 56
The ethogenic perspective 56
Problems with ethogenics 61
Discourse analysis and the study of scientists' rules 64
Testability, soccer violence and the analysis of rules 71

4. Accounts in sequence 74
Accounts and social psychology 74
Conversation analysis and accounts 80
Accounts in court 87
Discourse and accounts 93

5. Speaking subjects 95
Traditional images of the self 95
Towards a new conception of the subject 101
The ideological self 108
Discourse analysis at work on the self 110

6. Categories in discourse 116
Social psychology and social categories 117
Problems with traditional categorization research 120

    Prototypes and variability   122
    Motives and membership categories   126
    Categories, content and community   132
    Categories and the construction of discourse   136

7. From representations to repertoires   138
    The theory of social representations   139
    Problems with social representations   142
    Interpretative repertoires   146
    Language, representation and repertoire   155

8. How to analyse discourse   158
    Philosophy, sociology and methodology   158
    Ten stages in the analysis of discourse   160
    Conclusions   175

9. Controversial topics and future directions   177
    Discourse and the world 'under the skull'   177
    Discourse and the world 'out there'   180
    Discourse and reflexivity   182
    The development of discourse analysis   184

Appendix: transcription notation   188

References   190

Index   205

About the authors

Jonathan Potter is Lecturer in the Department of Social Science, University of Loughborough, Loughborough, LE11 3TU. Margaret Wetherell is Lecturer in Psychology, Faculty of Social Sciences, Open University, Walton Hall, Milton Keynes, MK7 6AA. They are the authors (with Peter Stringer) of *Social Texts and Context: Literature and Social Psychology* (1984) and many scholarly articles.

Acknowledgements

As with any work of this kind many people have contributed directly or indirectly to the final product. We would particularly like to thank those people who have read and commented on versions of chapters: Dominic Abrams, Charles Abraham, Mick Billig, Paul Drew, Nick Emler, Nigel Gilbert, Quentin Halliday, Dennis Hilton, Ruth McFadyen, Andy McKinlay, Mike Mulkay, David Myers, Gün Semin, Heather Smith and Rod Watson.

We have also benefited from an Economic and Social Science Research Council Grant, which enabled us to conduct some of the interviews which are discussed in the book. Bridget Rothwell retyped chapters and Diane Millar the references. Farrell Burnett at Sage has made many helpful suggestions about the content and organization of the work.

We are grateful to Academic Press for permission to reproduce a table from G. Semin and A. Manstead (1982) *The Accountability of Conduct*, London: Academic Press; to Paul Drew for permission to reproduce data extracts from J. M. Atkinson and P. Drew (1979) *Order in Court: The Organization of Verbal Interaction in Judicial Settings*, London: Macmillan/SSRC; and to Cambridge University Press for permission to reproduce data extracts from G. N. Gilbert and M. Mulkay (1984) *Opening Pandora's Box: A Sociological Analysis of Scientists' Discourse*, Cambridge: Cambridge University Press.

Introduction

This book is about language and its importance for social psychology. It looks at the subtle ways in which language orders our perceptions and makes things happen and thus shows how language can be used to construct and create social interaction and diverse social worlds.

We will be concerned with social texts of all kinds; that is, the conversations, newspaper stories, novels and soap operas which are a central and inescapable part of everyday life. Indeed, the term 'text' will be used in a broad sense, to include not only writing prima facie but also the written record of the spoken; the transcript of an interview will be as much our concern as the prepared narrative.

We had three main goals in writing this book. First, to illustrate the breadth of understanding which has emerged from research on social texts in the last few years. We deliberately chose to discuss examples of work which asks different sorts of questions of highly varied types of discourse. Second, we hoped the book could serve as a resource for those interested in doing their own research on social texts. To this end, we have tried to provide a full description of certain studies rather than a completely comprehensive, but more superficial, coverage of the entire area. In addition, Chapter Eight is devoted entirely to the analytic issues which arise in this kind of work. Third, we hoped to demonstrate how some of the most fundamental theoretical notions in traditional and more radical social psychology can be illuminated by an analysis of discourse. In fact, we will suggest that the *failure* to accommodate to discourse damages their theoretical and empirical adequacy. Overall, we hope that this work might encourage others to recognize the importance and interest of analysing social texts.

The book is organized as follows. In the first chapter, the theoretical roots of discourse analysis in linguistic philosophy, ethnomethodology and semiotics are described. In Chapter Two we overview the perspective of discourse analysis, and illustrate its utility with respect to the social psychological notion of attitudes. Then follow five substantive chapters which deal in turn with the theoretical concepts of rules, accounts, the self, categories and social representations. Chapter Eight then describes the practical stages through which research on social texts progresses, and discusses the issue of validity. Finally, Chapter Nine tackles some broader issues and identifies future research directions.

Before we begin, however, there are two things we want to do. We would like to discuss three simple examples of discourse to illustrate some of the phenomena with which we will be concerned throughout the book.

This should give a preliminary sketch of what we mean when we say social texts play a *constructive* role in our social lives. Then we will give a brief account of our rationale for the research included in the book, and describe some of the potentially confusing terminological issues which bedevil this area.

Three illustrative examples

Example one

The first example is a reflexive one in the sense that it is an instance of the kind of text social scientists themselves might write. This passage of discourse could, in fact, have stood perfectly sensibly as the first paragraph of this book.

> In the last fifteen years a revolution has taken place in social psychology. This revolution, sometimes known as the 'Crisis in Social Psychology' (Elms, 1975), was the consequence of deep dissatisfaction with the state of research and theory. Works like Harré and Secord (1972), Israel and Tajfel (1972), Gergen, (1973) and McGuire (1973) asked fundamental questions about the nature of the discipline and, in particular, about its strongly positivistic reliance on experiments as the main research method. In the aftermath of this radical reassessment there is now a need to develop systematic methods of analysis which...(from an earlier draft of this book)

When reading research papers, reviews and books we are constantly faced with writing of this kind which we recognize as providing a helpful introductory orientation or context for the reader. But we could also view this piece from a very different perspective, focusing on its nature as a *social text*, and analysing how it constructs a specific reality.

The first thing to note is that this passage is itself an enormously ambitious piece of social psychology, identifying social categories (social psychologist), states of belief shared by the members of the category (deep dissatisfaction), causal processes (dissatisfaction leading to change) and events (revolution). This ambitiousness is hidden, partly by the apparent simplicity of the description and partly by its conventional and familiar nature. But there is a great deal going on even in a short text such as this.

The category 'social psychology' is far from straightforward. It could refer to a set of ideas, a body of writings in journals, textbooks and so on, or to a group of people. Referring to social psychology is not quite like referring to doughnuts in the bun shop, as in 'I'll have that one with the extra jam'. The state of belief is equally difficult. How is the claim that there was general and deep dissatisfaction in social psychology in the early 1970s to be checked? It is most unclear what a 'deep' dissatisfaction is. Perhaps the dissatisfaction *must* have been deep because it led to revolution – but this is just circular. The idea of revolution itself fits in well, of course, because it follows on from the notion of deep dissatisfaction.

The point is, then, that even in an apparently simple passage the idea of plain reference to pre-existing entities does not do justice to the complexity of the material. From the many possible ways of characterizing the relevant group of people, sets of beliefs, and processes this particular one was chosen. During the course of this book we will repeatedly point out the ever-present possibility of alternative descriptions and categorizations.

A description of this kind involves a whole set of choices, and these choices may have many consequences. Take the use of the term 'positivistic'. There is a lot of debate about what precisely should be counted as positivist research – is it confined to the idea that science progresses through the accumulation of facts, or does it include all research which involves the conversion of data into numbers? At the present moment there is much more agreement that being 'positivistic' is a bad thing. It is a term which comes ready packaged with its evaluation. Another theme which will regularly recur in this book is the close interdependence of descriptive and evaluative language.

We can also look at how the passage is organized as an effective introduction. It offers a narrative of the development of the discipline so that our present project (writing a book on the analysis of discourse) becomes both a proper and important thing to do. In this sense it serves as an initial justification of our activity. Again, we will see that justification of various kinds is a very general feature of accounts given in a wide range of situations, and one which, on the whole, psychologists have been rather slow to pick up on.

These phenomena are not, of course, unique to scientific texts. Far from it. Texts are not part of some natural process like a chemical reaction or electrons moving around a circuit. They are complex cultural and psychological products, constructed in particular ways to make things happen. In the course of this book we will argue that any social text can become the object of research. Even our own writing should not be immune from this kind of examination.

Example two

The following passage comes from a conversation where Ruth is discussing an acquaintance who is supposedly mentally ill (transcription symbols are explained in the Appendix).

Ruth: He was a racing driver and [] he had one particular special car which he'd never let anybody else go in. But he used to take my mum out for drives in it, and, you know, everybody felt that that was alright and everything. Looking back on it they decided, my grandmother decided, that she should have realized that there was something odd about it. Because [] he wouldn't let anybody else near that car. And my mother was very very naive about everything at that stage. [] And he suddenly said to her in the kitchen one day: 'I think we'll have to stop meeting like this'. And she had no idea what he was talking about. It just completely baffled her. And then he started writing really strange, long, long, rambling letters – very abusive letters – to my grandfamily, who realized [] that something must be up. (Mi trans 4:1)

Just as with Example One, there is nothing peculiar or nonsensical about this section of discourse. As readers we do not have any difficulty in reading it as a literal description of someone who is starting to 'go mad'. Yet there is a lot more to notice about it. One of the interesting things about this account is that it is an account of an account. Accounts of accounts are a chronic feature of ordinary life: we read a story in a newspaper and then describe it to friends, or we gossip to Kevin about what Carol told us about Jane and Steve. Accounts are often versions of versions. The present one is Ruth's version of events; but it is not a first-hand version, it is based on her grandmother's version of what went on. And it is clear that even the grandmother's version is not first hand; her account of what occurred in the kitchen is presumably based on the mother's statement.

Another interesting feature of this piece of talk is its status as a description. In fact it is part of a much longer response to the question 'have you ever known anyone who you thought might be mentally ill?' Three features of the man's behaviour are singled out for comment: taking the mother for drives, the episode in the kitchen and the letters. Part of what makes these features evidence of mental illness is their inappropriate or unusual nature. The listener is not provided with a rational story to integrate them together and so they function effectively in an anecdote about mental illness. However, there are many ways to read texts and it is possible to look for other plots or patterns which might fit.

This account could be seen as a classic story of a love affair where the parents disapprove. There is nothing odd, let alone mad, about taking your loved one out for a lot of drives. Neither is the statement in the kitchen – 'I think we'll have to stop meeting like this' – unexpected in this kind of narrative. Using a clichéd jokey formulation is one way of broaching delicate questions about a relationship. People are often in situations where they raise topics obliquely to test the water before giving their whole-hearted linguistic commitment to something. And in this version the abusive letters make sense, because later in the account we find the letters only started after the grandmother had forbidden her daughter to see the man.

It is quite possible to erect a version which does not depend on the idea that the man has departed from the world of the sane. In doing this we are not, of course, claiming we can tell what 'really happened', but by displaying the possibility of alternatives we can start to look at how different readings are produced. Throughout the book we will encounter variability of this kind between versions, and in Chapter Five we will look specifically at how selves or types of people come to be constructed in discourse.

Example three

We will take one more brief example, from another area altogether. The following piece is from the beginning of a newspaper article.

Islamic Terrorists Blow Up Plane

In Beirut last night the hijackers of the British Airways 727 finally released the passengers and crew. As the gunmen left they detonated a large quantity of explosive and the plane was quickly gutted by fire. This followed a period of intense negotiation in which the authorities made it clear that they were not going to meet the hijackers' main demands.

Perhaps one of the most striking things about an account of this kind is its familiarity. It conforms to a standard pattern and we could probably give a reasonably detailed speculation about both the events leading up to those described and how this story will continue. There is a standard, virtually stereotypical, narrative which accompanies the events we categorize as 'hijackings'. As competent newspaper readers we can generate this scenario just from the term 'hijack'; the specific story that follows becomes a variant on a general theme rather than a uniquely new event.

As in the first example, some of the terms in this story come ready evaluated. This is true of 'the gunmen', 'hijackers' and, most especially, 'terrorists'. All are constantly used with negative associations in texts such as the above. A cursory look at the use of these terms might lead us to expect that they have a precise reference – small groups of politically motivated people who blow things up and create terror – and that the negative connotations are generated by repeated association of the term with horrific events. However, it is important to be aware that the evaluation comes into the system at a much earlier point.

It is well known that when such people are seen as acting in a good cause they are described not as 'terrorists' but as 'freedom fighters'. Often this goes along with evaluating their acts as 'necessary for encouraging social change' rather than 'causing pointless carnage' and evaluating their motivations as arising from 'moral and political ideals' rather than 'warped personalities'. The contrasting accounts of the African National Congress given by Western liberals and the South African government are prime examples of such a split. Here the political conflict is exactly paralleled by linguistic conflict. It is important to immediately dispel any illusions that the study of language is the study of a calm, idealized realm beyond politics, argument and conflict.

In discussing these three examples we have tried to provide some initial simple illustrations of the sort of phenomena which are the subject of this book. We have tried to show how social texts do not merely *reflect* or *mirror* objects, events and categories pre-existing in the social and natural world. Rather, they actively *construct* a version of those things. They do not just describe things; they *do* things. And being active, they have social and political implications. We have seen how description is tied to evaluation and how different versions of events can be constructed to justify or blame these events. As we will see, this approach to language has profound implications for the practice of social psychology which, in many cases, presupposes that language is unproblematically and simply descriptive.

Definitions of discourse analysis

Perhaps the only thing all commentators are agreed on in this area is that terminological confusions abound. The problem arises because developments have been happening concurrently in a number of different disciplines (psychology, sociology, linguistics, anthropology, literary studies, philosophy, media and communication studies), using a panoply of theoretical perspectives. For example, the label 'discourse analysis' has been used as a generic term for virtually all research concerned with language in its social and cognitive context (Brown and Yule, 1983; Coulthard, 1977; van Dijk, 1985), as a description for studies focusing only on linguistic units above the level of the sentence (Stubbs, 1983), as the correct term for research concerned with cohesion and connectedness across sentences or turns of talk (Tannen, 1984; van Dijk and Kintch, 1983), and to cover developments stemming from structuralism and semiotics (Foucault, 1971; Pecheux, 1982). It is a field in which it is perfectly possible to have two books on discourse analysis with no overlap in content at all (cf. MacDonell, 1986; Stubbs, 1983).

In line with these differences, the term 'discourse' itself has been used in many varying ways. Some researchers take 'discourse' to mean all forms of talk and writing (Gilbert and Mulkay, 1984), others take the term to apply only to the way talk is meshed together (Sinclair and Coulthard, 1975). While at the other extreme, some continental discourse analysts such as Foucault take 'discourse' to refer to much broader, historically developing, linguistic practices (Foucault, 1972). Some workers make a contrast between discourse analysis and conversation analysis on the basis of different theoretical and methodological strategies (Levinson, 1983), while others want to make a very different contrast between discourse analysis and text analysis with the aim of separating the study of underlying theoretical structures from actual linguistic performance (Halliday, 1978). All in all, there is a great deal of potential for confusion.

It is important, then, to clarify what we mean when we use these terms. We will use 'discourse' in its most open sense, following Gilbert and Mulkay (1984) to cover all forms of spoken interaction, formal and informal, and written texts of all kinds. So when we talk of 'discourse analysis' we mean analysis of any of these forms of discourse. We will give a fuller account of the nature of discourse analysis, as we understand it, in Chapter Two. For the moment, it is important to emphasize that our concern is not purely with discourse per se; that is, we are not linguists attempting to add social awareness to linguistics through the addition of the study of pragmatics. We are social psychologists expecting to gain a better understanding of social life and social interaction from our study of social texts.

By focusing the book in this way we have excluded three main areas of work. First, we have avoided research concerned with the interface between discourse and cognition. This includes work on the comprehension of texts, their mental organization when stored in memory, and the role of schemata and scripts for discourse processing (e.g. Bower and Cirilo, 1985; Frederickson, 1986; van Dijk and Kintch, 1983). Second, we have avoided research which is mainly concerned with what we see as primarily linguistic questions; for example concerning the way reference is made from one sentence to another (e.g. many of the volumes in the series *Advances in Discourse Processes*). Finally, we have not covered socio-linguistic work concerned with the study of variations in the language use of different social groups (e.g. Labov, 1972a; Milroy, 1980) and the psychological intergroup dynamics associated with these (Giles, 1977; Giles and St. Clair, 1979).

Even with these exclusions, there is still a huge amount of relevant research left (for the most comprehensive collection, see van Dijk, 1985). From this work, we have selected our topics according to what fitted best into our scheme of presentation in terms of the social psychological concepts we wish to cover. Naturally we have also been guided by our value judgments as to what is the most productive and interesting. Others will look at the field differently, but we hope that no one will be offended by either exclusions or selections.

Discourse analysis is a relatively new approach in social psychology. It should not, however, be thought that the approach fell out of the air. It has its roots in a variety of more established perspectives in philosophy, sociology and literary theory. We will start the book with a review of certain developments in these disciplines which have laid the foundations for our current understanding of the operation of social texts.

1

Foundations of discourse analysis

There are a number of very good reasons why psychologists should be interested in language. Language is so central to all social activities it is easy to take for granted. Its very familiarity sometimes makes it transparent to us. Yet imagine conveying a complex idea such as 'meet me Thursday in my room for a discussion of semiology' without language. It is not easy to see how it could be done.

Communication of this kind which involves abstract notions, actions and events removed in time and space, delicate shades of meaning, and logical distinctions depends on people sharing a complex symbolic representational system. Moreover, language is not just a code for communication. It is inseparably involved with processes of thinking and reasoning. Just as it is difficult to imagine sophisticated communication without language, it is hard to see how complex abstract reasoning could be performed by people without a language.

The study of language is particularly vital to social psychology because it simply is the most basic and pervasive form of interaction between people. We spend a lot of our social lives talking to each other, reading the papers, watching movies and writing shopping lists. Most forms of social interaction involve people talking together or reading each other's scribblings. Furthermore, when raising issues of the nature of culture, on the one hand, and the nature of the self, on the other, it is virtually impossible to clearly disentangle them from questions about language and its role in human affairs. As we will see shortly, it is clear that a large part of our activities are performed *through* language; our talk and writing do not live in some purely conceptual realm, but are mediums for action.

Despite the importance of language, it has not always been a topic which has interested psychologists. Indeed, it only really took off as a major field of study in the late 1950s and 1960s under the influence of the linguist Noam Chomsky. The best way to understand the developments discussed in this book is to contrast them initially with the very different Chomskian psycholinguistic tradition which predominated in psychology during the 1960s and 1970s.

Chomsky and psychology

Noam Chomsky (born 1928) developed his linguistic ideas at the University of Pennsylvania and latterly at the Massachusetts Institute of Technology.

His basic concern was to produce a generative grammar, that is, a limited set of rules which generates grammatical sentences and only grammatical sentences (cf.Chomsky, 1965).

Chomsky's work was crucially important for psychology because he viewed these rules not merely as a more economic form of description, like the Library of Congress system of cataloguing books say, but as psychologically real cognitive structures. He took the rules as representations of what speakers must actually know, that is, as representations of their cognitive systems. Indeed, Chomsky has suggested that these rules may actually be a part of every person's genetic make-up, inherited at birth (Chomsky, 1966).

The details of this at times highly technical theory are not of interest here. Our concern is more with the general nature of Chomsky's linguistic programme. We can best show the contrast between his work and discourse analysis by concentrating on three topics: the competence/performance distinction, the role of speakers' intuitions, and the importance of speakers' creativity.

The competence/performance distinction

Chomsky argued that it is possible to distinguish between, first, the underlying ability to produce grammatical sentences and, second, the actual production of particular sentences in particular situations. More formally, he distinguished between the set of rules which allows the speaker to generate grammatical sentences and the performance itself, which is subject to a panoply of speech errors, lapses of memory, distractions and effects due to context. Quite apart from the question of whether this theory is empirically correct (and it has not fared well on the whole – for a review of experimental work on the theory see Johnson-Laird, 1974) there are conceptual difficulties with this kind of approach.

The most fundamental of these centres on the problem of thinking of competence independently of performance. How does the researcher get directly at the underlying rules if not by way of performance data; via actual language of various sorts? In fact there is no independent access. But Chomsky skirts round this problem by working from idealized sentences and using these to make inferences about the nature of competence. The linguist John Lyons (1967) notes that there are three senses in which Chomsky's speech data are idealized compared with ordinary speech. First, the data is *regularized* so that the pervasive errors, hesitations, self-corrections and so on are removed. Second, it is *standardized*. That is, it takes no account of variations in pronunciation, say. Third, it is *decontextualized*, separating the sentences out from any specific context in which they might be used.

A theory whose data are transformed in this way is in danger of slipping into circularity. It is as if one did research on the visual system using only vertical lines as stimuli, and concluded that the visual system was especially adapted for the perception of vertical lines. Only certain data are admitted as 'proper' performance data, and from this base an ordered set of generative rules is produced. It is not at all clear, however, if these rules could cope with natural performance data, with ordinary talk in ordinary situations. The problem is not idealization per se; after all, Newton's laws of mechanics are exact only for ideal frictionless environments. The worry is that the idealizations Chomsky used miss essential features of natural speech and informal everyday conversations (for an excellent critique of these kinds of idealizatons in linguistics generally see Harris, 1980). There is, however, an interesting response to this point built into the Chomskian approach, which is to stress the importance of speakers' intuitions.

Speakers' intuitions

Chomsky indentifies the linguistic performances which are suitable for analysis on the basis of speakers' *intuitions* about which sentences are well-formed and which are not. What this means is that he does not try to find out what utterances conversationalists themselves treat as well-formed or badly constructed, rather he uses his own intuitions about what is and what is not a 'proper' sentence. If his general perspective is correct, this is a sensible and appropriate procedure because Chomsky holds that *all* of us, himself included, know what is grammatical and what is not. If we all have a linguistic competence, a set of rules for the production of grammatical sentences which also enables us to tell when other people are speaking grammatically or non-grammatically, then it seems perfectly sensible to use these intuitions to decide on appropriate speech data.

The problem with this assumption is that it risks compounding the existing circularity with another. This process of relying on intuitions is acceptable only if Chomsky's theory is correct. And when idealization is combined with reliance on intuitions it becomes hard to see how the theory could ever be falsified. Data which might potentially overthrow the theory are likely to be excluded tout court.

Against this background, the idea of looking at naturalistic speech data (transcripts of everyday conversations or documents of various kinds) as discourse analysts suggest, is a radical one. With its emphasis on competence and speakers' intuitions, Chomskian psycholinguistics does not accept this as a necessary step. But there is more to it than that; for the Chomskian perspective maintains ordinary language performance data will in any case be unmanageable because of the *creativity* of speakers.

Speakers' creativity

One of the central tenets of Chomskian psycholinguistics is that speakers are capable of producing an *infinite* number of sentences simply through the use of the various generative and transformational rules which make up a grammar. Chomsky identifies creativity as one of the most essential features of language use. The importance of this point should not be underestimated. At least in part, for Chomsky, it is the 'fact' of creativity which makes children's learning of a language so amazing, and which makes the behaviourist explanation of this learning, in terms of rewards, shaping and reinforcement schedules so unconvincing. If there is such a huge diversity of sentences in a child's environment, many of them novel, then how can the child possibly start to deal with them using the normal principles of associative learning? As is well known, Chomsky believes that only the presence of a genetically wired in 'language acquisition device' can make the surprising phenomenon of language learning possible.

The postulation of this radical creativity also has important methodological consequences. If we accept that speakers are *so* creative that many or perhaps the majority of their utterances will be unique then there would indeed be little point in looking at performance data, at open-ended ordinary talk. The task of systematizing such an infinite body would be daunting to the point of impossibility. The researcher could only achieve order by focusing on the speakers' competence or set of generative rules. Unlike performance data, these are manageable in complexity and number, and anyway are taken as providing an explanation of all possible performance data.

Natural language

The Chomskian approach is undoubtedly a very elegant one and its different facets fit together with a coherence unusual in a lot of psychology. It focuses specifically on the grammatical features of discourse and given this goal we would not wish to criticize it for failing to provide a complete explanation of language. Nevertheless, advances in language studies have depended on researchers questioning some of the presuppositions of this perspective. One of the most important stimuli for developing an alternative has come from natural speech data of various kinds.

If a verbatim transcript of real people having an ordinary conversation is examined, the Chomskian approach to the three issues above looks decidedly fragile. Take the following piece of transcript (slightly simplified from the original – the transcription symbols are explained in the Appendix).

```
N:  Anywa::y, =
H:  =pk! A:nywa ⌈ :y,
N:              ⌊ So:::,
    (.)
H:  .p=
N:  =You'll come abou:t (.) eight. Right? =
H:  =Yea::h, =
N:  =Okay
    (.2)
N:  Anything else to report,
H:  (.3)
N:  Uh:::::: m:::,
    (.4)
H:  Getting my hair cut tihmorrow, =
N:  =Oh rilly?
```

(Button and Casey, 1984: 168)

Genuine performance data of this kind seem very far removed from the idealized sentences used by generative grammarians. Even a successful generative grammar has virtually nothing to say about many of the features that are immediately relevant to those who analyse this kind of transcribed talk. For example, utterances are regularly ungrammatical in everyday talk without eliciting comment, they cohere into sequential discourse, and they are commonly the joint achievement of two or more people. All these features are apparent in the extract above.

Furthermore, the creativity evident in the natural language data examined up to now falls short of the unmanageable and unrestricted plenitude implied in the Chomskian tradition. Indeed researchers have found that much natural language use is highly stereotyped and quite predictable. Far from being impossibly unique, performance data is often boringly repetitive.

The fact that performance data *can* be systematically handled pulls out one prop from under the abstract psycholinguistic approach. A study of transcript also questions the central role played by speakers' intuitions. For verbatim transcripts are very different both from our intuitions about speech and from our later recollections of conversations. Part of the reason for this is probably the difficulty of escaping from our literary conventions for representing speech in written form. We tend to think we speak rather like characters in a play, but actual verbatim speech is not at all like play dialogue. And, as Sacks (1984) and other conversation analysts have shown, the detail that is edited out and lost in reconstruction and intuition is extremely rich and often vital for a full understanding of what is going on. This is not surprising, of course, because as lay talkers we almost never have to formulate how or what we do when we talk: we just talk.

In contrast to the Chomskian tradition, then, discourse analysis has embraced performance data in all its messy and ungrammatical complexity. It has not been cowed by a fear of impossible creativity, and it has let speakers' intuitions take a back seat. As a result, it has had to face up to the fact that language is not an abstract realm. Out there in the real world it is made up from particular utterances performed in particular contexts. Moreover, discourse becomes placed firmly in the arena of social behaviour. We become less interested in what is going on under people's skulls and a lot more interested in how people are actually using language with each other in the course of different kinds of interactions. Our research questions thus open out into a full-blown social psychology of discourse.

For a better understanding of the development of ideas about language function we now need to turn to events taking place in another discipline entirely, namely the philosophy of language. We need to look at John Austin's (1962) notion of speech acts.

Words as deeds: speech act theory

In 1955 at Harvard the psychologists were buzzing with excitement about the lectures being given by Noam Chomsky, although perhaps this had more to do with his outspoken criticism of B. F. Skinner's behaviourism than specifically his theory of Transformational Generative Grammar. Language in 1955 was interesting because, as we have noted, when children learn language they seem to defy the behaviourist, simple stimulus-response view of the world. In that same year the British philosopher John Austin (1911–60) was also at Harvard, presenting the prestigious William James lectures. A few psychologists drifted into these seminars. On the whole they were nonplussed by the urbane, faintly ironic manner of Austin's presentation, as well as being mystified by his apparently self-destructive procedure of first arguing *for* a distinction between two basic forms of utterance, and then, later, arguing *against* it. All the same, the general perspective on language Austin proposed ultimately had an enormous impact on a wide range of disciplines and has radically reshaped our view of language and its operation.

It is important for a clear understanding of Austin's ideas to have some indication of the situation in philosophy which he was both reacting against and commenting upon. His main target was the logical positivist view that sentences which cannot be verified, that is sentences for which there is no way of checking whether they are true or false, should simply be treated as meaningless. From this viewpoint, for instance, the statement 'God does not exist' should be treated as nonsensical since the truth of the statement can never be validated. In addition, Austin's argument was directed at a wide swathe of views of language which take it to be an *abstract system* whose central function is the *description* of states of affairs. What Austin set out to do was to undermine the notion that an understanding of 'truth conditions', states of truth and falsity, is central to an understanding of language, and in doing this he produced a model with far-reaching consequences.

Stating versus doing

Austin began with the observation that there is a class of sentences which are principally important for what they *do*, not because they describe things. For instance, the sentence:

I declare war on the Philippines

is not a description of the world which can be seen as true or false but an *act* with practical consequences; when uttered in the right circumstances it brings into being a state of war. Austin called sentences of this kind *performatives*. Other examples are:

I name this ship the Lady Penelope
Beware of the bull
I sentence you to six months hard labour

In each of these cases, the primary role of the sentence is not description as such but to make certain things happen; they are sentences performing acts.

Austin contrasted these kinds of sentences with others whose primary role did appear to be the description of states of affairs. That is, sentences making statements and assertions which can be checked as either true or false. Austin, who had a penchant for coining neologisms, named them *constatives* (in the hope of avoiding the ambiguity of 'statement' which could mean either a description or any spoken utterance).

One of the interesting features of performative utterances, as we have noted, is that unlike constatives, they cannot be straightforwardly true or false. But they can be defective in other ways. Think of the utterance used by a monarch when knighting.

I dub thee Sir Lancelot

There are various ways in which this utterance will fail to institute the act of knighting, or will make the act problematic in some way. For example, the person might have been misidentified: perhaps Merlin has mistakenly been caught tieing his shoe laces. Or perhaps the appropriate witnesses, the sword and so on are not present. It could even be that the whole thing is a joke set up to amuse the other Knights of the Round Table.

In each case, there would be a problem with the utterance but the problem is not with its truth or falsity in any simple sense. The crucial point is that certain conditions have to prevail for performatives to be accomplished successfully. These conditions are called *felicity conditions*, and they are listed schematically in Figure 1.1 along with an example violation of the conditions.

FIGURE 1.1

Felicity conditions

(A.i)   There must exist an accepted conventional procedure having a certain conventional effect, and further,

(A.ii) the particular persons and circumstances in a given case must be appropriate for the invocation of the particular procedure.

(B)   The procedure must be executed by all participants both (i) correctly and (ii) completely.

(C)   Often (i) the persons must have certain thoughts, intentions etc. which are specified in the procedure, (ii) the procedure specifies certain conduct which must be adhered to.

Violations

A(i)   Saying 'I find you guilty' to someone when seeing them shoplift in a supermarket.

A(ii)   Awarding an honorary degree to the wrong person.

B(i)   Saying 'OK' instead of 'I do' at a wedding.

B(ii)   Not saying 'you're on' when accepting a wager.

C(i)   A juror voting 'guilty' when she thinks the accused is innocent.

C(ii)   Making a promise and then not following it.

Austin's work is unusual in that he deliberately set out to test exhaustively his own notion that these two sorts of utterances can be distinguished. In the course of his William James lectures, subsequently published as *How To Do Things With Words*, he started with this notion of the two classes of utterance but went on to show that this is too unsophisticated a way of looking at things, that in fact *all* utterances have both performative and constative features. Take, for example, the suggestion that constatives can be true or false and that this distinction is not relevant to performative utterances. If we examine utterances like the following we can see some difficulties with this idea.

I bet you a pound that Ludwig wins the 3.15 at Kemptown

This is an utterance performing the act of betting; it is not describing the bet, but doing the bet. However, it becomes extremely problematic if there is no 3.15 race at Kemptown or if Ludwig is not a horse. Performative utterances are thus not entirely independent of matters of truth and falsity. On the other hand, descriptive statements – constatives – cannot only be true or false but can, like performatives, be infelicitous. There is something distinctly problematic, or as Austin put it, *unhappy* about this utterance:

That dog is called Lassie but I don't believe it

The problem here is not truth or falsity – the dog may or may not be called Lassie and the speaker may or may not accept this fact; the problem is the lack of the appropriate beliefs which go along with claims of this kind. In terms of Figure 1.1 it violates condition C(i) which states that people must have the appropriate thoughts, intentions etc. to properly carry out speech acts.

In the light of a large number of similar considerations Austin abandoned the simple distinction between two classes of utterance. However, the exploration of this distinction has raised some very important issues demonstrating, first, that sentences *do* as well as describe things and, second, that there are *conventions* or felicity conditions which link utterances and social activities. For example, in a ship-naming ceremony the force of 'I name this ship. . .' depends on a set of conventions concerning the correct sequence of events, the proper people who must be involved, the presence of the ship and so on. Austin replaced the performative/constative distinction with what he called the general theory of speech acts.

The general theory of speech acts

The general theory does not distinguish between sentences which do things and sentences which say things, between performatives and constatives, but casts this distinction in a different way. The fundamental tenet of the theory is that *all* utterances state things *and* do things. That is, all utterances have a meaning and a force. In fact, Austin suggested that with any utterance a speaker is simultaneously doing three sorts of things.

First, the speaker is uttering a sentence with a specific meaning – it has a certain sense and may refer to specific events, persons or objects. Second, the sentence is uttered with a particular force. We know what the words 'shut the door' literally mean, but they can be used with the force of an order, a request or even a question. Force is thus an element of utterances which is dissociated from their meaning, although it is often indicated by the use of a certain verb: promise, order, state and so on. The third feature refers to the effects or consequences of the first two. The sentence 'shut the door' may be uttered with the force of an order but it may have the effect of making the hearer shut the door or it may simply make the hearer annoyed.

This third feature is much less determinate than the first two. For instance, if the appropriate person in the right circumstances utters the sentence 'I declare war on the Phillipines' it is not really clear if the consequences are the initiation of the war, the entire set of military events which make up the war, or even those events and everything subsequently influenced by them. Austin has not provided a systematic way of deciding what precisely counts as the consequences of the utterance.

Austin's theory represented a radical departure from much of the previous philosophical work on language because instead of viewing it as an essentially abstract corpus, which can be dealt with in the same way as logic and mathematics, he recognized that language is a *human practice*. People use language, like a tool, to get things done, whether these things are bets, relief from the draught through an open door, or the start of a war. This feature of the theory makes it very attractive to social psychologists; as there is little in the psycholinguistic tradition which even begins to show how a researcher might deal with language function.

Austin offers a highly social view of language. He draws our attention to the role played by the web of social conventions in the achievement of actions through talk and thus sensitizes the researcher to features of the social *context* surrounding language use. Despite these positive aspects, however, his theory was primarily developed to combat alternative philosophical views and little consideration was paid to the practicalities of actually applying it to everyday talk in natural situations. In fact, the research tradition which Austin spawned has in many ways stayed as abstract and decontextualized as its Chomskian predecessor (cf. Searle et al., 1979). In contrast, the ethnomethodological research we will examine in the next section has been guided much more closely by detailed empirical studies.

'Doing' talking: ethnomethodology

As its name suggests, the subdiscipline of ethnomethodology is concerned with the study of (ology) ordinary people's (ethno) methods; the methods in question being those used for producing and making sense of everyday social life. Ethnomethodology treats the goals and aims of ordinary people as similar to the goals and aims of the social researcher. That is, people, like the scientist, are constantly attempting to understand what is going on in any situation and using these understandings to produce appropriate behaviour of their own. A central figure in the development of this per- spective was the sociologist Harold Garfinkel (born 1917 – see Garfinkel, 1967; Heritage, 1984). While working on the decision making of juries at the University of Chicago in the 1950s he was intrigued to note that jurors – just like social scientists – were interested in distinctions such as that between 'fact' and 'opinion' and in what one can and cannot do with evidence. Furthermore, they did not seem to learn these distinctions as a result of being a member of the jury but brought them into the court as part of an organized body of knowledge and skills used all the time (Garfinkel, 1974).

Ethnomethodology as a discipline is concerned with a wide range of features of the way social life is put together. However, it is of particular interest here because of the lessons it provides about how language is used in everyday situations. The best way to get to grips with these is through looking in detail at a classic ethnomethodological study by Lawrence Wieder (1974a and, most accessibly, in 1974b) which looked at life in a half-way hostel for narcotics felons.

Telling the code

Wieder's study was based on an intensive period of participant observation in the half-way hostel. The goal of the hostel programme was to help ex-convicts readjust gently to life in the outside world and lead them away from the world of drugs. In these terms it was a dismal failure. In fact only a third of the inmates left in the approved manner, the rest jumped parole or offended again and were rearrested. The research involved Wieder spending time around the hostel, watching what went on, and most importantly building up a rapport with the inmates and staff so he could spend long periods talking with them about their lives.

One of Wieder's objectives was to illustrate the difference between an ethnomethodological and a traditional social scientific approach to language use by displaying the shortcomings of the latter. To this end he first adopted the traditional social scientific ploy of identifying a set of informal rules operating in the institution. It is a commonplace finding in traditional research that prisons, hospitals and similar total institutions have a set of informal rules which are different from, and often oppose, the official ones (Becker, 1963; Goffman, 1961). In this kind of work the rules are seen as a template guiding behaviour, so if you could describe the rules you would have an explanation for the inmates' actions. Through his participant observation in the hostel Wieder was able to identify just such a set of rules – which he called 'The Code' (see Figure 1.2) – and he goes on to show how these rules *could* be considered as having motivational force.

In the first place, the narcotics felons had their own sanctions for those who departed from the Code. Inmates who deviated were categorized by their fellow inmates into a set of obnoxious social types; 'kiss ass', 'snitch' and 'sniveller'. 'Kiss asses' were too friendly with the staff; 'snitches' were informers and 'snivellers' constantly complained and pleaded with the staff These categories were backed up by verbal and sometimes physical abuse. In the same way, the rules could be used to explain certain styles of

FIGURE 1.2
The convict code

8 Basic Maxims
1. Above all, do not snitch.
2. Do not cop out.
3. Do not take advantage of other residents.
4. Share what you have.
5. Help other residents.
6. Do not mess with other residents' interests.
7. Do not trust staff – staff is heat.
8. Show your loyalty to other residents.

behaviour. For example, Rule Eight (show your loyalty to the residents) can explain why inmates avoided lively conversation with staff and the lack of enthusiasm for staff initiatives. Finally, the Code can sustain deviant behaviour, requiring that residents help those who flout the official rules, cover up for rule breakers and avoid informing staff about deviant goings on.

From resource to topic

Through first identifying this Code, Wieder was trying to demonstrate how the traditional social researcher might explain inmates' behaviour in the hostel. He goes on to suggest that we should now look more closely at how the Code is derived and, in particular, at how the rules of the Code are picked out in the course of conversations with residents and staff but are then abstracted from those conversations to serve as an explanatory resource for the researcher. In other words, how certain claims and categories deployed when the inmates talk in the institution come to be adopted by the researcher as the basis for a causal explanation of its workings. Wieder proposed, as an alternative to the traditional procedure, an analytic approach which takes this resource, the Code itself, as the *topic* of study and asks how the Code is used, in practice, in the hostel. We will describe a similar approach to rules in Chapter Three. This shift from using features of talk as an explanatory resource to looking at them as a topic for research in their own right is a standard one in ethnomethodology (Zimmerman and Pollner, 1971). In general, ethnomethodological researchers try to avoid simply adopting lay explanations and accounts as bulwarks for their own explanations. Rather they take them as the object of their study.

We can best see the distinctiveness of this move with an example. Wieder found his friendly conversations with inmates would sometimes be abruptly stopped by them saying 'you know I won't snitch'. Instead of immediately abstracting this comment as an indicator of an explanatory rule and part of the Code, Wieder asked what the utterance was *doing* and what it *achieved*. It occurred to him there were several different things going on at once. In part, this piece of talk was formulating the immediate social environment in constrained ways. First, it constructed what had just happened in the conversation as Wieder asking the inmate to snitch. It then allowed the resident to not answer Wieder's question because his demand was now characterized as illegitimate, and to respond would be morally inappropriate. Thus the resident had provided himself with a motive and reasonable explanation for not replying. Finally, this response reminded all concerned that this conversation was going on between an inmate and someone defined as an 'outsider' rather than a friend, for snitching only operates between inmates and outsiders. In this way the inmate's comment provided a version or definition of what was going on in the immediate circumstances; it established the interaction in one way rather than another.

In general, ethnomethodologists suggest that talk always has this quality. The nature of interaction does not arrive pre-packaged and pre-ordained but is reproduced on each occasion. To put it another way, the participants do not passively respond to what is going on but actively produce it. In this case, for example, Wieder and the resident are not just passively acting out the Code as a pre-written script for how inmates and outsiders should behave – rather that this role relation is reproduced for the occasion on hand by the inmate saying 'you know I won't snitch'; other pieces of talk might have reproduced other role relations.

As well as formulating what is going on, 'you know I won't snitch' also leads to certain practical consequences. First, it acts as a rebuff to Wieder by negatively characterizing his line of questioning as a request to snitch. Second, it calls for a stop to that line of questioning, and gets it. Third, because the question remains unanswered Wieder remains ignorant about the answer. Fourth, this utterance signals that the conversation might turn nasty if the questioning continued. If Wieder refuses to end this line of questioning he risks being seen as an incompetent, as someone who does not understand the Code.

Reflexivity

With these examples from his interaction with the inmates, Wieder draws attention to what he describes as the multiformulative and multiconsequential nature of talk. That is, the examples show talk is not merely *about* actions, events and situations, it is also a potent and *constitutive part of* those actions, events and situations. The utterance 'you know I won't snitch' is not just a *description* of a rule, it also *formulates* the nature of the action and the situation and has a number of practical consequences within that situation. Following Garfinkel (1967), ethnomethodologists refer to phenomena of this kind as *reflexive* features of talk.

As Wieder looked more closely at the use inmates and staff made of the Code in their talk, its reflexive character became more and more apparent. For instance, inmates often used the code with staff in order to encourage or discourage certain things happening. For example, when one resident was asked by a member of staff to organize a pool tournament the inmate replied 'you know I can't organize a pool tournament, because it would look like kissing ass'. By characterizing the act in terms of the Code it is displayed as something prohibited, and this justifies not performing the act. In fact, in his period of observation Wieder never saw a staff member following up a reply of this sort. Yet an excuse such as 'I haven't got the time' might well have been ineffective.

The etcetera clause

Another feature emphasized in the study was the 'open, flexible texture' of the Code. On most occasions the Code was only referred to in the most general of terms and at the same time was constantly being applied to novel sets of circumstances. Ethnomethodologists claim that all general rules or prescriptions are indeterminate in their application (Wootton, 1977; Zimmerman, 1971). That is, it is always necessary to elaborate on a rule and the nature of the circumstances to apply the rule in a definitive and clear-cut way (Mulkay, 1979a). In Garfinkel's (1967) terms, rules always embody an *etcetera clause* which allows novel or unforseen instances to be brought under the umbrella of the rule.

The presence of the etcetera clause and the open texture of the Code generate the possibility that inmates may characterize events in terms of the Code specifically to achieve the ends they desire. It might have been, for instance, that the inmate who got out of organizing the pool tournament by claiming it would be kissing ass was really just lazy, rather than concerned about following the rule. However, the fact that the Code has this open texture means that we cannot use it to decide what would count as proper adherence to it rather than strategic adherence. The inescapable etcetera clause built into rule systems means that these systems can always be used in a variety of ways to lead to a variety of ends for a variety of motives. The problem this ambiguity poses is that it undermines attempts to use the code in a clear-cut explanatory sense, for this draws upon the idea that rules work as a causal template (see Chapter Three).

Indexicality

A final feature of the talk in the half-way hostel is its indexicality. The basic idea, derived from philosophy (Bar-Hillel, 1954), is a simple one. If one person says 'my stomach hurts' and then someone else utters the same sentence, although the sentence is the same, the reference is different. Different stomachs are indexed by the same sentence. Or take 'it's a nice day' – this sentence could be used as a surprised description of sunshine or perhaps an ironic comment on further rain. In general, indexical expressions are expressions whose *meaning alters with their context of use* (Barnes and Law, 1976). One of the central claims of ethnomethodology is that the vast majority of expressions used are indexical. That is, their sense and reference are settled by looking at features of their context or occasions of use. Thus for virtually any utterance the listener will 'fill in' its meaning with the aid of information about, for instance, who the speaker is, what their status is, what they have said previously, what is likely to happen next and so on.

In the half-way hostel, then, to make sense of utterances, Wieder and the other residents had to sort out such issues as the identity of the speakers, whether they were staff or inmates, who they were talking to, and what the topic of the conversation had been. For example Wieder would have interpreted the statement 'you know I can't organize a pool tournament' quite differently if he had heard it said not by an inmate to a staff member but from one staff member to another, where it might have been taken to imply the speaker does not know enough about pool or something similar. Ethnomethodologists suggest that people in conversations are constantly engaged in *interpretative work* to *accomplish* the meaning of utterances using their knowledge of context to help them. Producing smooth conversation is a highly skilled art which only appears to be natural and unproblematic because we are so practised at it.

Overall, Wieder's study illustrates the difference between the ethno-methodological and traditional approaches to language and interaction. In particular, he shows the limitations of traditional work which has tended to treat references to rules basically as descriptions of external, objective constraints on behaviour and ignored the flexible application of these rules. In contrast to this Wieder looked in detail at what the inmates were *doing* with their talk of rules; he looked at the way language was operating practically, within the scene of the action. In Garfinkel's term, he looked at the reflexive character of talk.

Although speech act theory and ethnomethodology have been enormously important in the development of discourse analysis, and have turned attention to the functional, constructive nature of language, discourse analysis also has its roots in a third theoretical tradition – semiology – and it is to this we now turn.

Signs of structure: semiology

The Swiss linguist Ferdinand de Saussure (1857–1913) outlined the idea of a science of signs, or semiology, in three courses of lectures given at the University of Geneva shortly before he died. These ideas were not published during his lifetime, but after his death two linguists put together lecture notes taken by his students into an integrated book called *Course in General Linguistics* (1974). It is probably easiest to get hold of the basic idea of the notion of semiology through a non-linguistic example.

Imagine going into a restaurant and giving your order to the waiter. He brings the first course to you and – horror! – it is the Black Forest gateaux and not the vichyssoise. Clearly something has gone terribly wrong. But what would a semiologist say about this? The semiologist would suggest that the problem with the meal is exactly analogous to an ungrammatical sentence: a specific rule of combination has been broken, namely that in our culture, in this particular historical period, Black Forest gateaux fits into a slot towards the end of a meal and vichyssoise fits into a slot at the beginning. In between the two we might have Caeser salad or coq au vin and afterwards cheese and then coffee. There is a rule of order here concerning the way dishes can be combined into sequences or in Saussure's terms there is a *syntagmatic* rule. It is important to realize that it is not a *prescriptive* rule that is being identified here, of the kind criticized by ethnomethodologists. Syntagmatic rules set conditions for meaning; they do not regulate behaviour in the same way.

Back at the restaurant, when we are ordering our meal we know there are various options for each slot, perhaps prawn cocktail instead of the vichyssoise or paella instead of the coq au vin. There is another principle at work here, one of substitution rather than order. Semiologists call these rules of substitution *paradigmatic* rules. The power of this idea lies in the fact that with two simple rules it is possible to endlessly generate more or less acceptable meals. If we wished to research meals it would be important to identify these rules; they are a very economical way of making sense of the structure of any particular meal. The claim that an underlying system involving rules of acceptable sequences and combinations can generate and make sense of cultural phenomena is basic to semiology.

It is important to note Saussure's suggestion goes further than merely providing a convenient and less redundant way of organizing a mass of material. He argues that the underlying system is essential for full knowledge of the nature of given items. Or, to put it another way, we could not fully understand the nature of Black Forest gateaux, say, without an understanding of its place in the system of sequence and substitution which underlies meals. This may sound like a rather odd claim. After all, it might seem that the *essential* nature of Black Forest gateaux is the sweet, sticky, chocolate flavour on the tongue. Yet, while we tend to think that what tastes nice is a purely natural perhaps even an entirely physiological phenomenon, independent of culture and language, we only have to visit a few other cultures to be disabused of this idea. Saussure calls the principle lying behind these ideas the *arbitrariness of the sign*.

The arbitrariness of the sign

Basic to Saussure's thinking is a distinction between a concept and its associated speech sound. For example, on the one hand, there is the concept 'dog' (furry animals with four legs which bark), and there is the speech sound 'dog'. Saussure calls the speech sound the *signifier*, the concept the *signified* and the combination of the two the linguistic *sign*. The argument for the arbitrariness of the sign rests on the demonstration that neither the nature of the signifier, signified or their relationship is fixed or determined. This demonstration depends on producing examples to show that things could easily have been otherwise.

In the first place, Saussure suggests that there is no *natural* relation between the signifier and the signified, between the word 'dog' and furry animals with four legs which bark. The fact that other cultures use other speech sounds confirms this; in English where we use 'dog' the French use 'chien'. Any sound could be used as the signifier for dog, the choice is essentially arbitrary. Humans are capable of producing an immense range of sounds, and different languages use certain sounds for conveying meaning and ignore others. There is no necessity that certain sounds should carry some meanings and others not. The most controversial claim, however, is that signifieds, concepts, are themselves arbitrary. The examples used to support this claim rely mainly on linguistic evidence. For instance, in English a distinction is marked between sheep, the animal, and sheep meat, by the use of the two terms 'sheep' and 'mutton' while in French this distinction stays unmarked: the single term 'mouton' is used for both. In English the distinction between 'river' and 'stream' is basically related to size: rivers have more water flowing down them, while in French a distinction is made between 'rivière' and 'fleuve' where the latter flows into the sea and the former does not. The idea is that the world can be conceptually partitioned in endless different ways.

This, then, is what Saussure means by the arbitrariness of the sign. There is nothing which *determines* the nature of the signifier or the nature of the signified; there is no natural or intrinsic relationship between them. The radical consequence of this for Saussure is that using a language cannot be seen as a naming process, using a list of words each corresponding to the thing that it names. Instead it is always dependent, as with the nature of Black Forest gateaux, on a system of relationships.

Think of a railway timetable. What makes the 8.25 Geneva-to-Paris train what it is? It is not the physical nature of the train – it might have completely different coaches on it every day. Nor is it the time that it leaves – for it is still the 8.25 even if one day it leaves at 8.35 or even 9.30. What defines it is its place in *relation* to other trains, as indicated by the railway timetable. The timetable is the underlying system used to make sense of particular instances, particular trains.

It is this basic insight concerning the relationship between particular meanings and an underlying system of differences which led Saussure to suggest that a separate science of signs within society is conceivable. This science of semiology (named after the Greek work for sign) would not be concerned only with language but would study *any* human realm to which meaning is systematically applied (Culler, 1976). And indeed many studies have now been carried out on subjects as diverse as fashion (Barthes, 1985), road signs (Krampen, 1983), literature (Barthes, 1974), television programmes (Fiske and Hartley, 1978), rock music (Hebdidge, 1979), buildings (Broadbent et al., 1980) and many other cultural forms which can be considered sign systems.

Probably more than any other, the person responsible for developing this kind of work was the multitalented French semiologist Roland Barthes (1915–80). He was a central figure in Parisian intellectual life for three decades before he died. One aspect that Barthes stressed in particular was the possibility of additional levels of meaning in cultural semiological systems (1964, 1972).

Second level signification: myth

Saussure suggested that signifiers (speech sounds) and signifieds (concepts) are connected together in signs by the process of signification. Barthes makes the point that this process need not stop here; for a sign can take part in another level of signification where it becomes the signifier to a new signified. Thus the word 'Jaguar XJ6' signifies the concept of a specific car with a certain body shape, performance and so on. But this sign can itself become the signifier of a new signified at another level (see Figure 1.3). What is signified here is much more diffuse but is likely to include such notions as 'wealth', 'luxury', 'speed', 'glamorous living' and so on. If we see the line in a novel 'Mark got into his Jaguar XJ6 and drove off' we are provided with a set of expectations about the status, wealth and personality of the owner without any direct information concerning these things.

Throughout the mid 1950s Barthes wrote brief articles for a French newspaper on second-level signification, or myth as he called it (1972). He wrote essays on the semantics of trivia: wine, steak and chips, writers abroad, Einstein's brain, striptease. Yet their interest lie in displaying the

FIGURE 1.3
Second order signification – myth

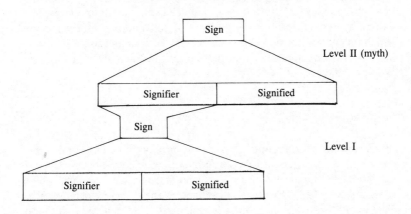

E.g. Level I – car, Jaguar XJ6; Level II – 'wealth', 'luxury', 'speed', 'glamorous living', etc.

complex meaning systems associated with such apparently simple cultural artifacts and, moreover, showing that these taken-for-granted meanings are not natural, inherent properties of these things but essentially arbitrary, culturally constructed conventions. Things could easily have been otherwise. Take the essay on wrestling. Barthes notes that it would be possible to think of a culture where wrestling is very much like boxing; it would be a sport where the goal is to demonstrate physical prowess. Yet in our culture wrestling is not like this at all. Why do people bet on boxing and not on wrestling? Why do wrestlers moan with agony and pain? And why do they continually break the rules? Barthes' answer is that there are two contrasting sets of meanings at work here.

Clearly there is pain in both wrestling and boxing but its significance is quite different. In boxing, the expression of pain is a sign of impending defeat which undermines the impression of excellence the boxer tries to portray. Boxers get up quickly when knocked down and try to minimize the appearance of hurt. Wrestling, however, has a moral dimension where the good guy fights it out with the bastard who flouts the rules. Pain here is part of the spectacle; it helps clarify the display of suffering, defeat and justice. To hide pain as boxers do would undermine the moment by moment intelligibility of the moral drama. Suffering and rule-breaking are part of this drama for without these things the essential element of justice would be lost.

Following on from Saussure's general argument, Barthes' essay reminds us that the meaning of wrestling or boxing does not arise *naturally* out of movements and behaviours. At the first level of signification, a particular fist movement may correspond to a punch, but at the second level of signification the meaning of that punch will depend whether it is thrown in a boxing match or a wrestling match. Thus ultimately its significance will be a product of the underlying set of conventions and distinctions which people use for decoding the meaning of actions and events (for a more detailed exploration of Barthes and the semiotics of wrestling see Webley, 1986).

Social study of language

In the last three sections of this chapter we have outlined some of the basic contributions of speech act theory, ethnomethodology and semiology to the study of language (for reviews and introductions to these fields see Levinson, 1983; Heritage, 1984; and Sturrock, 1986 respectively). This work turns away from the Chomskian/psycholinguistic tradition in which language is viewed as a formal system principally concerned with describing or representing the world. This work also retreats from the idea that language is best understood outside the specific occasions in which it is used.

Speech act theory and ethnomethodology both emphasize that talking is a species of action. In speech act theory this is enshrined in the principle that the same sentence, the same string of words, can be used in different ways: with the force of a request, an order, a question and so on. Ethnomethodologists have taken this idea even further by identifying a reflexive dimension to talk. While Austin concentrated on categories of action derived essentially from an analysis of English verbs, Wieder stressed that an utterance can formulate both the nature of the action it is performing and the relationship between the parties involved in the talking. In addition he noted that utterances typically do not have just one but a whole series of consequences for the talkers and subsequent interaction.

Rather than emphasize function in this way, semiologists have worked on undermining simple models of language which conceptualize meaning as a consequence of the relation between isolated words and objects. Instead semiology lays great stress on the existence of a system of oppositions and differences – 'la langue' – as a prerequisite for giving sense to individual words. This forces us to think about description in a rather more sophisticated way taking into account both the words which *are* used for description and those which *are not*. For semiologists have shown that what is absent is as important in providing meaning as what is present.

The treatment of language as action moves toward a more social perspective than traditional psycholinguistics. When language is conceptualized as a form of action performed in discourse between individuals with different goals we are forced to take the social context into account, likewise, with the notion that a web of felicity conditions or a system of distinctions is required for language to be used meaningfully. These things are not the property or creation of individual persons but are of necessity shared across collectivities (Harré, 1979). Taken together, these features suggest language should be of enormous interest to social psychology, although as yet there are only isolated and preliminary moves to put it at the heart of a programme of research. If we wish to know more about the way language is actually operating we are going to need to think about social psychological issues.

Despite their important insights, speech act theory, ethnomethodology and semiology are not without their flaws. They are not a fully solid basis on which to build a social psychological approach to language. But before we can start to develop a more viable approach we need an appreciation of both their insights *and* their problems.

Problems and limitations

Speech acts

One of the main difficulties with speech act theory is that it was developed as a philosophical thesis criticizing alternative philosophical perspectives rather than as a theory able to cope with the vicissitudes of real talk. As such, it mirrors much of the idealization of psycholinguistic work: it deals best with 'made up' sentences taken outside genuine contexts of use or highly ritualized speech forms in ceremonies like weddings and ship namings. In ordinary talk participants often do not make the act their speech is performing explicit. When we want the salt we often say 'can you pass me the salt?' not 'please pass me the salt'. Yet in this case we are not after information – although our request is couched in the form of a question – what we want is action: the salt to be passed. Attempts to try to deal with these problems by introducing a notion of indirect speech acts have appeared rather post hoc and have certainly reduced the heuristic power of the theory (Levinson, 1983).

When we try to apply speech act theory, to categorize a piece of transcript into speech acts say, these sorts of problems become acute. In particular, the idea that conversation is built out of discrete speech acts meshed together through sequencing rules (cf. Jacobs and Jackson, 1983; Labov and Fanshell, 1977; Sinclair and Coulthard,1975) is beset by a host of problems. For example, single utterances can perform a number of acts at once or acts may be spread over a number of utterances. Furthermore, in practice the decision about what act an utterance is performing is often made by referring to the response rather than to any features of the utterance itself. Thus if 'is it nine o'clock yet?' elicits the reply 'yes, just gone' it can be interpreted as a question; but if the response is 'alright, I'm just going to get the drink' it seems plausible to interpret it not as a question but as a request to carry out a pre-arranged duty (for a detailed discussion of these issues see Levinson, 1983: 286–94 and the important work of Grice, 1975).

Ethnomethodology

One of the difficulties with ethnomethodological research is that the kind of ethnographic study methods (Hammersley and Atkinson, 1983) adopted are prey to many of the same problems which ethnomethodologists identify in other work. For instance, Wieder's description of inmates' talk about the convict code is based on his interpretation of how they formulate what is going on and the resulting consequences. In this sense Wieder's work is not a great advance on the more traditional work. Although he is taking talk as the research topic, we find this talk pre-packaged when we read his work. Put another way, the reader of an ethnographic report of this kind is dependent on the researcher's description both for what they know about the data and for their evaluation of the researcher's analytic conclusions (Atkinson and Drew, 1979). Pretty much the same point has been made by discourse analysts in their criticisms of a whole range of sociological research (Mulkay et al., 1983; Yearley, 1984a).

In effect, it is often difficult to assess the findings of ethnomethodological work because it uses unexplicated commonsense assumptions (although it is unclear whether such assumptions could ever be entirely eliminated – Ashmore, 1985; Atkinson, 1985). Thus, even though ethnomethodologists have offered a much more subtle approach to language use, the empirical basis is unclear. As a response to this problem many ethnomethodologists have adopted a new analytic strategy known as conversation analysis based primarily on verbatim transcripts of interaction rather than on field notes or the researcher's remembered experiences. This will be described in Chapter Four.

Semiology

The empirical basis of semiological research has also been questioned (Culler, 1975). The problem when carrying out semiological research, of course, is adequately dealing with a system of distinctions where the vast majority might be absent in any one case examined. If we are concerned with the use of the category 'terrorist', for example, we need to look not only at those situations where 'terrorist' is used but also at those situations where some other term is used. The absence is as important as the presence. This is often a difficult thing to do and it is easy for the researcher to shirk this task and end up conducting traditional interpretative studies which attempt to get at second order signification through basically intuitive means. Indeed, Barthes' (1972) essays on mythology, although highly suggestive, can be criticized on exactly these grounds.

Semiology tends to produce, once again, static idealized analyses. This problem has been especially recognized by those who had previously been proponents of semiology. The emphasis on looking at structure ('la langue') rather than specific uses ('parole'), coupled with a focus on examining meaning at a single time rather than processes occurring over time, has ruled out a number of important and interesting questions. Continental analysts such as Barthes, Foucault and Derrida have suggested that some of the crucial insights from semiology could be maintained, particularly the stress on underlying structure, while paying more attention to language use and processes of change. This modified semiology (sometimes known as 'post-structuralism') has had a huge impact on literary theory and, as we will see, is now starting to penetrate social psychology, particularly in research on the self (see Chapter Five).

Overall, then, these perspectives from outside psychology embody important insights about language function and the organization of meaning. Although none have articulated a sustained empirical programme they provide the basis for this articulation, which we will turn to in the next chapter.

2

Unfolding discourse analysis

In the first part of this chapter we would like to begin the process of describing what we mean by discourse analysis although, of course, our description will only be complete when the book is finished. We hope to indicate how a new style of socio-psychological research can be erected on the foundations of speech act theory, ethnomethodology and semiotics.

Throughout this chapter, and the book as a whole, we will be assuming that discourse analysis will become more than a new field of study in social psychology – that is, discourse added to the list of attributions, altruism, bystander apathy and all the other topics which have interested social psychologists over the last thirty years. Discourse analysis is a radical new perspective with implications for all socio-psychological topics. The second part of this chapter will try to make this claim come alive through demonstrating how other socio-psychological methodologies have ignored or covered over the constructive, active use of language in everyday life and then the implications of this repression for the central socio-psychological concept of attitude.

It is important to emphasize at this stage, that we are not naively expecting all social psychologists to down tools and start working on discourse. The point is that discourse analysis asks important questions of conventional research, it provides a workable methodology and we will be satisfied if we can demonstrate that the study of social texts can, in itself, be a fascinating and potentially significant occupation.

Some major components of discourse analysis

Function, construction and variation

One of the themes strongly stressed by both speech act theory and ethno-methodology was that people use their language to *do* things: to order and request, persuade and accuse. This focus on language function is also one of the major components of discourse analysis. Function, however, cannot be understood in a mechanical way. Unfortunately, as we all know, when people are persuading, accusing, requesting etc. they do not always do so explicitly. When someone makes a request – perhaps they want to borrow your calculator – they do not always politely but explicitly ask: 'could I borrow your calculator this evening, please?'. Often they are less direct than this, perhaps couching the request as an abstract question:

'would you mind if I borrowed your calculator this evening?' or even more obliquely: 'it is going to drive me mad doing all those statistics by hand tonight' (Brown and Levinson, 1978). It may be to the speaker's advantage to make a request indirectly because it allows the recipient to reject it without making the rejection obvious (Drew, 1984). On the whole, people prefer to head off undesirable acts like rejections before they happen (Drew, 1986; and see Chapter Four).

The analysis of function thus cannot be seen as a simple matter of categorizing pieces of speech, it depends upon the analyst 'reading' the context. There is nothing intrinsic to a complaint about doing statistics by hand that makes it a request. It can only be recognized as this from the context.

In the calculator example one specific function is being performed: requesting. However, functions can also be more global, and this is the second point to make. A person may wish to present himself or herself in a favourable light, for example, or to present someone they dislike in a poor light. Global self-presentations can be achieved with particular kinds of formulations which emphasize either good or bad features. As with the previous example, it can be sensible to be inexplicit. For one thing, explicitness risks being less persuasive. To present yourself as a wonderful human being to someone, you perhaps should not say 'I am a wonderful human being', but you might modestly slip into the conversation at some 'natural' point that you work for charities, have won an academic prize, read Goethe and so on.

In general, we find that if talk is orientated to many different functions, global and specific, any examination of language over time reveals considerable *variation*. A person's account will vary according to its function. That is, it will vary according to the purpose of the talk. For example, if we take two descriptions of a particular individual, we will expect them to vary in accordance with the feelings of the person doing the describing. If you like a person you may, in the course of everyday gossip, describe particularly likeable characteristics out of the many available. Someone who dislikes that person may emphasize very different characteristics, or the same likeable characteristics may now become disagreeable. Alternatively, imagine you have to describe a person to a close friend on one occasion and to a parent on another. Again, what will be picked out for description will vary. For instance, you are probably not going to focus the parental account on this person's daring acts of delinquency, but this might be a more appropriate focus for a close friend.

What is happening in these cases is that people are using their language to *construct* versions of the social world. The principal tenet of discourse analysis is that function involves construction of versions, and is demonstrated by language variation. The term 'construction' is apposite for three reasons. First, it reminds us that accounts of events are built out of a variety of pre-existing linguistic resources, almost as a house is constructed from bricks, beams and so on. Second, construction implies active selection: some resources are included, some omitted. Finally, the notion of construction emphasizes the potent, consequential nature of accounts. Much of social interaction is based around dealings with events and people which are experienced *only* in terms of specific linguistic versions. In a profound sense, accounts 'construct' reality.

We do not wish, however, to make the process seem necessarily deliberate or intentional. It may be that the person providing the account is not consciously constructing, but a construction emerges as they merely try to make sense of a phenomenon or engage in unselfconscious social activities like blaming or justifying. It is important to note that in these cases, too, there is variability in accounts, because different forms of description may be right for different occasions, but the person may be just 'doing what comes naturally' rather than intentionally deciding this rather than that form of language will be appropriate. Indeed, we expect this to be the much more common situation in the hurly-burly of ordinary language use, and we are not beguiled into thinking that some classes of talk are merely descriptive while others are deliberately constructive. All language, even language which passes as simple description, is constructive and consequential for the discourse analyst.

Overall, then, discourse analysts' propose that people's language use is much more variable than is indicated by the widely held 'realistic' descriptive model of language – which treats discourse as a relatively unambiguous pathway to actions, beliefs or actual events. Researchers who presuppose the realistic mode assume that when people describe the same event, action or belief their accounts will, broadly speaking, be consistent. And, for methodological purposes, they will take consistent accounts to mean that events did happen as described. Brenner provides a good example of this realistic position when he claims that 'descriptions and explanations of events and experiences may be regarded as highly valid, when they are, by and large, the same across accounts' (1985: 156).

There are two basic problems with this. First, consistency in accounts is often overstated by the various aggregating techniques commonly used by psychologists, as we will indicate later in the chapter. Second, there is no reason to suppose that consistency in accounts is a sure indicator of descriptive validity. This consistency may be a product of accounts sharing the same function; that is, two people may put their discourse together in the same way because they are doing the same thing with it.

Discourse as topic

Discourse analysts have responded to the all-encompassing functional/ constructive nature of accounts by suspending the realistic approach and focusing on discourse as a topic in its own right. That is, we are not trying to recover events, beliefs and cognitive processes from participants' discourse, or treat language as an indicator or signpost to some other state of affairs but looking at the analytically prior question of how discourse or accounts of these things are manufactured (Gilbert and Mulkay, 1984; Potter, Stringer and Wetherell, 1984).

Take the idea of attitudes. If someone espouses attitude x on one occasion and the contradictory attitude y on another, the analyst clearly cannot treat the existence of attitude x or y as an unproblematic guide to what the person actually believes. But it is possible to treat the account containing the expression of the attitude as the focus itself, asking: on what occasions is attitude x rather than attitude y espoused? How are these attitude accounts constructed? And what functions or purposes do they achieve? It is questions of this kind which are at the heart of discourse analysis.

To summarize, then, this first stage, discourse analysts are suggesting that:

1. language is used for a variety of functions and its use has a variety of consequences;
2. language is both constructed and constructive;
3. the same phenomenon can be described in a number of different ways;
4. there will, therefore, be considerable variation in accounts;
5. there is, as yet, no foolproof way to deal with this variation and to sift accounts which are 'literal' or 'accurate' from those which are rhetorical or merely misguided thereby escaping the problems variation raises for researchers with a 'realistic' model of language;
6. the constructive and flexible ways in which language is used should themselves become a central topic of study.

So far we have illustrated the need for an analysis of participants' discourse from theoretical principles, although we have been guided by the research associated with the positions discussed in the last chapter. Nevertheless, it is clear that our perspective depends on an empirical claim as its mainstay, namely that there is considerable variation in participants' accounts; or, more specifically, that there is sufficient variation in accounts to cause problems for the realistic approach.

We intend to provide documentation for this claim later in this chapter and in subsequent chapters. However, readers may be wondering why, if this variability is as common as we have suggested, it does not feature widely in the current empirical literature of social psychology. How can it have been overlooked? There are two answers to this question. The first is that it *does* feature in social psychological research – but it is not understood within the broad discourse analytic framework. The second answer is that variability in accounts is managed through analytic strategies of restriction, categorization and selective reading. We will take these facets in turn.

Variable discourse and traditional social psychology

There are a number of strands of experimental social psychology which illustrate account variability. The areas of social perception, impression management, cognitive dissonance and speech accommodation have in particular brought inconsistencies in language use to the fore.

Social perception

In the field of social perception, studies such as Duncan's (1976) have demonstrated that people provided with the same kind of scenario will nonetheless describe that scenario in quite different ways. Duncan showed his experimental subjects a film in which either a black or a white man shoved another person. In each case it was exactly the same action, all that changed was the race of the protagonists. The viewers, who were white students, then had to categorize this event, for example as 'playing around' or as 'aggressive behaviour'. Duncan found that his subjects were much more likely to describe the event as aggressive behaviour when it was the black who was doing the shoving, thus apparently indicating the effect of their stereotypes on their perception of events.

This study certainly shows variability in accounts – even where people have seen the same kinds of actions with their own eyes. This finding is generally interpreted, however, according to theories of social perception as an example of how racial prejudice and stereotypes can *distort* perception. Account variability of this kind is not taken as a more general and normal phenomenon, as is the case with discourse analysis. Moreover, no attempt is made to look at the construction of the accounts or their possible function. Indeed, this kind of analysis is precluded by the experimental design which allows participants only an extremely limited range of descriptions, and provides these descriptions for the participants in advance.

The point we wish to make is that people are *always* constructing versions and re-describing events, not merely when prejudiced or stereotyped. The study of social perception largely concerns how people talk about other people; it is a linguistic study as much as an investigation of visual processes. Descriptions of others are inevitably 'distorted', not simply occasionally, but perenially, in the sense that they are always constructions for some purpose. Different pieces of talk and prescription have, of course, different functions and different consequences. A racially prejudiced description is highly pernicious in its effects but other descriptions are no less functional and constructive. This point is overlooked by social psychologists who investigate 'bias' in information processing, assuming a realm where some descriptions will simply and neutrally reflect reality. The meaning of the variability found in these studies is thus frequently misunderstood.

Self-presentation

There is a large literature in social psychology concerned with people's self-presentation or impression management (Baumeister, 1982; Tetlock and Manstead, 1985). One of the most reliable findings in this area is that people modify their behaviour, including their talk, in accordance with different social contexts. To ingratiate themselves, people often resort to gross flattery and insincere compliments directed towards those they wish to influence. When they have succeeded in their aim, the compliments may be replaced by hostility. Variation in self-presentation is particularly relevant, of course, in experiments where subjects can change their actions to please experimenters or in line with the researcher's subtle cues, meeting the demand set up in the experimental situation (Orne, 1969; Rosenthal and Rosnow, 1969).

Once again, account variability is illustrated in social psychology, but the theoretical perspective is rather different. Discourse analysts see variation in accounts as a consequence of people performing a whole range of different acts in their talk. Some variations may be due to considerations of face saving and creating a good impression, but, as we will shortly try to demonstrate, others will result from the need to construct discourse to achieve an effect – a blaming, say – or arise from a broader concern with making accounts locally coherent, where there is little sense in talking of active self-presentation. Variability is confined to a narrow area of social life, if we see it as resulting merely from impression management.

Cognitive dissonance

Research in social perception and self-presentation actively stresses variation. Cognitive dissonance or cognitive consistency theories, on the other hand, focus on people's desire to appear consistent and invariant to themselves and others. Festinger (1957) argued that if a person perceives dissonance or inconsistency between two or more of their cognitions they will experience an unpleasant state of psychological tension and will be motivated to reduce the tension by changing their attitudes and thoughts so they are once more consistent. For instance, if someone trying to lose weight also fancies having a cream cake for afternoon tea, they may rationalize the contradiction by telling themselves that they will go without dinner as compensation. The dissonance perceived is reduced by the new self-stricture. In this perspective variability is not seen as a normal or natural feature but as a psychologically unpleasant state.

It is often the case that if people become aware of contradictions or inconsistencies immediately, as they are talking, they will attempt to gloss over or make sense of the inconsistency. In our society inconsistency is rarely a desirable way of presenting oneself. However, discourse analysis also demonstrates that these cases of self-conscious recognition and repair of variability are relatively small in number. As we will try to show in the last section of this chapter, variability is still pervasive in people's accounts. Given just a small separation of accounts in time, across one or two turns of talk, people cease to attend to the variation in their language use. It will become evident, in other words, as we progress through the book that variability is an expected usual feature of conversation and social texts despite the fact that people often try to reduce it when it is pointed out to them or when it becomes salient for some other reason.

Another point should be made here. Namely, the type of inconsistency described by cognitive dissonance theory is not a formal or strictly logical inconsistency. It is a psychological inconsistency. Something may be perceived as inconsistent by a logician but not by the person concerned, and vice versa. Consistency and inconsistency are highly negotiable occasioned phenomena, in fact. On some occasions some variations in accounts will be seen as inconsistent, on other occasions the same variations will be seen as sensible and rational after all. To put it crudely, consistency and inconsistency are variable states themselves and one of the things which interests the discourse analyst is how they are used, variably, as argumentative or rhetorical strategies.

Speech accommodation

Work on speech accommodation in social psychology has looked at the factors that surround speech and the variability in this domain. How, for instance, speakers modify their accent, dialect or intonation pattern etc. in different group contexts (Giles, 1977; Giles and St. Clair, 1979). For example, Welsh speakers have been shown to broaden their accents when talking to an upper-class English speaker, with the goal of emphasizing their group distinctiveness (Bourhis and Giles, 1977). Variability in these kinds of speech dimensions can readily be related to the context and function of speech. What distinguishes discourse analysis, however, is that we also study variability in linguistic *content* in relation to function and give this a priority.

Overall, therefore, there are research topics within experimental social psychology which document variability in accounts. But none of this research addresses the broader implications of variation. Comparison with these research areas clarifies our perspective. We are concerned with the functional aspects of *all* kinds of talk, not just that seen as 'biased' in some way, or involved in impression management. All types of variation are interesting, not simply logical inconsistencies or variations people recognize immediately, and we examine linguistic content or *what* people say and write rather than *how* they say it in terms of phonology, intonation and so on.

The suppression of account variability

Social psychology not only tends to play down the issue of variation in areas crucially concerned with it, but it is also the case that the procedures psychologists regularly use for dealing with discourse have, often inadvertently, acted as management strategies for suppressing variability. For the sake of simplicity, we can distinguish three broad strategies which obscure variability in accounts. These involve restriction, gross coding and selective reading.

Restriction

The restriction strategy involves techniques which prevent the variability in participants' discourse becoming in any way apparent. Experiments use restriction very effectively, because the control exerted over the subjects and the situation to measure the effects of the independent manipulated variables also works to exclude information which might potentially throw up variability in discourse. Of course some experimental work can highlight variations in language use, as our discussion above indicated, but typically, very restricted parts of participants' talk are sampled in very constrained circumstances.

Experiments normally take place in social psychological laboratories; the experimenter sets up a scenario within the laboratory for the subjects who are asked to respond to it in a way which can be numerically quantified. For example, they may have to play a game and choose between specified options where the number of choices for one option across the sample becomes the dependent measure. The experimenter's goal is to constrain the situation in such a way that it can only be perceived by the subjects as the researcher intended. Other interpretations must be ruled out, although it is clear that this ruling out is frequently ineffective and controversial (cf. Mixon's, 1972, discussion of Milgram's, 1963, obedience research).

The subjects' reaction to the situation must also be as constrained as far as possible if the experiment is to be successful. There must be no ambiguity about this reaction, responses must fit into pre-categorized entities. Subjects cannot behave in just any way, they must select their response according to the options offered by the experimenter. Similarly they cannot usually give more than one response, they cannot choose two or three options or mark several points on a scale, and their response is generally measured only once. That is, it is not usual for the experimenter to return ten minutes later and say to the subject 'what do you think now?' There is usually no scope for recording uncertainty of response, varied reactions or changes in opinions. In other words, experiments are situations where the value placed on consistency of behaviour in our culture is made particularly salient to participants. In general, experiments are designed to wipe out variability of interpretation and response, indeed, that is supposedly their strength and rationale, although they may be obscuring one of the most interesting and important features of social life in the process.

In surveys or opinion poll research, restriction arises similarly from collecting a very constrained selection of participants' discourse on one discrete occasion. It is often only possible to respond 'yes', 'no', 'don't know' or 'agree', 'strongly agree' etc. to a survey question. The possibility of a respondent giving *contrasting* views on a topic is again precluded; ambivalence, the expression of flexible opinions tailored to the context and inconsistent responses are ruled out by the response format.

As with experiments, these restrictive practices do not *prevent* information pertinent to people's variable language use appearing altogether. For instance, there is a considerable literature showing that subtle variations in question wording can lead to large differences in responding (see Marsh, 1982) and that people contradict themselves and make 'incoherent' claims when responding to opinion questionnaires (Kinder and Sears, 1985; Schuman et al., 1983; Turner and Krauss, 1978). Unfortunately, these phenomena are rarely treated as theoretically interesting indications of the way people deploy their language, but are generally treated as obstacles to the production of reliable research findings.

Both experimentation and survey research came under sustained attack during the 1970s; experiments because of supposedly unwarranted assumptions about the causal constraints on behaviour (Harré, 1979; Harré and Secord, 1972) and doubts about the generalizability of findings (Argyris, 1975; Gergen, 1978); survey research because of the severe limitations on the responses it is possible to make (Rosier, 1974; Harré, 1979) and because of the difficulty of deciding on the proper interpretation of those responses which are produced (Cicourel, 1974). In the light of these kinds of criticisms, considerable interest was expressed in the use of open-ended interviews and procedures based on the interpretation of documents, which had been more common in areas of micro-sociology (Plummer, 1983) and ethnography (Hammersley and Atkinson, 1983). With the advent of this work, the variability in participants' discourse could no longer be dealt with merely by restriction; new strategies – which we will call gross categorization and selective reading – had to be adopted.

Gross categorization

The technique social psychologists have traditionally used to deal with participants' open-ended discourse is content analysis (Holsti, 1968; Mostyn, 1985). This involves the generation of categories which can be reliably coded and imposed over the data for the purposes of hypothesis testing. For instance, in McLelland's (1961) well-known research on 'achievement motivation', content analysis of achievement themes in books was used as an index of the stress on achievement in a particular society. Coders were trained to reliably categorize themes stressing high achievement so the prevalence of achievement themes could be correlated with broad indicators of national development such as gross national product. In principle, there is nothing wrong with this procedure. Yet, in practice it is more suited to research where the discourse is understood primarily as an indicator of something lying beyond. If we adopt a theoretical perspective in which language is seen as an essentially functional medium, where the meaning of terms is closely related to their particular context of use, content analysis is less helpful.

Function is a problem for content analysis because of the difficulty of dealing with the sheer subtlety of a situation where participants may be constructively using their language to produce different sorts of effects. As ethnomethodologists have emphasized, when a person is trying to persuade, for example, part of their effectiveness may well depend on producing their talk in a way which conceals that it is an attempt to persuade; for what could be more persuasive than the 'mere description of facts'? Context is a problem because, if the meaning of a section of discourse depends on the context in which it appears, the criteria for what counts as an instance in a particular coding category may become impossibly complicated.

More importantly for the present argument, the broad categories often used in content analysis (e.g. achievement themes) can easily obscure theoretically interesting differences in discourse. Broad categories are particularly likely to be used when researchers expect consistency. At the same time, the fact that different coders can reliably operate the same category – the acid test of a well-conducted content analysis – does not resolve this problem. For two coders, trained in the same way, can persistently repeat the same confusions and categorize together different sorts of utterances. This leads to a big problem in evaluating content analytic research, because even in the most detailed research report very few examples of the application of the category to the discourse or the training of coders are reproduced (Abraham, 1984).

Selective reading

Problems of this kind have led some social psychologists, notably Rom Harré (see Chapter Three), to advocate qualitative research which works with the accounts themselves as opposed to a numerically transformed version of them. This approach has been commonplace in micro-sociology (Bogdan and Taylor, 1975; Plummer, 1983) and when adopted it is certainly more difficult to ignore variability in participants' discourse. Nevertheless, if the analyst is operating with a commonsense 'realistic' model of language, the model can be sustained by selective reading.

One form of selective reading takes place when the analyst handling interviews or texts selects out those which *appear* to be significant when listening to the tape or reading the document. The great danger here is that the researcher making selections will simply mirror his or her prior expectation. In this situation the data can be used to simply buttress the favoured analytic story rather than being used to critically evaluate it.

If the researcher does notice variability he or she can use another form of reading which selectively *reifies* and/or *ironizes* the discourse. Reification refers to the process where abstractions are treated as material things or, in this case, where words referring to objects or processes are treated as guarantees of the actual existence of these objects or pro- cesses. For example, a spoken account of an event which describes it as a quarrel might be taken to indicate that the event was in fact a quarrel. Ironization is the reverse. Irony occurs, of course, when a meaning different or opposite to the literal one is intended. Ironization refers to the process where descriptive language is treated not as genuinely descrip- tive but as having another purpose or as a deception. The notions of reification and ironization can be combined to create a selective reading of accounts and thus eliminate variability once again.

With these two approaches to reading at their disposal, analysts working with open-ended discourse find it relatively easy to construct one coherent story of events, processes or beliefs out of the material at their disposal. Versions which are in line with their preferred story can be reified and others, which conflict with it, can be ironized. Reification and ironization can be very subtle, but nevertheless can be revealed by a careful and critical examination of the way analysts draw upon participants' discourse (Mulkay, 1981; Mulkay et al., 1982; Potter and Litton, 1985; Potter et al., 1984). In the next chapters we will demonstrate how a classic ethogenic study based on Harré's perspective adopts these devices.

Overall, it is possible to see how the use of these three strategies – restriction, gross coding and selective reading – can suppress the variability discourse analysts claim is inherent in social texts. These strategies *pre- suppose* the 'realistic model' of language use by obscuring any data which might throw it into doubt. What is required is an analysis of discourse which focuses on variability and the construction of accounts. However, before making any more moves we must illustrate in more detail how a discourse analyst approaches accounts. This goal can be attained by demonstrating how we would deal with one of the most fundamental social psychological notions: attitudes.

Attitudes in discourse

Our approach to attitudes should reveal that distinctiveness of the discourse position and put some flesh on the notion of variability in accounts along with the idea that accounts are constructed to have specific consequences. These are some of the themes which will recur frequently in later chapters. First, let us clarify what social psychologists mean by the term 'attitude'.

The concept of attitude is one of the oldest theoretical ideas in social psychology and, in manifold ways, has supported a huge body of some-times disparate research. Despite this history, the exact meaning of the notion has remained somewhat obscure. Indeed, in a classic overview Gordon Allport (1935) suggested that the very imprecision of the meaning of attitude is one of the features which has made the notion so popular, because it glossed over difficult theoretical conflicts. A recent review (McGuire, 1985) also describes a number of radically different perspectives on the nature of attitudes, and we will return to the most important of these later. However, McGuire goes on to suggest that it is possible to formulate a working definition which would command a wide degree of consensus.

McGuire claims that empirical studies of attitudes work with, at least implicitly, the following basic definition. When people are expressing attitudes they are giving responses which 'locate "objects of thought" on "dimensions of judgment"' (McGuire, 1985: 239). That is, when they are speaking or acting, people are taking some idea or object of interest and giving it a position in an evaluative hierarchy. We will describe a concrete example to make this concept sharper.

Traditional approaches to attitudes and racism

In 1976 a British researcher, Alan Marsh, asked a random sample of 1,785 people to express their attitude to 'coloured immigrants' by placing a mark on a scale which ran from 'completely sympathetic', through to, 'no feelings about them either way', to 'completely unsympathetic'. In McGuire's terms the object of thought would be the 'coloured immigrants', while the dimension of judgement would consist of the 'sympathy' which the respondent can offer or refuse. Marsh's survey resembles myriads of other surveys, the techniques he used are extremely common in attitude research. Having collected his responses, Marsh went on to split his scale up 'logically' into categories. These are labelled 'very hostile', 'hostile', 'neutral' and so on (see Figure 2.1).

FIGURE 2.1

Distribution of sympathetic and unsympathetic feelings towards coloured immigrants

Completely unsympathetic		No feelings about them either way				Completely sympathetic
0	1–20	21–45	46–55	56–79	80–99	100
12%	13%	17%	25%	20%	10%	3%
Very hostile	Hostile	Unsympathetic	Neutral	Sympathetic	Positive	Very positive

No. in sample: unweighted = 1,785, weighted = 1,482; 'don't know' (excluded = 4%).

Source: Marsh, 1976.

From the point of view of a discourse analyst, there are a number of interesting points to be made, both about McGuire's minimal definition of attitudes and the kind of practical research procedures illustrated by Marsh's scale; we will concentrate on three issues.

First, there are obvious problems with the status of 'coloured immigrants' as an object of thought. One way of looking at the term 'coloured immigrants' would be as a simple category label for a group of people, in fact those people who fit the descriptions 'coloured' and 'immigrant'. However, things are a lot more complex than this. For example, there is no clear-cut neutral way of deciding how to apply the category 'coloured immigrant'. That is, there are no objective criteria for category membership (this is a theme which will be explored in detail in Chapter Six).

The proper application of 'coloured' is dependent on unstated theories of race and biology. But modern theories of genetics and population give no support to the idea that 'races' of people can be distinguished in terms of unambiguous, underlying physical, and ultimately genetic, differences (Husband, 1982). In addition, 'immigrant' means (in the dictionary sense) a person who comes into a foreign country as a settler. Yet Marsh (1976) does not address the problem of splitting 'coloured immigrants' from 'coloured residents', and it is clear that he takes the term 'coloured immigrant' as a bland descriptive category covering both these groups. In fact this is reflected in the very title of his article, which is called 'Who hates the Blacks' not 'Who hates those people who are both recent settlers in Britain and black defined'. His terminology is not neutral. If you have lived in a country for the whole of your life you might be concerned if people start calling you an immigrant – a term often used to connote aliens or outsiders (Reeves, 1983; Sykes, 1985).

A second problem arises when we examine the transformations which Marsh makes to his subjects' responses. If we look at Figure 2.1 we can see that Marsh has transformed one dimension, running from 'completely unsympathetic' to 'completely sympathetic', into a more complex set of labels: 'very hostile', 'hostile', 'unsympathetic' etc. There is no coherent justification for making transformations of this kind. For example, it is probably wrong to suggest respondents mean the same thing by the words 'very hostile' and 'completely unsympathetic'. For one thing, the term hostility is often used to imply an *active* disposition, while if someone lacks sympathy, they are *without* a certain kind of active disposition. By making this transformation the analyst is riding roughshod over subtle distinctions that may play a crucial role in the participants' discourse, and certainly in their methods of making sense of the survey questions.

A third problem also concerns translation: in this case the researchers' translation of participants' responses into the underlying theoretical category of attitude. The aim of attitude scales is not merely to show how people fill in these scales, but to identify attitudes. That is, in McGuire's terms, to identify where on a specific dimension a person locates an object of thought; in the current example, where the respondents locate 'coloured immigrants' on the dimension of 'sympathy'. The crucial assumption of attitude researchers is that there is something enduring within people which the scale is measuring – the attitude.

Discourse analysis points to many difficulties with this. We need to ask, for instance, whether people filling in an attitude scale are performing a neutral act of describing or expressing an internal mental state, their attitude or whether they are engaged in producing a specific linguistic formulation tuned to the context at hand. From the discourse analytic perspective, given different purposes or a different context a very different 'attitude' may be espoused. Put another way, if a certain attitude is expressed on one occasion it should not necessarily lead us to expect that the same attitude will be expressed on another. Instead there may be systematic variations in what is said, which cast doubt on the enduring homogeneous nature of the supposed internal mental attitude.

How, then, should we deal with these three problems which are by no means unique to Marsh: first, the meaning of interpretation given to the terms in the attitude scale; second, the translation between participants' discourse and analysts' categories; and third, the treatment of linguistic products as transparent indicators of underlying objects or dispositions.

More generally, what might a study of participants' discourse tell us about phenomena traditionally understood in terms of attitudes? The time has come to get down to the nitty-gritty of accounts and perform our own analysis.

Discourses of immigration

In the remainder of this chapter we will indicate how a discourse analyst might go about researching attitudes to constructed categories such as 'coloured immigrants'. We will closely examine some accounts produced in a less organized environment than Marsh's survey, but which, nonetheless, are easily recognizable as evaluative expressions concerning race and immigration. All the accounts we shall analyze have been extracted from open-ended interviews with white, middle-class New Zealanders. These interviews discussed generally 'controversial' issues in New Zealand society.

The goals of our analysis will obviously differ from those determining traditional attitude research. Broadly speaking, discourse analysts are interested in the different ways in which texts are organized, and the consequences of using some organizations rather than others. So our aim will be to look at the different forms taken by evaluative discourse about minority groups, and the effects of these forms. At the same time, the analysis will try to avoid the three problems we identified as endemic in traditional attitude research, namely presupposing the existence of the 'attitudinal object', making translations from unexplicated participants' discourse to unexplicated analysts' discourse, and treating utterances as indicators of the presence of enduring, underlying attitudes. We shall try to show why the concept of an enduring attitude is theoretically redundant.

Context

Perhaps the first thing which becomes apparent when embarking on this task is the sheer complexity of working with extended sequences of talk rather than the brief isolated utterances which make up responses to attitude questionnaires. Take the following interview extract for example.

1. *Respondent.* I'm not anti them at all you know (Benton: 26).

We do not have any trouble in reading this as a relatively positive statement of the speaker's position on 'them' – in this case, in the New Zealand context, 'Polynesian immigrants'. In attitude terms, the 'object of thought' is 'Polynesian immigrants', the 'dimension of judgment' lies from pro to anti, and the position espoused is pro. Following standard attitude theory, we would treat this speaker as possessing a specific attitude. If they had to fill in Marsh's questionnaire they might endorse the 'sympathetic' end of the scale – or so the traditional account would have it.

Yet, when we look at more of this sequence, the simplicity starts to fall away. Here is the entire turn of talk from which Extract One was taken.

> 2. *Respondent*. I'm not anti them at all you know, I, if they're willing to get on and be like us; but if they're just going to come here, just to be able to use our social welfares and stuff like that, then why don't they stay home? (Benton: 26).

There are a number of interesting features here which immediately question our first interpretation. To begin with, the 'pro immigrants' claim is made contingent on immigrants exhibiting a willingness 'to be like us'. Thus we can no longer read it as an unqualified expression of sympathy. Moreover, the whole statement is organized within a complex linguistic structure of conditionals and contrasts. This can be shown clearly if we rearrange the extract.

> 2b. A1 If [they're willing to get on and be like us]
> A2 then [I'm not anti them]
> but
> B1 if [they're just going...to use our social welfares]
> B2 then [why don't they stay home]

In technical terms, contrast structures are now revealed. Taken in isolation, the consequences of these kinds of contrast structures are not easy to ascertain. However, it is notable that studies of the way public speakers, such as Margaret Thatcher and other politicians, elicit applause have found that constructions of this sort are very effective in producing audience appreciation (Atkinson, 1984a; Heritage and Greatbach, 1986). And it may well be that this kind of construction is commonplace in everyday discourse because it helps package the message to make it more convincing.

A further feature of Extract Two also highlights its persuasive orientation. It draws upon what Pomerantz (1986) has called the *extreme case* formulation. For example, if someone is asked why they carry a gun and they respond, '*everybody* carries a gun', they are providing an effective warrant. Gun-toting is depicted not as a notable or restricted activity but as normative, something shared by everybody. Extreme case formulations take whatever evaluative dimension is being adopted to its extreme limits. Thus if it is a question of numbers, then it is 'everybody' or 'only one', things are 'very' or 'terribly' bad etc. In the second part of Extract Two the speaker produces an extreme case formulation of this type: 'if they are *just* going to come here *just* to be able to use our social security and stuff'. The repeated use of the word 'just' paints a picture of people whose *sole* purpose in coming to New Zealand is the collection of social security, a selfish motive much more blameworthy than, say, coming to provide essential labour but being laid off due to economic recession. By representing it in this extreme way the criticisms are made to appear more justifiable.

Finally, if we look back to the first part of Extract Two – 'I am not anti them at all' – we can see that this operates as a *disclaimer*. Hewitt and Stokes (1975) define a disclaimer as a verbal device which is used to ward off potentially obnoxious attributions. Thus, if someone says 'I am no sexist but. . .' they are aware that what they are about to say may sound sexist, but are trying to head off such an attribution. In this case, the speaker is disclaiming possible attributions of racism consequent on the suggestion that immigrants should 'stay home'.

Now, these interpretations of Extract Two are tentative. They are not based on a systematic study of many instances but on a detailed reading of a single one. But they suggest two things. First, that even a small amount of additional information about context can throw into question what, at first, appears to be a reasonable interpretation of a person's utterance. Second, that discourse has an action orientation; it is constructed in such a way that particular tasks – in this case blaming and disclaiming responsibility for the obnoxious effects of this blaming – are facilitated. This is, of course, just what is expected in the light of developments described in Chapter One.

These points have important implications for attitude scale research. If the person filling in the scale is viewed as merely *describing* or *expressing* their attitude, things seem quite clear-cut. Yet, if we start to view their response as a discursive act, which it always is, things become murkier, because there is a great deal of scope to perform different kinds of acts when filling in the scale. For example, a person might fill in the scale to perform the task of disclaiming by marking the 'sympathetic' pole; or they might perform the task of blaming by marking the 'unsympathetic' pole. They might hesitate because they see themselves as sympathetic and unsympathetic at the same time – 'I'm not anti but. . .'. Two people putting the same mark on the scale could well be doing very different things with their discourse. If the opinion pollster is coordinating an interview rather than requiring paper and pen responses the person might offer the whole utterance to the pollster and how it emerges, in terms of the category scales, will depend on the pollsters current method of scaling.

One way we could proceed, given this line of argument, is to suggest that attitude measurement might survive in its present form if it became a more subtle business, more sensitive to the different acts performed. We should note, however, that this continues to assume that there is such a thing as 'an attitude' or an enduring, underlying state expressed in talk and behaviour. This position becomes extremely difficult to maintain when we look at the variations which appear in participants' accounts.

Variability

The following example is typical of the sort of variation in accounts which has now been documented in a wide swathe of different kinds of discourse. These two extracts are taken from subsequent pages of the interview transcript.

3. *Respondent.* What I would li. . rather see is that, sure, bring them ['Polynesian immigrants'] into New Zealand, right, try and train them in a skill, and encourage them to go back again (Pond: 17).

4. *Respondent.* I think that if we encouraged more Polynesians and Maoris to be skilled people they would want to stay here, they're not um as uh nomadic as New Zealanders are (*Interviewer*. Haha.) so I think that would be better (Pond: 18).

The contradiction is stark. In Extract Three the respondent states that they would like Polynesian immigrants to be trained in New Zealand and then to return to the Pacific Islands. In Extract Four the respondent claims it would be better if Polynesians were encouraged to become skilled and then stay in New Zealand. What are we to make of this variability? The problem is particularly acute for the attitude researcher because of the conflict between versions. An attempt to recover the person's 'underlying attitude' is not going to get very far.

The discourse analyst's reponse is rather different from the attitude researcher. We do not intend to use the discourse as a pathway to entities or phenomena lying 'beyond' the text. Discourse analysis does not take for granted that accounts reflect underlying attitudes or dispositions and therefore we do not expect that an individual's discourse will be consistent and coherent. Rather, the focus is on the discourse *itself*: how it is organized and what it is doing. Orderliness in discourse will be viewed as a product of the orderly *functions* to which discourse is put.

If we return to the accounts quoted above, and provide a bit more of the context, we can illustrate how a functional analysis might begin.

5. *Interviewer.* [Do] you think that, say, immigration from the Pacific Islands should be encouraged [ ] to a much larger extent than it is? It's fairly restricted at the moment.
Respondent. Yes. Um, I think there's some problems in, in encouraging that too much, is that they come in uneducated about our ways, and I think it's important they understand what they're coming to. I, what I would

li. . .rather see is that, sure, bring them into New Zealand, right, try and
train them in a skill, and encourage them to go back again because their
dependence on us will be lesser. I mean [ ] while the people back there
are dependent on the people being here earning money to send it back, I
mean, that's a very very negative way of looking at something. [ ] people
really should be trying, they should be trying to help their own nation first
(Pond: 17–18).

6. Polynesians, they are doing jobs now that white people wouldn't do. So
in many sectors of of the community or or life, um, we would be very much
at a loss without them, I think. Um, what I would like to see is more effort
being made to train them into skills, skilled jobs, because we are without
skilled people and a lot of our skilled people, white people, have left the
country to go to other places. I think that if we encouraged more Polynesians
and Maoris to be skilled people they would want to stay here, they're not
as, uh, nomadic as New Zealanders are (*Interviewer*. Haha.) so I think that
would be better (Pond: 18).

Now we have a bit more of the context available we can see that the
question of Polynesians returning to the Islands is related to a different
issue in each extract. In Extract Five returning is related to the problem
of 'dependence'. The speaker expresses concern that if Polynesians stay
in New Zealand they will become dependent upon their incomes to support
people in the Pacific Islands. The speaker suggests it would be better if
they returned with skills to contribute to their 'own nation'.

In Extract Six, on the other hand, returning is related to problems with
the New Zealand workforce. The speaker suggests that Polynesians are
doing dirty jobs disliked by 'whites', so their leaving would precipitate
economic problems. Moreover, she goes on to claim, the emigration of
skilled whites has left a hole in the labour market which Polynesians should
be trained to fill. So the speaker's two different versions of whether
Polynesians ought to stay or not can be seen to flow logically and naturally
from the formulations in the surrounding text. It is, of course, only sensible
to adjust one's response to a topic according to the context. However,
this kind of adjustment tends to be overlooked by the attitude researcher
who would expect the speaker to be able to articulate on a decontextualized
scale a static constant attitude regarding whether Polynesians should stay
or return. If it is not static and constant then much of the point of this
kind of measurement technology disappears.

Constitution

In traditional attitude theory, the attitude is considered to be separate from
the 'object of thought'. The entire logic of attitude measurement, where
a scale is used to compare different people's attitudes to the same object,

is based upon this. If the object is not the same for different people there is no sense in comparing attitudes and the notion ceases to have utility. However, when we come to look at the detail of people's accounts this separation becomes virtually impossible to sustain. Far from the object of thought being a simple already present entity, the object is formulated and constructed in discourse in the course of doing evaluation.

Take the following extract, for example, which is part of an answer to a question about Polynesian crime.

> 7. *Respondent.* Then again, it's a problem of their racial integration. They've got a big racial minority coming in now and so they've got to get used to the way of life and, er, perhaps rape is accepted over in Samoa and Polynesia, but not in Auckland. They've got to learn that. And the problem's that a lot of people coming in with mental disease I think it is, because there is a lot of interbreeding in those islan. . islands. And that brings a big, high increase of retards and then people who come over here, retards perhaps and they//
> *Interviewer.* // and that causes problems?
> *Respondent.* And that's pretty general I know (Johnston: 20–1).

In this passage the speaker is not just giving his views *about* 'Polynesian immigrants', he is formulating the very nature of the Polynesian immigrant. That is, he is not working with a neutral description of an object and then saying how he feels about it; he is constructing a *version* of the object. It is in this way evaluation is displayed. His version of the object carries off his evaluation. Polynesian immigrants are floridly depicted as a group who are involved in rapes and are carriers of 'mental disease'. It is implied they are from a culture which cannot control its desires properly, something they will have to learn to do before settling in New Zealand.

A central feature in this speaker's construction of 'Polynesian immigrants' is his use of broad explanatory principles. He does not rest at merely describing phenomena, he explains them too. Specifically he accounts for the prevalence of mental disease in terms of simple farmyard genetics; it is a consequence of 'interbreeding'. This drawing together of description, evaluation and broad systems of explanation is dramatically illustrated in the next extract from another speaker.

> 8. *Interviewer.* Yeah, so [crime] is partly sort of immig., its related to immigration?
> *Respondent.* Yeah, we don't, seeing them coming through, off the aircraft at night, half of them can't speak English. Um, if they can't speak English they're not going to be able to get a job, they're going to go and be in their little communities and they're not going to be able to contribute anything. And they're going to get frustrated because they're going to get bored. And they're going to, you know, there's nothing for them to do so the kids are going to start hanging around in the streets. At home Mum and Dad can't

speak English and so the kids can't speak English. They go to school and suddenly they are confronted with English – 'we can't speak that, and what do we do?' – nothing. And so by the time they get to fifteen they just drop out. They have had it up to here with school and it's not the school's fault. They have brilliant lives, they have brilliant lives back in, family lives, back in the Islands and that is where they should be (Jones: 16).

There are many fascinating features of this passage as a rhetorical construction. But the central thing to note is the way the final claim – that potential immigrants should stay in the Islands – is warranted through the use of an elaborate psychological and sociological story starting with a charged image of Polynesians slipping off the plane at night, going through language difficulties encountered by immigrants, which is taken to cause unemployment, and, eventually, the children's alienation from school. All this is contrasted with the 'brilliant family lives' available if they had not come to New Zealand. Throughout the passage we see a complex intertwining of description, explanation and evaluation.

Crucially, what we find when we examine naturally occurring discourse in detail is that the distinction between 'object of thought' and position on a 'dimension of judgment' becomes virtually impossible to make. It seems this distinction is an *artifact* of the way attitude scales are put together: all respondents are supposedly reacting to the same object of thought. Yet, as we can see from the extracts discussed in this chapter, sameness of wording does not necessarily mean that respondents will understand the terms or formulate the object of thought in an identical way. We have seen how different respondents formulate 'Polynesian immigrants', and how the *same* respondent might reformulate this notion on different occasions. If a researcher really wishes to get to grips with racism then a vital part of their activity must be the investigation of how description and explanation are meshed together and how different kinds of explanations assume different kinds of objects or supply the social world with varying objects.

One way out of this dilemma might be to argue that Extracts Seven and Eight simply illustrate the use of stereotypes of 'Polynesian immigrants' by people with 'prejudiced attitudes'. However, this interpretation relies on the idea that the speakers are using a distorted picture (the stereotype) of an unproblematic objectively identifiable category of people (Polynesian immigrants). Unfortunately categories are as complicated as 'objects of thought' (as we will illustrate in Chapter Six), and psychologists do not have access to the true, factual nature of Polynesian immigrants to allow them to assess the distortion in participants' versions (Potter and Litton, 1985: 82–4).

Rather than look at racism in terms of distorted perception, we are more concerned with looking at the racist consequences of different forms of accounting (Billig, 1987; Reeves, 1983; Wetherell and Potter, 1986, forthcoming[a]). Theories of stereotypes presume that people carry around these biased images and reproduce them on demand, while discourse analysts have noted how the same person can produce quite different stereotypical categorizations depending on the demands of the situation (Wetherell et al., 1986).

Beyond attitudes

Earlier in this chapter we illustrated three problems plaguing traditional attitude research using Marsh's study of attitudes to 'coloured immigrants' as an example. The problems were: the status of the 'object' which the attitude assesses; the dubious translation from participants' terms to analysts' categories; and the assumption that attitudes are enduring entities which generate equivalent responses from occasion to occasion. We have seen how discourse analysis deals with these problems. We will now quickly review some of the responses attitude theorists might make to the variation demonstrated in this analysis.

Marsh adopted a simple one-dimensional scale in his study; other workers have produced multidimensional scales which are intended to measure many different aspects of racist attitudes (McConahay, 1985). However, while this path to increasing methodological sophistication may provide a measure with a number of different facets, it does not avoid the general problems raised above. The variability in people's discourse cannot be explained merely as a product of a more *complex* multi-faceted attitudinal structure which a more complex scale can assess, because the views expressed vary so radically from occasion to occasion. It is impossible to argue that the claim, Polynesian immigration is desirable and the claim that it is undesirable are merely facets of one complex attitude. The notion of enduring attitudes, even multidimensional ones, simply cannot deal with this.

A social psychologist familiar with attitude research might argue that there is yet another way the attitude theorist can cope with variability and maintain the basic concept of attitude. There is, for example, the complex theory generated by Fishbein and Azjen (1975) which tries to explain why attitudes frequently fail to predict behaviour. It is commonly found in attitude research that people will say one thing, or express one kind of attitude, but then will behave in a way which is inconsistent with this attitude (Wicker, 1969). This kind of variation differs from the variation discourse analysts note as we are suggesting that what people say or their attitude will not be static either but just as variable as their behaviour. Nonetheless, we should not ignore Fishbein and Azjen's contribution.

Fishbein and Azjen (1975) argue that the path between attitudes and behaviour is indirect and muddled. When people decide to act in a certain way, their decision is only partly influenced by their relevant attitudes; it is also influenced by their judgements of the normative desirability of the action (what will other people think?) and so on. The expression of an attitude in a particular behavioural form will always be modified by many other variables. Presumably the same argument could be extended to discursive acts. The question is, can a theory of this kind explain the phenomena discourse analysis demonstrates? Do the New Zealanders we interviewed actually have underlying consistent attitudes, although they say many contrasting inconsistent things in practice? This is difficult to resolve. How can we tell, for example, which expression is the 'genuine' one, and which is merely 'normative'? There is always the danger of massive post hoc interpretation to preserve the notion of attitude. Given enough modifying variables huge flexibility in response can be explained, although there must come a point when it is no longer useful to continue stressing the underlying attitude. Our view is that a much more powerful explanation can be given if the researcher looks at the organization of discourse in relation to function and context. This kind of analysis usefully supplants attempts to decode general afunctional decontextual principles such as attitude.

In summary, a brief analysis of some extracts from interviews has highlighted the importance of a number of phenomena which have been relatively neglected in traditional attitude research. We stressed first the importance of examining context. Contextual information gives the researcher a much fuller understanding of the detailed and delicate organization of accounts. In addition, an understanding of this organization clarifies the action orientation of talk and its involvement in acts such as blaming and disclaiming.

The second phenomenon we illustrated was variability. A high degree of variation in accounts is a central prediction of the discourse approach: widely different kinds of accounts will be produced to do different things. On the other hand, considerable consistency must be predicted if participants are producing their language in the light of sets of attitudes which are stable across different contexts. Variability of the kind seen in detailed studies of discourse is thus a considerable embarrassment to traditional attitude theories.

The third phenomena we noted was the construction of the attitudinal object in discourse. The customary view is that attitudes are about distinct entities. Attitudes to immigrants, for instance, should concern an existing out-there-in-the-world group of people. Yet when we examined actual discourse this simple 'word and object' view of attitudes became unworkable. It is clear that the attitudinal object can be constituted in alternative ways, and the person's evaluation is directed at these *specific* formulations rather than some abstract and idealized object.

In response to these difficulties, the discourse approach shifts the focus from a search for underlying entities – attitudes – which generate talk and behaviour to a detailed examination of how evaluative expressions are produced in discourse. Two central and novel questions become dramatized. How is participants' language constructed, and what are the consequences of different types of construction? Whether at the end of this examination space is found for some modified notion of attitudes is, as yet, unclear (cf. Lalljee et al., 1984). All we have done in this chapter is indicate how an analyst might begin to address these questions. However, we hope we have given an initial demonstration of some of the limitations of traditional research and the promise of discourse analysis.

3

Making rules work

During the last fifteen years, as we noted in previous chapters, there has been considerable debate about the adequacy of the experimental method and the form of explanation prevalent in social psychology. The critics have castigated traditional researchers for displaying a number of vices, such as attempting to ape mythical versions of what goes on in the natural sciences, explaining all social processes by reference to the cognitions of individuals, and tending to treat all human action as a consequence of causal mechanisms. The most coherently articulated alternative to traditional research which emerged from this debate within social psychology is known as ethogenics (or the identification of the generative 'mechanisms' which give rise to behaviour) and is associated with Rom Harré and his colleagues (Harré, 1979; Harré, Clarke and De Carlo, 1985; Harré and Secord, 1972; Kroger, 1982). Instead of experiments, the methodological approach these workers advocate relies largely on the investigation of accounts; and rather than searching for causal laws, the aim is to identify the rules and conventions used by social actors to generate their behaviour.

In this chapter we are going to concentrate on one central facet of ethogenic theory: the identification of rules. Our aim is to highlight the difficulties which arise when ethogenists – or indeed any social researcher using this analytic strategy – try to extrapolate sets of rules from people's talk which are then used to explain their behaviour. It will become clear that the primary problem with this form of analysis arises from its unsystematic approach to discourse. We will start by giving a brief general introduction to the ethogenic approach and then will look in detail at one study which purports to identify social rules: Marsh et al.'s (1978) *The Rules of Disorder*; a piece of research which examined the closed and seemingly violent world of British football fans. This study will be contrasted with research conducted by discourse analysts on scientists' use of rules when choosing between different theories. Throughout the chapter we will be emphasizing the fundamental importance of making a detailed study of participants' rule discourse.

The ethogenic perspective

Linguistic competence and social competence

The clearest way to approach ethogenic theory is through its use of the basic distinction between 'competence' and 'performance'. We met this distinction in Chapter One when we discussed Chomsky's (1965) contrast between the speaker or hearer's *knowledge* of language (competence) and the actual way people *use* language in concrete situations (performance). According to this model, if we have properly identified a speaker's linguistic competence we have a means of explaining how the speaker can produce grammatical sentences – although this by no means provides a complete explanation of their speech.

Harré duplicates this argument for social life in general. He suggests that all action, whether it is performed through talk or otherwise, should be explained by reference to the actor's *'social competence'*. The possession of this social competence sets limits on the acts one can perform in social situations and determines what will be accepted as the correct performance of these acts; although, just as with linguistic competence, we need to know many additional things before we have a complete explanation of the performance of actions. As an example of this notion we can consider the actions involved in having a dinner party. The hosts are usually socially competent, in Harré's sense, that is, they know how to behave in this situation, just as an English speaker generally knows whether a sentence is grammatical or not. The guests, too, know which acts are suitable and which are not. When discussing the dinner party the next day with friends, guests and hosts can draw once more on their stock of social knowledge to give an intelligible description of what happened and to evaluate the success or failure of the party.

The central ethogenic hypothesis, therefore, is that people possess a *store* of *social knowledge* which enables them to both act and to give accounts such as explanations or justifications of their action. Important methodological consequences flow from this hypothesis. Most notably, because the same set of cognitive resources are thought to underlie *both* actions and their description/justification, it should be possible to identify the nature of specific actions by using the actor's accounts. The analysis of accounts will reveal features of people's social competence which, in turn, will reveal the significance of their acts. Thus from listening to people talk about dinner parties, the anthropologist from a non-Western society can learn the underlying social competence and thus understand what is happening when next invited to dinner.

At this point one might object that surely it would be much more straightforward to *observe* the behaviour directly, rather than follow this roundabout route of getting people to give an account of it. Unfortunately, according to Harré, this simplicity is beyond our grasp, because the actions of human beings within a culture are far more than mere movements which could be easily described and catalogued. Movements and behaviour only take on meaning in the context of specific, and often very local, social conventions. To an observer it may seem obvious that two people shaking hands are greeting one another. But this obviousness is not due to any natural relationship between the movements involved in shaking hands and the act of greeting; rather it derives from the fact that both the people shaking hands and the observer understand the same social conventions. It is these shared conventions which allow them to see the movements of hand shaking as an act of greeting.

The local nature of our conventions can be seen when we think of the problem of identifying greeting conventions in very different cultures. The observer might well think that two Maoris from New Zealand rubbing noses together were expressing intimacy – yet those familiar with the conventions of Maori culture would know that they were simply greeting each other. An untutored observer of a greeting between two British soccer fans might well conclude that they were witnessing not a friendly act but an exchange of insults. The general point ethogenists are making here is that actions have a semiological character (Swartz and Swartz, 1982; Totman, 1980). That is, the relation between brute movements and their meaning is not a natural one, but is dependent on the existence of a network of social conventions which allow certain movements to be seen as the performance of a particular act. As we saw in Chapter One, when reviewing semiology, even the basic human movements we regard as expressions of pain can mean different things in different contexts, for example when produced in a wrestling rather than a boxing match. For this reason the social researcher is dependent on the accounts, there is no way people's interpretations of their actions and understanding of social conventions can be bypassed through mere description of what goes on.

In Chomsky's theory linguistic competence is taken to be a speaker's mastery of an underlying set of rules. Harré makes the same case for social competence. He argues that it is made up from knowledge of sets of social rules which enable people to act proficiently and rationally and, furthermore, to display that proficiency and rationality (Harré, 1974, 1977b). One of the main goals of ethogenic research is thus the elucidation of the rules that make up the social and conventional knowledge of a person, subculture or society.

These rules fall into two basic classes (Collett, 1977). There are *regulative rules* which are used to guide behaviour down appropriate pathways. This concept very much resembles our everyday notion of rules: 'do not walk on the grass', 'remove your hat in church'. On the other hand, there are *interpretative rules*, which allow people to assign meaning to movements and events. The rule in games of soccer which states that kicking the ball between two white posts counts as a goal is this kind of rule: it is not just guiding behaviour, telling players how they should play soccer, it is saying that one sort of movement of the ball is to be interpreted as the act of scoring. Harré's suggestion, then, is that people draw upon a set of cognitive resources – their shared social competence made up of regulative and interpretative rules – to produce effective and legitimate social activity, and to mesh their activity with other people's actions.

Rules to order disorder

The implications of these ideas will become more vivid if we describe a specific research project. We will look at Marsh, Rosser and Harré's (1978) study of the social world of British soccer fans, one of the most elaborated examples of ethogenic research which illustrates extremely clearly the centrality of rules in this type of explanation of behaviour (Marsh, 1982).

Soccer fans and violence at football matches featured very prominently in the news media throughout the 1970s, and now in the 1980s debate still rages about causes and solutions. For many people, soccer violence seems to breach civilized values, expressing almost animalistic, aggressive drives. The principal goal of Marsh et al.'s research was to show that the apparently unrestrained, aggressive behaviour of the football fans is, in fact, tightly structured and rule bound; and thus what seems like a threatening chaos of disorderly actions is in fact closely guided by a social competence shared by the fans. If this analysis was correct, it would suggest, controversially, that soccer violence has been radically misunderstood.

The starting point for the research was a body of accounts (interviews and conversations between fans) and videos made of the fans' behaviour on the soccer terraces. From this material Marsh et al. built up a picture of the normal events in the life of a football fan and, in particular, confrontations between rival groups of football fans which provide the arena for soccer hooliganism or football violence. Confrontations typically take place between the fans who support the home team and those who have travelled to support the opposition, or the away team. The point of these confrontations seems to be to try and take over the other group's 'territory' (usually home and away fans are seated in different parts of the ground) or to make the opposition fans run away when threatened, thus acknowledging the superiority and valour of the successful group of fans. Marsh et al. argued that in the various confrontations which occur between rival groups a complex structure of rules was operating. These rules helped organize any conflict in such a way that few fans were actually hurt. Actual incident or injury, they suggest, are rare given the number of confrontations taking place, despite the picture of violence and mayhem painted in the newspapers. In their view the newspaper stories considerably overestimate the extent of the violence.

For example, Marsh et al. claim that fights between rival fans are often ended by the loser ceasing hostilities and looking downwards and away from his opponent (the participants in this study were overwhelmingly male). This display of submission would, in most instances, stop the aggression before either party was hurt. In many confrontations, there was no actual physical contact at all; both sides could satisfy the requirement that their honour be maintained by a ritual chase. The fans who did the chasing would gain the highly visible, symbolic victory of seeing the opponents off and the fans running away could often gain face or honour because of the patently tactical and risky nature of their retreat. Indeed, it seemed likely that often the point was not to catch the fleeing fans at all, because doing so might result in an actual fight. Rather, chasing was more an expressive than practical activity (Harré, 1979) – it demonstrated willingness to fight without the damaging consequences which might result from actually fighting.

Although Marsh et al. could deduce this orderly rule-guided view of events from the fans' accounts, these accounts also at times confirmed the opposing newspaper view of soccer hooliganism, namely that a great deal of actual violence does take place, many people do get hurt, and soccer matches are inherently dangerous places which sensible people should avoid. Sometimes these two sorts of accounts appeared closely intertwined in the fans' accounts.

Questioner.   What do you do when you put the boot in?
Fan A.   You kicks 'em in the head don't you?...
              Strong boots with metal toe-caps on and that.
Questioner.   And what happens then?
              [Quizzical look]
Questioner.   Well what happens to the guy you've kicked?
Fan A.   He's dead.
Fan B.   Nah – he's all right – usually anyway.

(1978: 83)

In this extract from Marsh et al.'s data Fan A formulates a picture of violent and dangerous struggle, while Fan B interrupts with a much more placid picture. The researchers, however, treat these two versions in fans' accounts very differently. They regard the placid, rule-bound picture as a more or less literal version of what goes on, as indicating the social competence, while they maintain that the violent, disorderly version presents a very inaccurate representation of football supporting. The fans know that it is not really that dangerous; indeed, the authors suggest that they are simply reproducing in part of their talk the dramatic and exaggerated story telling of the mass media evident in headlines such as 'Smash these thugs', 'Clobber boys on the rampage'.

At this point Marsh et al. make a very subtle and interesting analytic suggestion. They claim that it is the *combination* of the two kinds of accounts – one stressing disorder and violence, one stressing order and safety – which keeps the fans acting the way they do. The accounts which emphasize violence and destruction make sure that when the fans get involved in the action it will be exciting: they seem to be risking their lives! They have a rich vocabulary for constructing stories after the match about their glorious and exciting actions. Yet, at the same time, they also know it is really safe. They are not put off taking part by fear of injury. Thus, paradoxically, the fans' accounts of disorder play an essential and purposeful part in the maintenance of their local social order; they make up a functional rhetoric (Harré, 1985a) in contrast to the fans' more descriptive vocabulary, which stresses order.

For Marsh et al., then, the fans' accounts have a crucial place in the analysis of their activities in line with ethogenic research principles. Through these accounts the researchers are able to reveal the structure of rules and thus the social competence which regulates and gives meaning to the fans' action. These researchers concur with discourse analysts in finding it analytically fruitful to pay close attention to the variability in participants' discourse or the divergencies in the accounts given by the fans. Yet despite the shared focus on people's language use, and emphasis on variability, there are important differences between this ethogenic study and the perspective a discourse analyst would adopt for data of these kinds. In particular, there are damaging inconsistencies in the way discourse is interpreted in this study, as we shall now attempt to demonstrate.

Problems with ethogenics

One area in which discourse analysts and ethogenic researchers are in accord is in emphasizing the range of purposes to which language is put. It is used for explaining, justifying, cajoling, persuading; to present the speaker as worthy and competent or to accuse another. As we noted in Chapter Two, the problem for any analyst who is concerned with people's accounts is that they do not come ready labelled with the goals they are designed to achieve. Quite the reverse, unfortunately. Often accounts are constructed specifically to keep their aims hidden or, equally often, the consequences of some accounts may not be immediately clear to participants. The kind of literal and explicit speech acts which Austin focused on – 'I hereby accuse you of lying' – are very much the exception rather than the norm. This does not necessarily mean that listeners who are part of an interaction have difficulty in detecting the upshot of accounts, but their embedded, inexplicit nature presents the analyst with great problems.

The soccer fan researchers treat different parts of the fans' discourse in very different ways. For them, some parts reveal what is *actually happening* on the football terraces, while others are broadly functional: they serve to create a frisson of excitement and danger. Now, the authors claim that they are not trying to determine the *truth* of accounts, for there is no, one, true, literal account of an event; any event can be characterized in numerous different ways. Nevertheless, they treat the accounts of order as indications of the *genuine* structure of the fans' activities (although they do not take them as directly truthful). This portion of the fans' discourse is used to reveal a social reality beyond itself. Marsh et al. state:

> [The] apparently disordered events on the football terraces [ ] can be seen as conforming to a very distinct and orderly system of roles, rules and shared meanings. Action is neither chaotic nor senseless but rather is structured and reasoned. (1978: 97)

In contrast, the other set of accounts, which emphasizes senseless violence, is treated as a rhetoric which is more important for what it does than what it says. These are conspiratorial accounts, derived largely from press reports, which the fans use to retain an exciting sense of danger and as a resource for valorous display. The authors contrast what the fans really 'know' about what goes on with their rhetorical 'construction' of events.

> Since fans 'know' that this is not the case – they are aware and can tell you that few people get hurt even when things 'get out of hand' – they must conspire to construct disorder. And because there is an easy rhetoric at hand – the rhetoric of the media which insists that events at football matches are *in fact* disordered, the conspiracy is an easy one to conduct. (1978: 97)

The crucial problem, however, is that Marsh et al. offer no method or criteria for making this division into genuine and rhetorical accounts, nor do they conduct an analysis which shows that one set of accounts is important for its acute description of the fans' social world and the other for the largely imaginary sense of danger it produces. Their division is plausible – but then so is the alternative. We could easily imagine the fans drawing on the vocabulary of rule use and order to rationalize and justify their part in what is in reality a violent, senseless and potentially dangerous activity! The point is not that this alternative is any more likely to be correct, it is that Marsh et al. have not provided a principled way of deciding between them.

Observation and triangulation

At this point traditional researchers generally offer one of two solutions for overcoming the problem of deciding which of the various available accounts should be taken literally. They suggest either observation or triangulation. With observation, the accuracy of accounts is checked by comparing them to the researchers' observations; the correct accounts are those concurring with these observations. In psychology, ecological researchers have placed the most stress on this observational method (Wicker, 1979). Triangulation suggests that a variety of different accounts from different sources should be collected to allow the researcher to determine the correct version of events. This approach has been popular in areas of micro-sociology (Bogdan and Taylor, 1975; Denzin, 1978).

The first thing to note about observation is that if it were sufficient to simply observe the actions and events taking place there would be no need for the extremely complicated and time-consuming process of collecting participants' discourse. Psychologists could just watch what went on and have done with it. However, this forgets the point made earlier concerning the semiological character of action: the connection between movements and particular actions depends on knowledge of shared social conventions. This idea is fundamental to ethogenic theory, and thus observation is not an approach open to Harré and his fellow researchers.

The second point to note about observation is the assumption that actions have one, intrinsic, unitary meaning. Yet even ethologists, who have based a whole science of animal behaviour on observational research of various kinds, note that visually identical behaviours may be serving quite different functions, while visually dissimilar behaviours may be serving the same functions (Hinde, 1975). When we are dealing with humans, their linguistic and interpretative abilities make things many times more complicated. The same movements may be interpreted as performing different actions by different people, or the nature of the movements may be reassessed and reinterpreted over time (Gergen, 1982; Schutz, 1972). An event may be a demonstration to some people and a riot to others; a person may initially view a comment as a joke but later come to view it as an insult. These phenomena are a pervasive and important part of social life – they cannot be circumvented by observational research.

Triangulation or the use of 'multiple partial indicators' (Denzin, 1978) has been suggested as the other way of defusing the problem of variability in accounts. Indeed, Harré himself suggests something like this when describing the soccer research (Harré et al., 1985: 87–8). The term triangulation is, of course, derived from navigation. In the B movie, the exact position of the damaged bomber limping back from Germany is always found by triangulation. The direction of its radio signal is assessed by two geographically separated receivers, allowing an exact fix to be made on its position. In the same way, it is thought that the researcher can use discourse collected from different sources to 'home in' on the facts of the matter and thus show up some accounts as distorted or rhetorical.

This is an appealing solution. However, as we shall see in this and later chapters, when discursive data from a number of sources are examined in fine detail the information does not allow the researcher to home in on the correct version of events. The detailed studies of discourse reviewed in this book overwhelmingly indicate that the close study of documents and accounts from different sources and settings *compounds* rather than reduces the variability between participants' claims and descriptions. Indeed, in the course of attempting to triangulate the result is more often than not 'homing out', resulting in the proliferation of more and more inconsistent versions (Gilbert and Mulkay, 1984).

So we are forced back to the fundamental question. If observation and triangulation are not the solution, how should we respond to the variation between accounts? As we indicated in Chapter Two, the solution adopted by discourse analysts is not to try and resolve the variation between accounts but to make that variation a way into analysis. In the case of rules, our approach is to look at how participants' rule accounts are constructed and organized to try and reveal what is achieved by different accounts. We do not have access to Marsh et al.'s data, and so cannot undertake this exercise on the discourse of soccer fans. Discourse analyses of rules, however, have been conducted on the language of scientists, and it is to these that we now turn.

Discourse analysis and the study of scientists' rules

Why science?

It might seem odd that discourse analysts have taken scientific language as one of their central topic areas (Brannigan, 1981; Bazerman, 1984; Gilbert and Mulkay, 1982; Myers, 1985). You might think that science is an abstract, technical and precise realm, and as such can tell us little of value about the social and psychological processes operating in language. Yet it is exactly these features which make scientists' discourse such an attractive research topic. If interesting discourse processes can be found even in this rarefied environment it is extremely likely that they will also be found, probably in more exaggerated forms, in everyday conversation, newspaper stories and in all the other kinds of talk we will encounter. Science is a useful hard case where discourse analysis can hone its claims.

There are other good reasons for studying scientists' discourse. For one thing, a large proportion of scientists' discussion and writing is encoded in highly explicit forms and is readily available for research. It is fairly easy to collect scientists' discourse without disturbing their social fabric; journals and books are full of publicly available accounts and it is often possible to obtain records of naturally occurring interactions such as conferences and workshops. By collecting material in this way the researcher is able to amass what is basically a slice through the social life of one discrete realm of human activity.

With respect to the theme of this chapter, science is a place where rules abound. At one level, there are the more or less explicit practical rules and guidelines for experimentation, analysis of data and writing up results. At another level, the philosophical and sociological literature concerning the operation of science often suggests that what distinguishes scientific discussions are their adherence to generalized norms. For example, there is a norm or rule that scientists should assess all knowledge claims sceptically and independently of the status of the claimer (Merton, 1973; Zuckerman, 1977). There are in addition particular rules for the selection of theories like always select the simpler, or more testable of a pair of theories (Kuhn, 1977; Popper, 1963). Just as Marsh et al. claim that the distinctive culture of soccer fans is managed and reproduced by following a limited set of rules, so Popper, for example, suggests the same is true for science. Its distinctive culture is produced through conformity to rules such as formulate testable theories and try to refute them (Mulkay and Gilbert, 1981).

Discourse analysts have conducted a number of studies on rules and theory choice in the natural sciences (Mulkay, 1979a; Mulkay and Gilbert, 1981, 1985) but to make things more interesting we will concentrate on a study of rules in the discourse of researchers who are much closer to home, namely psychologists (Potter, 1984). The data for this study consisted of the transcripts of discussions at a major five-day international psychology conference concerned with fundamental theoretical issues. It was a particularly fertile setting for the study of rules because, at conferences, scientists are continually describing and justifying their acts of theory choice under the critical scrutiny of experts within their own field, who may respond by supporting, modifying or challenging the propriety of choices. Here scientists try to negotiate a more or less stable scientific reality, and it is exactly in this kind of situation that we ought to see them identifying the rules which, supposedly, guide and sustain their theoretical commitments.

We will concentrate here on the rule or criterion for theory choice which specifies testability. Roughly stated, this is the rule that scientists should always adopt theories which are open to empirical test and, conversely, they should never select theories which are untestable. As well as being a rule deemed fundamental by many philosophers and sociologists of science (Crane, 1980; Popper, 1963; Quine and Ullian, 1970), references to it appeared repeatedly in the data transcript.

Versions of the testability rule

The first step in the analysis of the conference data was to select from the transcript all references, however oblique, to testability or the related notions of refutability and falsifiability. It became immediately apparent from this exercise that there was no consensus in this scientific grouping with respect to either the nature or the importance of testability. In fact, the conference participants provide a whole range of different versions. For example, in the following extract we see a psychologist stressing the crucial importance of testability. (In all the extracts which follow pseudonyms have been adopted to protect the identity of those involved.)

> 1. [A] means of testing your explanation – [ ] of course that is the absolute, cardinal feature of scientific work, scientific explanation. And that's not just pointing to something that you say is important. It has the following critical value: it allows us to make progress; we can discard theories which have proved useless. (Norton: 3)

This is a very strong account of the role of testability. The speaker claims that a theory which cannot be tested is simply not scientific; for testability is not merely important but essential. Progress happens through testing explanations and rejecting those which fail these tests.

The next account is very different. The possibility of any clear test of theories is questioned because of the way data can be reinterpreted.

> 2. We can negotiate the meaning of any particular observation in virtually any direction. So that, for example, we talk about aggression, and yet it's not clear when we ever have an instance of aggression. [ ] Virtually any activity, I suspect, that I engage in any day, could be looked at as an instance of aggression in some form. [ ] it depends on the set of social agreements of what things are called. And those agreements, it seems to me, are negotiable over time, and they can be disagreed upon and writhed round in any case. So that, in effect, any theory can be sustained so long as you have a capable negotiator of reality. (Leary: 278–9)

In this view, theories can never be clearly tested against observations because the meaning of any observation is dependent on conventions which can be interpreted in different ways. The scope for flexibility is so great that a 'capable negotiator of reality' can indefinitely shape observations into line with theories. Testability is thus virtually irrelevant to scientific progress, because what is seen as a test will depend entirely on the negotiated conventions for interpreting observations.

These two illustrative extracts are comparable to the different kinds of accounts given by Marsh et al.'s soccer fans. They demonstrate that within a given social group there is no consensus about the constraining role of rules. Just as some of the football fans' accounts suggested different versions of the way rules guide activity on the terraces, so it is with these scientists' accounts. In Extract One the testability rule acts as a potent constraint on the choices of scientists; yet, in Extract Two, the very possibility of applying testability as a potent, clear-cut rule of choice is denied because of the ever-present option to reinterpret the nature of potentially falsifying data. In the case of the soccer fans, of course, Marsh et al. found that not only would different fans draw upon two inconsistent versions of rule operation but the *same* fan would describe rules variably in his or her talk. As we examine further extracts we will see that this is also true of our psychologists. There was not only variation between the psychologists' accounts of testability, there was also variation *within* psychologists' accounts.

The illustration of variation between accounts is analytically useful because it reminds us of the dangers of taking accounts at face value as accurate descriptions. If we had examined either one of these extracts alone, we might have taken it as a description of the role played by the criterion of testability in the scientific specialty we know as psychology. However, when we examine such contradictory extracts together the folly of this approach becomes clear. Testability cannot be *both* a clear-cut, potent criterion *and* a rule which can be interpreted to fit any set of data.

Nevertheless, the identification of these sorts of variations is only a preliminary stage in discourse analysis. On its own, it provides no way of inferring the sorts of functions performed by different passages of discourse. To get to a functional level of analysis much more attention must be paid to the patterning or organization of different versions and the way they are constructed. To achieve this end we looked in this study at the varying accounts given of testability when speakers are depicting the criterion with respect to their own work and then work they disagree with.

The organization of variation

The following extract illustrates a phenomenon which appeared repeatedly in the conference transcript we analyzed. It is interesting and illuminating because the speaker characterizes testability very differently at different stages in his presentation. Because rather more detailed interpretations than we have made up to now are required, we will number the sentences so that the separate parts of the extract can be referred to accurately. Thus (3–4) is a reference to some features of sentences 3 and 4 of the extract.

3. (1) I would like to return to this game of I am more refutable than you.
(2) I said *refutable*, not reputable, although you can be forgiven for misunderstanding that. (3) [laughter] [ ] (4) Um, they all, everyone pretty

well has paid lip service to refutation. (5) It is interesting to notice the strat, the different strategies that people, er, have used. (6) Um, since Norton spoke such a lot it is a pity he is not here. (7) It's, I would like to draw attention to his, which is very clearly to say: [changes tone of voice] 'leave me alone, I am doing very well in my own small corner' – you know – 'go and die in your own'. (8) [laughter] (9) Although he says that every-body has a duty to [create large-scale theories] he is not trying to produce, um, larger, more ambitious models which are, of course, much easier to, er, refute, er, than the less ambig, ambitious ones. [ ]

(10) The good guys are the ones who *are* leaving hostages to fortune, who really *are* laying themselves open to being knocked down in all possible ways. (11) The good guys are the people who are putting up the biggest possible theory that they can imagine and, um, hoping that, um, it won't be knocked down too quickly. [ ] (12) Among these people I would put Squire, um, Chester – I apologize if I have missed anybody else out – I can't remember all the things that have happened in the, in this meeting. (13) But I can, of course, remember what I said, and I am one of the good guys. (14) [laughter] (Young: 270–2).

In this extract, the same speaker, Young, draws upon two rather different versions of theory choice, resembling the different versions documented in Extracts One and Two above. In the first version – in, roughly, sentences 1–9 – the criterion of testability is said to be used strategically (5); it is depicted as being inconsistently invoked in support of Norton's theory at the expense of others (7–9). In contrast, in relation to the speakers' own theory, the criterion is depicted as an effective constraint on action. Refutation is removed from the speaker's sphere of social control; all he can do is hope that his theory will not be undermined by the evidence – it is a 'hostage to fortune' which will be rejected or retained by virtue of the data alone (12–13). Unlike Norton, he is unable to influence whether or not his theory will be found wanting.

It is worth pointing out that this kind of combination of strong criticism and self-praise is tricky to manage – it can easily be heard as persecution and boasting (McKinlay and Potter, 1987; Pomerantz 1978; 1984). In this extract we see Young skilfully using humour to deflect any potentially negative attributions of this kind (Mulkay and Gilbert, 1982a).

So, what is the significance of these two different versions? What is Young doing with these two ways of formulating the rule? To address this question we can look at the way Young presents his own and Norton's agency. On the one hand, the rule of testability is depicted as operating on Young's own theory quite *independently* of his agency. In effect, he stands back and waits to see if the data overthrow the theory which is a hostage to fortune. The rule of testability is applied impersonally and allows clear-cut decisions to be made. Young thus represents his own position, albeit humorously, as fully conforming to the canons of empirical science where the data are the most crucial consideration in theory choice and personal interests become irrelevant. In this way, the account provides strong legitimation for his scientific claims.

On the other hand, Young also depicts the rule of testability as open to Norton's strategic manipulation. Norton is said to inconsistently invoke the rule to support his own theory at the expense of others, producing theories so small in scale that they are not likely to be overthrown by the evidence. The nature of the rule is thus seen very differently in this case; testability is no longer a clear-cut and impersonal constraint on the scientist's actions but part of a rhetorical display. By depicting Norton's theoretical claims and actions in this fashion, the account undermines them.

As with earlier extracts, if we examined this passage of Young's talk in isolation we might well interpret it as an unproblematic description of the way the testability rule has been applied to two different theories. When we compare this account to others, however, the inconsistencies are such that one cannot conclude that Young is simply correctly describing the difference between his own and Norton's theories. For example, in the next extract we will examine, Norton's theory is presented as unambiguously open to testing and Squire's as resistant to this testing – the very *reverse* of Extract Three!

But before going on to discuss the implications of this next step in the functional analysis of rule discourse it is worth briefly pointing out one of the procedures that discourse analysts have used to confirm claims of this kind. (A more detailed discussion can be found in Chapter Eight). This procedure is best described as confirmation through exception.

Confirmation through exception

In our analysis of the rule of testability we seem to have found a regularly occurring pattern of accounting. The testability rule is not used equally with all theories, one's own theory tends to be described as unproblematically testable while other scientists are portrayed as strategically attempting to avoid this rule. We hypothesized that this regularity can be explained in terms of the functioning of the accounts for the criticism of others versus self-justification. However, what of exceptions to the regular pattern? If the proposed functional hypothesis is correct it ought to make sense of *both* the pattern regularly found in the data and the exceptions. That is, the analyst must predict that there will be special features of the organization of the exceptions which allow them to fulfil the required function in some other way. If these predictions do not work out, of course, then the analyst will need to start reassessing the adequacy of their explanation.

In the study of the testability rule in psychologists' conference discourse we found just one exception to the pattern of own theory described as testable, other theory described as resisting testing. The exception can be found in Extract Four. Unusually, in this passage, the speaker fashions an account which depicts his own theory as actually *less* testable than certain other theories. Although it is a rather long extract, it repays detailed examination as it is a superb rhetorical construction.

4. Could I just say a quick word about falsification, because I think it is really a rather important topic. And I think part of the troubles that arise in trying to get a handle on it, as a practical working scientist, is that it is quite different, it has a quite different character depending upon the type of theory that you are operating with. If you are operating with a theory which has a well-established deductive structure then the, er, the refutatory process is, relatively speaking, logical [ ]. Now that's okay, and that's I think the structure of what we have been calling mini-theories, i.e. theories which are sufficiently small-scale to be articulatable in that deductive form. [ ] But I think the case that's much more interesting is the sort of theorizing at the level of which I was talking of this morning: molecular theory of gases; evolutionary theory; [Squire's own theory]; those kind of theories which contain the [specified] structure [ ]. And it may be that a really powerful theory contains within itself enough, as it were, potential material, as indeed the molecular theory of gases did, to go on with, through a great deal of traditional refutatory procedures and still survive as the theory in the field. And Darwinian theory has also been through the same kind of game. Now the theory I was trying to outline this morning has just that character; that is, it is a theory for providing a conceptual system. But it does have – although Young, of course, sees it as having pseudopodia which are put a fair way into the, into the refutable world – at least I would also claim for it that it has a certain measure of elasticity and that *it is not going to be too darn easy to refute.* (Squire: 273–4)

The first thing to note about this passage is that it is an almost total inversion of the previous extract we considered. Like Extract Three, it employs two very different images of the way the testability rule operates: as a clear-cut, logical process which effectively constrains theory choice, and as a flexible, negotiable process where no data on their own can force choice. However, the attribution of the two images is reversed. Opponents' theory choices are depicted as resulting from the impersonal, data-driven rule, while the speaker characterizes his own choice as negotiable and less dependent on experimental findings: in effect, less testable.

When we spell it out in this bald way, it is hard to reconcile this with our suggestion that these scientists are depicting their own theories as testable to justify them. Perhaps our analysis is confused or, worse, perhaps it is wrong! A close examination of the passage suggests another interpretation. We can see that Squire fashions a wide-ranging historical account of the nature of theories in science to display a lack of testability as a *positive* feature of certain theories. He does this by characterizing classic theories from the natural sciences, such as the molecular theory of gases and evolutionary theory, as not being clearly refutable. The charge that all theories ought to be refutable is thereby made equivalent to the extremely implausible claim that certain classic and profound theories are not properly scientific. And by characterizing his own theory as a member of this class Squire equates it with theories which are usually seen as the very pinnacle of scientific achievement and, at the same time, indicates that its lack of refutability is an asset rather than a fault.

When we look at the detailed structure of this exceptional extract, then, we can see it is performing the same justificatory function as the previous one. The speaker is depicting his own theory as the better, more powerful, more scientific one. It inverts the idea that better theories should be more testable, but warrants this inversion by offering 'lessons' from the history of science. The very fact that the speaker feels it necessary to provide this detailed warrant shows that he is orientating to the expectation that better theories should be more testable. Thus a close examination of this exceptional passage provides further confirmation of the operation of the more standard pattern of discourse.

Squire's difficulty in sustaining this non-standard version of testability can be seen when he is faced with a theory which he feels has been undermined by empirical findings. Here his non-standard view would make it hard to criticize the theory and so Squire reverts to the more familiar pattern.

> 5. The survival by a thousand qualifications ah, is, er is what goes on. And certainly [the specified] theory is a beautiful example of that. The more the theory got refuted the more distinctions that were made. Now, of course, that is a technique which you can use. But it has, as it were, nothing to do with the logic of the case. And one would then query the motives of the people engaged. (Squire: 276)

When Squire's *own* theory flexibly avoids refutation that is a good thing; it is only doing what great theories have done in the past. When the same procedure is followed with a theory Squire opposes, he suggests that this is not an acceptable, rational process, but a situation where motives should be questioned.

Testability, soccer violence and the analysis of rules

We have now indicated how a discourse analyst might approach the topic of rule use. The analyst would start by examining the manifold ways rules are formulated in participants' discourse and then go on to look at the organization of these different accounts. With respect to the rule that theories should be testable we found an important asymmetry between accounts of the rule with respect to the speakers' own theories and those of their opponents and critics. This asymmetry was understood in terms of the functions served by the different accounts in buttressing speakers' own positions and making opponents' positions problematic. In addition, these findings have important implications for the philosophy and sociology of science, but that is another story (Potter, 1984).

Although Marsh et al. reached the stage of showing variability in accounts of the rule-bound nature of life on the terraces, they did not go on to look at the *organization* of these different accounts. They speculated about functions but did not attempt to reveal them through systematic analysis. Instead they introduced the idea that some accounts are simply rhetoric for generating excitement in order to resolve the difficulty of providing a coherent explanation of hooliganism at soccer matches when faced with the variable and contradictory nature of fans' accounts. Their resolution works by dismissing one subset of accounts as fantastical while treating another as providing genuine information about what the fans actually do.

The variation which discourse analysts have found in rule accounts of scientific theory choice is very similar to that found in soccer fans' discourse. Some accounts stress the constraining force of rules and others claim the rules have little practical effect. However, instead of assuming that one of these versions is correct and attempting to choose between them, discourse analysts have tried to demonstrate that *both* serve important functions and thus explain them in this manner. Of course, without a full study of football fans' talk we cannot say that this will necessarily be true of the soccer discourse, but it is at the very least a plausible alternative to the explanation provided.

The findings from these studies of scientists' rule use are quite consistent with Wieder's research on the convict code described in Chapter One. Both pieces of research emphasize the reflexive dimension of rule talk: talk is not just *about* actions and events but it is also a potent working part of these things. The realistic model which would treat this talk as basically a descriptive medium is flawed. It would be impossible to integrate the highly divergent versions we saw in Extracts One and Two into a single set of facts, or to sensibly accommodate the many subtle differences between Extracts Three and Four. It is only when we start to look at the functions to which the talk is put that we can begin to fully understand what is happening in social life. The scientists are using the rule of testability just as the inmates are using 'the Code' – to persuade, justify and criticize.

Both studies also indicate how participants draw upon rules in an occasioned fashion. That is, the meaning of the rule is expressed in a way appropriate to the speaker's context. It is not the case that rules somehow carry implicit instructions for their precise and proper application; the way they are applied is, in fact, as much dependent on people's constructive use of language. The inmates in Wieder's study creatively depicted certain of their actions as governed by the code to achieve a whole range of goals (Heritage, 1984). The scientists flexibly drew on the notion of testability to construct a coherent and convincing version of the way their own and others' theories were chosen. The degree of flexibility possible was graphically shown in Extract Four where, in an impressive rhetorical construction, Squire inverted the evaluation of testability which was standard elsewhere. In each of these studies, then, rules are seen to operate not as templates or mechanical guides, as part of a 'competence', but as symbolic resources used to perform specific tasks.

The general problem for researchers such as Harré, who wish to explain behaviour through the control of rules, is that there can be no neutral, disinterested statement of rules and how they are applied. Harré sees rules as part of a person's social competence, but this competence can only be revealed through a study of performance data, namely talk. And, given the reflexive and contextualized nature of rule talk shown in Wieder's work and analyses of scientists' discourse, any extrapolations from performance to competence require extreme caution. The danger is that the researcher will fall into their subjects' trap and adopt the factual view of the world they offer. To prevent this, we need the much more comprehensive study of rule talk provided by discourse analysis.

4

Accounts in sequence

So far in this book we have used the notion of accounts to refer generally to any passage of talk or writing. However, there is a more restricted technical sense of this term marking out the discourse produced when people are explaining actions which are unusual, bizarre or in some way reprehensible (Scott and Lyman, 1968). If you are caught doing something which appears odd – perhaps someone walks into your room while you are wearing your underwear on your head – you will want to *account* for your behaviour; you might, for example, explain that you are exploring possibilities for Saturday's fancy dress ball. If this account is successful your behaviour will seem rather less odd.

These kinds of accounts are intrinsically interesting because they are such a habitual feature of language use; they are notable, too, because social psychologists have recently paid some attention to this topic area (Semin and Manstead, 1983; Snyder et al., 1983). We thus have an opportunity to evaluate the achievements of current experimental methods and social psychological theories when they are turned on a central area of language function. These achievements can be compared with those emerging from the discipline of conversation analysis which takes a more naturalistic orientation to the study of discourse and accounts. This chapter will hence serve the dual function of describing some mainstream social psychological research while introducing an increasingly important analytic perspective on language.

Accounts and social psychology

Austin's work is undoubtedly the best place to begin any examination of accounts. We should particularly note his influential article, 'A Plea for Excuses', which appeared in 1961, as this paper acted as a basic starting point for many of our contemporary ideas about this subject.

Austin's plea for excuses

Austin claimed that there are two important reasons why we should study excuses. First, as excuses occur in situations where there has been some failure or breakdown in normal conduct, their study may clarify the nature of the normal. As Austin put it, excuses 'help us penetrate the blinding veil of ease and obviousness that hides the mechanisms of the natural successful act' (1961). Some light might be thrown on the way social order is produced in a society. The study of *fractures* and their *repair* should illuminate how social frameworks emerge.

The second reason for studying excuses is their significance for understanding the *causes* of action. Austin argued, for example, that a major breakthrough might be possible with the perennial philosophical problem of free will if it were refocused on the kinds of things which people treat as interfering with their actions. He suggested that rather than discuss free will in abstract terms we should look at the procedures people use when *accounting* for freedom and constraint in those cases where breakdowns occur and excuses or justifications are required. We are all familiar with the apocryphal defendant in the dock who explains their crime by saying 'I am just a victim of a broken home, Your Honour'. This defendant is providing an excuse or an account but his statement could also be taken as evidence for the causes of his behaviour. Austin advocated a systematic conceptual investigation of talk of this kind, rather than naive acceptance of its import.

Both of these points are mirrored in the way ethnomethodologists have organized their research. Garfinkel (1967), notoriously, sent his students out on exercises which involved disturbing the social fabric in an attempt to understand it better. For instance, they were asked to barter in shops for fixed price items like toothpaste (this could be surprisingly effective) or to imagine that they were strangers in their own home. The idea is not unlike the goals of high energy physicists when they shoot protons at matter and study the tracks of the breakdown particles. Or imagine taking different parts out of a car engine – the air filter, say, or the horn – to see the effect on its running. In addition, ethnomethodologists have commonly used the strategy of taking issues typically construed from a philosophical perspective and looking at their importance for participants themselves. For them also, the problem of free will should be translated into the question of how people depict constraints on their actions when giving accounts and excuses, how they *formulate* freedom or constraint, and what these formulations achieve.

Austin's paper contained a wealth of interesting ideas about the language of excuses. However, his most important legacy to social psychology was the clear distinction he made between two main species of accounts: justifications and excuses. Austin observed that when someone is accused of acting in a bad, untoward or shocking way, these two alternative strategies are open to the person: they can provide either a justification or give an excuse.

Excuses are accounts which admit the relevant act was bad in some way, but claim performance was influenced or caused by some external agency.

Thus you might excuse late arrival at a meeting by noting that the alarm clock failed. Justifications, on the other hand, do not involve the denial of responsibility, instead they claim certain actions are in fact good, sensible or at least permissible in the circumstance. A person might justify stealing by the suggestion that all property is theft and it is a good thing to redistribute wealth.

Accounts and typologies

Austin's basic distinction between justifications and excuses was later taken up by two sociologists, Marvin Scott and Stanford Lyman, in their 1968 paper on accounts. Scott and Lyman made a number of interesting although often rather speculative points, but their main goal was to produce a typology of accounts. Hence they identified different species of excuses such as the appeal to accident ('I tripped up'), to mental elements ('I forgot'), to natural drives ('I was so hungry, I couldn't help myself') and scapegoating ('Kevin caused me to do it'). In addition, Scott and Lyman followed Sykes and Matza (1957) in identifying a number of different techniques of justification: denial of injury ('I can't see what the fuss is about, it's only a scratch'), denial of victim ('she deserved everything she got') and appeal to loyalties ('I owed it to Brian'). They stressed that both justifications and excuses are highly conventional acts: they take certain standard forms and are couched in certain socially approved vocabularies (Mills, 1940). The point is that people are not inventing these accounts anew but drawing from a range of pre-existing resources.

The next development we should note in the study of accounts arose from a more social psychological perspective and is associated with the work of Gün Semin and Tony Manstead (1983) who provided an extremely useful integrative overview of the field. They, too, emphasized the conventional nature of accounts and saw the generation of a comprehensive and systematic typology as an important task. Their typology added three new categories to excuses and justifications: *apologies* (Goffman, 1971; Schlenker, 1980; Tedeschi and Riess, 1981), *requests* (Goffman, 1971) and *disclaimers* (Hewitt and Stokes, 1975).

Apologies are the kind of accounts which neither mitigate responsibility for the suspect act nor attempt to justify it. Instead the apology acknowledges that an offence has taken place and implies that the transgression will not recur. Requests are accounts used before the act occurs in an attempt to licence what might be perceived as a violation. Like apologies, they admit the potential offence. For instance, if you simply take a cigarette from someone else's pack this could be highly offensive – but it can be transformed by the use of a request: 'do you mind if I cadge one of your cigarettes?' In fact, it is not easy to turn down requests of this kind without seeming miserly or unfriendly.

Disclaimers are the third new category. As we noted in Chapter Two, these are pre-accounts which attempt to ward off anticipated negative attributions in advance of an act or statement. To recapitulate, the typical form for a disclaimer might be: 'I am no sexist but . . .' followed by a negative comment about women. People use disclaimers when they are about to do or say something which is likely to be interpreted as coming from someone with a particular identity, in this case a sexist. The disclaimer attempts to prevent the listener interpreting the talk in terms of this noxious identity by acknowledging the possible interpretation and then denying it (Hewitt and Stokes, 1975).

Semin and Manstead integrated these various genera of accounts into a sort of super-typology intended to cover all possible excuses and justification. A shortened version of the typology is reproduced in Figure 4.1. This is an extremely useful exercise, but, as they themselves note, taxonomies need to be supplemented by research on the use and effectiveness of accounts.

Accounts and experiments

We will briefly describe just two experimental studies on the effects of accounts, because our concern is more with the general style of research than the detailed findings, and the great difficulties facing any researcher who attempts to sensibly capture this subtle form of discourse in an experimental manipulation. The studies selected illustrate two common trends in this line of research: the use of written stories – 'vignettes' – and the attempt to look at accounts in more realistic settings via field work.

Schlenker and Darby (1981) presented people with a written scenario or vignette concerning bumping into others in a public place and then asked them to imagine they were the central character. The scenario was manipulated to show the offender – the person doing the bumping – as having either high or low responsibility and the consequences as either serious or trivial. The subjects' task was to select the appropriate response from a list including apologies, excuses, justifications and simple acknowledgements.

Not surprisingly, Schlenker and Darby found that apologies were the most favoured response and as responsibility for the incident and the damaging consequences increased the apology became more elaborate and self-blaming. Merely saying 'pardon me' was satisfactory for a slight bump, while a more extended apology was given for a painful knock.

Another study staged in a Toronto metro station, involved a briefcase being kicked over (Ungar 1981). The offender who did the kicking was either high or low status (they wore different sorts of clothes in each condition) and there were three different levels of excuse: the offender

FIGURE 4.1
A synthetic typology of accounts

A   Excuses

A1   *Denial of intent* ('I did not intend to produce these results')
       Accident
       Unforseen consequences due to:
          lack of knowledge, skill, motivation or environment
       Identity of target person mistaken

A2   *Denial of volition* ('I did not want to perform this act')
       Physical causes
          temporary (e.g. fatigue)
          semi-permanent (e.g. paralysis)
       Psychological causes originating in:
          self (e.g. insanity)
          others (e.g. coercion)
       Lack of authority ('I would like to help, but I do not have the
          authority')

A3   *Denial of agency*
       Mistaken identity ('It wasn't me, honest')
       Amnesia ('I can't remember anything about it')
       Joint production ('It wasn't only me who did it')

A4   *Appeal to mitigating circumstances* ('I am not entirely to blame')
       Scapegoating – behaviour was a response to others
       Sad tales – arrangement of facts highlighting dismal past

B   Justifications

B1   *Claim that effect has been misrepresented*
       Denial of injury (no harm done)
       Minimization of injury (consequences only trivially harmful)

B2   *Appeal to principle of retribution*
       Reciprocity (victim deserving of injury because of his/her actions)
       Derogation (victim deserving of injury because of his/her qualities)

B3   *Social comparison*
       (Others do same or worse but go unnoticed, unpunished or even praised)

B4   *Appeal to higher authority*
       Powerful person(s) commanded
       Higher status person(s) commanded
       Institutional rules stipulated

B5   *Self-fulfilment*
       Self-maintenance (catharsis, psychological or physical health)
       Self-development (personal growth, mind expansion)
       Conscience (acted in accordance with)

B6   *Appeal to principle of utilitarianism*
       Law and order
       Self-reliance
       Benefits outweigh harm

B7   *Appeal to values*
       Political (e.g. democracy, socialism, nationalism)
       Moral (e.g. loyalty, freedom, justice, equality)
       Religious (e.g. charity, love, faith in deity)

B8   *Appeal to need for facework*
       Face maintenance ('If I hadn't acted like that I would have lost credibility')
       Reputation building ('I did that because I wanted to look tough')

Source: Semin and Manstead, 1983: 91–2. Slightly shortened.

either simply walked away after kicking the case over or said 'you shouldn't have left it there, someone might have tripped over it', or a confederate – a person acting the role of an ordinary bystander – said, 'she shouldn't have left it there, someone might have tripped over it'.

Following the staged incident, someone nearby who had witnessed the event was selected and asked about the extent of the offender's blame for the incident. Any disparaging remarks were noted down as an index of derogation. Ungar found the offender was blamed less when an excuse was provided but that the status of the offender did not effect the amount of blame, although it did cut down the number of derogatory remarks.

As we indicated in Chapter Two, there has been a great deal of discussion in social psychology concerning the general adequacy of the kind of experimental methods used in these two studies. It is not our intention to rehearse the various positions in this controversy here. Indeed, in the light of recent philosophy and sociology of science, we would suggest there are no perfect methods and the use of any technique involves a complex balancing of pros and cons (Barnes, 1982; Chalmers, 1980; Collins, 1985). Nonetheless there are some points which should be made specifically in relation to language function. These concern the naturalistic status of the research, the anonymity of participants and the way the context was conceptualized.

Drawbacks to experiments on accounts

The problem of experimental naturalism, or ecological validity as it is often known (Brunswik, 1955), is a thorny one. While some workers have expressed worries about the possibility of adequately duplicating 'real world' phenomena in the laboratory (Harré and Secord, 1972: 44–66), others have argued that the quality of experiments does not depend in any way on successfully mimicking aspects of social life. From this point of view the crucial issue is the skilful operationalization of variables which might appear in very different forms outside the laboratory (Turner, 1981). The difficulty with experiments on accounts lies at a rather more basic level.

The problem with research using vignettes, as Schlenker and Darby themselves admit, is that data are essentially dependent on participants' *theories* of how they would behave in the circumstances detailed in the vignette. The dependent measure is not what the participants *actually* do or say in a real situation but what they *imagine* they would do or say. And there may be all the difference in the world between being confronted with a situation in a vignette and in real life.

The same sort of problem arises with Ungar's study. However, here the crucial imaginings belong to the researchers and confederates when they *construct* a naturalistic scenario for their experiment in the real world. Are participants responding simply to the bald provision of an excuse (the identified dependent variable) or to some more subtle feature of the way the confederates of the experiment design their conduct? The problem when dealing with accounts is that any wooden style of presentation or bad acting might be construed as a sign of the inauthenticity of the excuse giver. That is, it might be taken to indicate they do not really mean what they say. Furthermore, as we will see later in the chapter, participants pay close attention to the *delay* in responding when accounts are relevant to events that have just happened and this is the sort of variable which is difficult to properly control in contrived field experiments.

The second problem with these studies of accounts is a classic one in social psychological experiments – the participants are predominantly strangers to one another. Exactly why this is crucial for the study of accounts becomes clear when we consider the close association with issues of politeness and formality. If you don't account for some item of misconduct people may well think you are rude; in formal settings when strangers are present accounts may be particularly elaborate and ceremonial. Both the form and content of accounts may be very different when produced between friends or between acquaintances and strangers (Brown and Levinson, 1978).

The third problem concerns context. The experiments described above abstract particular linguistic forms – excuses and justifications – from their contexts of use and treat them as basic variables. That is, accounts are viewed outside the specific sequences of talk in which they are typically produced and examined in terms of their relationship to predefined outcomes. This neglects both the detailed organization of accounts and their position in particular ongoing sequences of discourse. As we will see, it is precisely these phenomena, overlooked in traditional experimental studies, which are vitally important in understanding the nature and use of accounts. These problems suggest that it may be useful to take an alternative analytic approach to the study of accounts, and conversation analysis is one alternative which has grown increasingly important in the last few years.

Conversation analysis and accounts

Conversation analysis is a youthful discipline focused on people's talk. It is concerned with how the contributions of different speakers are meshed together in conversations and the way different types of actions – blamings, greetings, excuses – are produced and managed. Its initial development owes much to the late Harvey Sacks and his collaborators Emanuel Schegloff and Gail Jefferson. Like other notable twentieth-century figures, such as Saussure, Austin, George Mead and Wittgenstein, Sacks had published relatively little before his premature death. Much of his impact has thus been due to his lecture notes which were copied and privately circulated.

The principal locus of this work is the events of everyday, mundane conversation. Everyday conversation may be simple chatter but it is by no means trivial. In terms of the historical origins of language, conversation predates the development of written forms of communication. In developmental terms, the ability to take part in conversational exchanges seems to be a crucial part of becoming a person (Garvey, 1984; Shotter, 1984). Moreover, conversation is all-pervasive. When we are not working, sleeping or watching television what we are doing mostly is nattering away to one another. Sacks argued (and a similar point is made by Moscovici, 1984a – see Chapter Seven) that this talk has an essential part to play in the creation and maintenance of our social worlds, and would be a good candidate for the primary psychological reality, if one were looking for such a thing (Beattie, 1983).

Conversation analysis is very much an outgrowth of ethnomethodological research, and shares a number of its main concerns (Heritage, 1984). However, its analytical approach is rather different. It concentrates on what are, at first sight, the minutiae of naturally occurring conversations represented in verbatim transcript. Typically, analysts will study a number of instances of one phenomenon and try to elucidate its systematic properties. As studies have accumulated it has become possible to describe the elaborate and detailed architecture of conversation (Levinson, 1983).

This perspective gives us a very different path to understanding accounts. Instead of attempting to experimentally relate them to broad variables such as the severity of the violation, or status, accounts are examined as they occur, in context, embedded in conversational sequences. Conversation analysts argue that to find out how accounts work, they must be studied in terms of their sequential position in talk. It is necessary for us to become familiar with some of these basic sequential properties so we can see the point of the analysis conducted in this tradition. For the next few pages we will go on a detour to illuminate the primary conversation analytic notions of 'adjacency pairing' and 'preference structure'. Only then will we return, better equipped, to the topic of accounts.

Adjacency pairs

Conversation analysts have observed that many of the more general properties of dialogue and the way it is meshed together can be explained in terms of a small set of principles which govern the changeover of speakers (Sacks et al., 1974). Changeovers are remarkably orderly with speakers predicting the ends of utterances in such a way that there is usually not much overlap of talk or many gaps between utterances. Typically, there are more gaps *within* a speaker's turn of talk than between turns. Within this general turn organization conversational analysts have noted a further structural feature known as *adjacency pairing* which is relevant to the specific acts performed in the discourse.

At first glance the phenomenon of adjacency pairing seems hardly startling. Typical examples of adjacency pairs are questions and answers, greetings and return greetings, offers and acceptances, assessments and second assessments. These have a first part produced by one speaker and a second part produced by another. They are also *typed*, so that a particular first – a question, say – requires a second from a restricted range of utterances – most likely an answer (Schegloff and Sacks, 1973). It is tempting to think that this is exactly the sort of truism which gives social scientists a bad name. But these rather simple initial observations serve as a base allowing conversation analysts to describe complex organizations of talk which are far from obvious.

The first thing to note about adjacency pairs is that the adjacency should not be interpreted strictly. The second part of the pair is not always exactly adjacent to the first. For instance, *insertion sequences* are commonly found. Thus in the following extract certain things have to be sorted out before the question is answered.

1. Q1. Kevin. What's on next?
   Q2. Jane.   On this channel or Four?
   A2. Kevin. Four.
   A1. Jane.   Ah, it's that thing on the Sandinistas.

Before Jane answers Kevin's question she checks on its specific meaning; a second question/answer adjacency pair is inserted into the first. As everyone knows, sequences of this kind can get quite complicated as, at times, a considerable number of things have to be dealt with before the second part is offered.

So adjacency here does not mean the second part will immediately follow the first; instead conversation analysts suggest the relation is one of *conditional relevance* (Schegloff, 1968). That is, given that the first part of an adjacency pair has been uttered, the second part is immediately *relevant* and *expected* – although its actual production may depend on sorting out a variety of other things. The first and second parts are not bound together by a strict rule; the uttering of the first sets up normative expectations to which speakers must attend (Goffman, 1981; Heritage, 1984).

The operation of these expectations can be seen in sequences like the following (the figures in brackets are pauses timed in seconds – see the Appendix for a full glossary of transcription conventions).

```
2. A:  Is there something bothering you or not?
       (1.0)
   A:  Yes or no
       (1.5)
   A:  Eh?
   B:  No.
```
                        (Atkinson and Drew, 1979: 52)

The fact that A repeats the question is evidence that an answer is expected (and the truncated form of the repeat shows that A does not think B has merely not heard). Indeed, the question is repeated twice until an answer is (grudgingly) forthcoming. It is possible to point to many of these phenomena which show the conditional relevance of adjacency pairs (Atkinson and Drew, 1979) and suggest this is a central organizational principle of conversation.

The usefulness of this notion seems rather blunted by the observation that there are often quite a wide range of potential second parts available (Levinson, 1983). For example, if the first part of the pair is a question, apart from an answer the second part might be a protest of ignorance ('haven't a clue'), a re-route ('ask Dick'), a refusal ('I'm not commenting') or a challenge to presuppositions ('I think you are barking up the wrong tree'). On the face of it, this means the adjacency pair is a rather looser organization than it first appeared. But, there is a further organizational principle at work which allows us to order these different possibilities, known as *preference structure*.

Preference structure

Preference structure is the idea that the second parts of adjacency pairs can be ranked into responses which are preferred and responses which are dispreferred. Thus the preferred response to questions is an expected answer while the dispreferred response is a non-answer or unexpected answer. The preferred response to an invitation is an acceptance and the dispreferred a refusal. It should immediately be emphasized that the notion of preference is not meant to describe psychological desires or dispositions. A speaker may be personally very keen to refuse an invitation but this does not stop the refusal being, in normative terms, a dispreferred act. The concept of preference is used to indicate a *normative ranking* of different responses exhibited in the organization of talk.

The following question/answer sequence is typical of those where the second part of the pair is preferred (the large bracket indicates the point where one speaker's talk starts to overlap the talk of another speaker).

```
3. Hanna:  Is Wednesday definitely early closing ⌈ day?
   Alan:                                         ⌊ Umhum
```

The first part of the pair is a question and the second an expected answer; that is, an answer related closely to the possibilities raised in the question. There are a number of features of the way the answer is delivered which are characteristic of preferred responses. First, the response is produced with a minimum of delay, in fact in this case Alan's answer is given in slight overlap. Second, it is a brief response, which means the answer component of the turn is delivered straight away – the speaker does not add any extraneous material before introducing the answer. Third, there is no qualification or hedging in the answer – it is clear-cut and positive.

We can contrast this with a sequence involving a dispreferred second. The following comes directly after Extract Three (for clarity, Alan's response has been split into different components).

4. Hanna:	1.	There's no point in going then at all
	2.	(1.0)
Alan:	3.	Well
	4.	not uh I mean
	5.	the major shops will probably be open

Here Alan disagrees with Hanna's assessment about the shopping trip (the preferred second part of this pair would, of course, have been agreement). Again, there are characteristic features to the delivery. First, there is a delay component (2). Alan only starts to respond after a pause of about a second. Then the response is prefaced by the term 'well' (3). This both marks the dispreferred status of the response and increases the delay before the disagreement is broached. Third, when disagreement is formulated (4) it is done so rather weakly – contrast 'not uh I mean' with the 'no' or 'certainly not' which Alan could have said.

At this point we can return to the central topic of this chapter: accounts. There is a fourth feature which distinguishes preferred and dispreferred seconds; dispreferred seconds almost invariably include an account. This extract is no exception. Alan *justifies* his disagreement by providing information about the quality of the shopping (5). That is, rather than simply do the disagreeing and leave it at that, he *accounts* for his disagreement with Hanna. In general, accounts are a recurrent and routine component of dispreferred seconds. The detailed content of dispreferred seconds may be extremely varied but their organization is highly regular. In most cases an account is included, usually in the same position as Extract Four.

Take another example. In this case the first part is a question and the dispreferred response is the refusal to answer the question (note that = indicates words run together, (.) indicates a short but noticeable pause, : indicates extension of vowel sounds). The speakers are talking about a film called *Justice for All*.

5. Dave: 1.   What's in *Justice for=All*
           2.   (0.3)
   Paul: 3.   Its (.) ah (.) its about
           4.   (1.0)
           5.   Well
           6.   you've got na:h I'm not going to tell you
           7.   (1.0)
           8.   'cos you wo:n't belie:ve the reason I like the film

Again we see Paul's response is initiated only after a delay (2–4), it is
marked as a dispreferred second by his use of 'well' (5), his refusal to
answer is a hesitant and softened one (6), and finally he offers an account
of the non-answering (8). This extract also shows evidence of the conventional, expected character of accounts. Another interesting feature of this
extract is the full one second delay after the refusal to answer in which
none of the other speakers cut in. This suggests they are *expecting* an
account to be offered, as indeed it is. A pause of one second may not
sound like a long time when thinking about it in the abstract, but as
conversation analysts have demonstrated, it can sound like a yawning
chasm in the fast flow of conversation.

The fact that even a very short delay is a reliable discriminator of
preferred from dispreferred seconds means that speakers can use the
occurrence of delay as a cue that a dispreferred second is about to be given
(Davidson, 1984; Levinson, 1983). Witness the following extract.

6. A: 1.   C'mon down he:re=it's oka:y

        2.   (0.2)
   A: 3.   I got lotta stuff=I got be:er en stuff

                                                    (Davidson, 1985: 105)

The speaker makes an invitation (1) and then there is silence for a fifth
of a second (2). This very short delay is taken by the speaker as evidence
the response will be a refusal – that is, a dispreferred second – and he
then provides further information which makes the invitation more attractive: when the listener arrives they will find lots of stuff (food?) and beer,
with emphasis on the beer.

The demonstration that speakers both closely monitor the silences in
conversation, and use their occurence to make inferences about the acts
being performed, has important consequences for the experimental social
psychological work on accounts. In studies where subjects are assessing
the adequacy of excuses and justifications from written vignettes (such
as Schlenker and Darby, 1981) it is not possible to convey details of the
manner of delivery. Yet if this is crucial to the interpretation of accounts
– and the conversational analytic work we have examined here suggests
it is – doubt is cast on the generality of the findings. Moreover, in field

experiments (such as Ungar, 1981) it may be the style of delivery that is mediating the effectiveness of the account; yet this is virtually impossible to examine in research of this kind.

We have seen, then, that in everyday conversation accounts commonly appear in certain kinds of turns, namely in the second parts of adjacency pairs where the second part is dispreferred. Conversants use their knowledge of the delivery features of these turns – knowledge about delay for example – to make judgements about the kind of act being performed. However, conversation analysts have pushed on beyond this to study the relation between the specific type of account which is offered and the particular adjacency pair in which it appears.

Offers and accounts

John Heritage (1984) has provided a useful discussion of accounts presented in the context of offers and invitations. When someone makes an offer, to lend you something perhaps, or to invite you to a party, the preferred response is an acceptance. As we have seen, this response is preferred in the sense that it will typically be given with little or no delay, it will be positive and will be produced early in the turn of talk. However, if you refuse the offer or invitation you will be making a dispreferred response, and you are likely to do this in the standard way with delay, marking and an account. In principle you could use all kinds of different accounts when making this response. Yet Heritage noted that accounts in this case overwhelmingly cluster around the issue of ability (Drew, 1984; Levinson, 1983; Merritt, 1976). Thus you don't turn down the party invitation because the host's friends are so boring (at least not to the host's face) but because you have another, more pressing, arrangement.

The following is a typical refusal of an invitation.

> 7. Mark: We w're wondering if you wanted to come over Saturday, f'r dinner.
>   (0.4)
>   Jane: Well (.) .hh it'd be great but we promised Carol already.

The invitation is refused using the standard dispreferred format. It contains an account which makes reference to an earlier commitment. The advantage of an account like this is its 'no blame' quality. It avoids the implication that the invitation is unwanted or unattractive. Furthermore, as it invokes new information (the commitment to Carol) it does not imply that the person giving the invitation is being unthinking. Since there is no way the inviter could know of this commitment they can not be accused of making an invitation which they knew would be turned down. Finally, the knowledge drawn on in the account is hard to dispute: the person inviting is unlikely to know about the recipient's future commitments.

This kind of account, then, is carefully designed to achieve a number of different goals; it does the refusal while avoiding as far as possible any negative or critical consequences. Of course, the speaker is very unlikely to be thinking about these things or spending time on complex planning – they are probably just using the conventional refusal format which comes naturally. Yet close attention to the considerations outlined above helps us understand why such a refusal format might have evolved into a taken-for-granted social convention.

Conversation analysts have extended this work on accounts in everyday talk to make sense of more formal situations. We will take a detailed look at one example: Max Atkinson and Paul Drew's (1979) research on how accusations and defences are managed in courts of law, an example which reveals a great deal about social influence processes at work in courts.

Accounts in court

When we know how speaker changeover is achieved, how conversation on a topic is sustained and how corrections are managed in everyday mundane settings we have more of a handle on things happening in formal institutions: when a teacher is controlling a class (Mehan, 1979), when positions are formulated in a TV news interview (Heritage, 1984), when a scientist graciously accepts the Nobel Prize (Mulkay, 1984a) or when a 'charismatic' politician such as Margaret Thatcher attempts to solicit applause from an audience (Atkinson, 1984a). In each of these cases everyday conversational practices are refined and modified to fit the requirements of the situation. Atkinson and Drew's work is a good illustration of what can be achieved here. They effectively demonstrate how an understanding of informal, unconstrained conversation can aid understanding of interaction in a more formal situation.

Questions and accusations, answers and rebuttals

Atkinson and Drew began by noting two basic ways in which the examination of witnesses in court differs from the conduct of ordinary conversation. First, the turn *order* is fixed – on the whole, who speaks next is not managed locally on a turn by turn basis, but is pre-ordained: counsel speaks, then witness, then counsel and so on. Second, certain *kinds* of turn are preconstituted. In witness examinations it is normally the case that turns should be question and answer pairs with the counsel asking the questions and the witness answering. Moreover, each turn of talk should be, at least minimally, a question or an answer.

Within these restrictions, however, talk is managed in basically the same way as in everyday conversation. Participants use their turns to do different kinds of things, to bring off different sorts of goals. Being a court of law, one of the goals of the prosecuting counsel is to make accusations and challenges. Counsel does this by deploying some sequences of questions rather than others. Witnesses, on the other hand, often wish to rebut accusations, and thus they offer particular types of answers. Put simply, the counsel constructs accusations out of sequences of questions and the witness constructs rebuttals out of sequences of answers.

We are all familiar with the conversational phenomenon where one general form of talk is used to achieve a different purpose. For example, we may couch a request in the form of a statement (see Chapter Two), or an invitation in the form of a question as in the following case.

8. A: Why don't you come and see me some ⌈times
   B: ⌊I would like to
                                  (Atkinson and Drew, 1979: 50)

Although A's utterance takes the syntactic form of a question, the response is not one which fits a question, i.e. an answer, it is an acceptance. The recipient, B, treats A's utterance as an invitation.

In courts, this packaging of acts into question and answer sequences is a delicate matter. For if the counsel is seen to stray too far beyond the minimal requirement of asking questions they may be reprimanded by the judge. On the other hand, if witnesses make statements which are seen to exceed mere answers to the question they may be struck from the record. Thus accusations, denials etc. have to be carefully managed within the broad question/answer adjacency pair.

So, how do counsels produce accusations in the course of constrained questioning? The following extract comes from the proceedings of the Scarman Tribunal on the 1969 disturbances in Northern Ireland. This tribunal was set up to investigate police practices after a disturbance in which Protestants invaded a Catholic area, burning and looting. The police were subsequently accused of being too lenient with Protestant offenders and even abetting their activities, in line with general uneasiness about the role of the largely Protestant Royal Ulster Constabulary in keeping order in Northern Ireland. As with the other extracts we will use from Atkinson and Drew, our first extract records the examination of Royal Ulster Constabulary (RUC) officers by counsel and focuses particularly on why they did not intervene to quell rioting and assault (C is counsel, W is witness, the 00.55 hours referred to is an entry in a police station log book).

9. C: Was there firing in Sandy Row that night?
   W: Not to my knowledge
   C: Will you look at 00.55 hours: 'Automatic firing in Sandy Row'.
   W: No, that is not correct.

(1979: 70)

The important thing to note about this extract is the order of the counsel's questions. The first elicits information from the witness while the second question provides apparently *discrepant* information. The effect of this second question is to *challenge* the testimony of the witness. This is not simply Atkinson and Drew's theoretical interpretation, but how the witness sees things too; his reply displays his understanding that the sequence is a challenge. Instead of noting the log book entry and waiting for further questions he issues an explicit rebuttal. By questioning the correctness of the log book entry the witness attempts to undermine the force of the challenge to his evidence.

One of the features of the restriction of turns to questions and answers is that it is very difficult to allocate blame directly. Indeed, it normally takes two (as in Extract Nine) or more turns to achieve a blaming. This opens the possibility of the witness deflecting blame before it has been properly assigned. The counsel may then have to recover the deflection to restart the blaming sequence and so on. It also means that the witness has a choice of where to produce their defence. They can give it *before* the blaming is completed or *after*. Despite this difference both kinds of defence tend to orientate to the same objectives; first, to avoid allocating blame to oneself; second, and less obviously, to minimize disagreement with the information provided by the counsel in the prior question.

One of Atkinson and Drew's most interesting findings concerns the difference between these two kinds of defence as witnesses use contrasting strategies to achieve the two objectives.

Defences made before blaming is completed

As we have noted, the general question/answer constraint means that the counsel has to build up to blamings and accusations over a number of turns. In the Scarman Tribunal the blameworthy issue was the *failure* of RUC officers to do certain things (arrest rioters, protect property), so a blaming is produced when the counsel makes this failure noticeable. However, the build up to making the failure to act noticeable provides the witness with an opportunity to produce a defence before the accusation of failure to act is completed.

The general form of these defences *plays down* the importance or severity of the events in question. The witness manages to imply that action against rioters was unnecessary. This kind of defence is illustrated in the next extract.

10. C: You saw this newspaper shop being petrol bombed on the front of Divis Street?
    W: Yes.
    C: How many petrol bombs were thrown into it?
    W: Only a couple. I felt that the window was already broken and that there was part of it burning and this was a rekindling of the flames.

(1979: 137)

The counsel has not yet asked the witness why he did nothing to stop the bombing – but this accusation is anticipated and the witness produces a description of the scene which minimizes the need for action. We can note the use of 'only' to qualify the number of petrol bombs used and the description suggesting damage had already been done, with the implication it was not worth bothering about. The overall upshot of the defence is that there was no point in further action as nothing could be done to rescue the shop. In terms of Semin and Manstead's typology, defences of this kind would best be classified as a species of justification, namely a claim that an effect has been misrepresented (see Figure 4.1). These kinds of claims, of course, need to be extremely carefully managed: 'what's a couple of petrol bombs more or less' might begin to sound like black humour.

In addition to giving an account which underplays the damage, these defences can deflect attention away from matters where blame could *potentially* be allocated. In this case, the witness concentrates on the issue of property, ignoring the issue of whether he should have tried to arrest the people throwing petrol bombs. In this way, he attempts to select the ground from which to conduct the defence.

This, then, is the first type of defence, occurring before the counsel displays to the court the RUC man's failure to take action. The second major type of defence occurs *after* the blaming has been completed, and involves a very different type of account.

Defences made after blaming is completed

In Atkinson and Drew's data, defences following completed blamings had two components – a rebuttal and an account, and these components could either be produced in a single turn or in separate turns. The following extract (actually a continuation of Extract Ten) is a typical example of this kind of defence.

11. C: What did you do at that point?
    W: I was not in a very good position to do anything. We were under gunfire at the time.

The rebuttal is the first part of the response to the counsel's completed accusation. The aim is to counter the presupposition of the prior question that the witness *should* and *could* have done something; for example, stopped the crowd throwing petrol bombs. It does not, however, disagree with the presupposition that this action *might* have been relevant.

The second part of the defensive response is the account, supplying an excuse for inactivity. It supplants the idea that the witness did not want to do anything or was not trying to do anything by suggesting a powerful constraint. Who is going to try and stop a crowd throwing petrol bombs when they are being shot at? In Semin and Manstead's terms, this form of account is a denial of volition – the witness intended to do something, but was thwarted by the physical danger from gunfire.

In these cases it seems the effectiveness of the account depends on making the constraints on action as strong as possible. Given that the witness did nothing, the greater the constraint the less the blame. If we examine the extract below we see an extended passage of talk from the witness which gives a powerful picture of causal constraint.

12. C: Did you know the mob were liable to follow you on this occasion?
    W: What I knew and what actually took place are two quite different things. I was *powerless* to prevent quite a lot of things that did happen. In fact we were *just a drop in the ocean* with *so few in number*. I realized certainly that there would be some of them following behind. I could not do anything to prevent that. I saw damage caused and tried to prevent it. I realized *it was bashing my head against a brick wall* really; we were *completely ineffectual*.
    (1979: 164 – emphasis added)

We see the witness constructing a version of events using a number of rhetorical devices to maximize the impression of causal constraint. We have already come across the use of 'extreme case' formulations (Pomerantz, 1986) in Chapter Two. This account joins several of these together, as well as drawing on metaphorical constructions such as 'drop in the ocean' and 'bashing my head against a brick wall'. Overall, the witness undermines the blaming by displaying himself as having the best of intentions, someone who tried as hard as he could, but was unable to do anything because of the weight of constraint.

One way of looking at constraint in psychology is to look at the *actual* constraints and limits on people, while a second very common procedure is to look at people's *attributions* of constraint. That is, to look at the beliefs people express about causal processes when they give explanations (Heider, 1958; Jones and Davis, 1965; Kelley, 1967). In this chapter, and indeed in the book as a whole, we have described a third important approach. This concentrates on the construction of *versions* of constraint in discourse. Atkinson and Drew's work has illustrated the connection between the version of the world put together in cross-examination and the accounting work it was intended to perform. In this case, they have shown how descriptions are manufactured to achieve rebuttals.

At first examination, this kind of conversation analysis concerned with turn taking, adjacency pairs and preference structures may seem to have little to offer the social psychologist. Social psychology is generally thought to be about broader questions, and the study of excuses or accounts and sequential structure seems to have more to do with etiquette than social issues. In this respect Atkinson and Drew's research provides a salutory lesson. It points to some exciting new lines of research and demonstrates the relevance of conversation analysis.

Over the years the study of social influence has formed one of the main research areas of social psychology and recently this work has been extended to the study of influence and court juries. Generally research has focused on relatively macro-variables such as the status and physical attractiveness of defendants (e.g. Kulka and Kessler, 1978; Sigall and Ostrove, 1975). The impression a jury member forms of a witness will also, however, be based on their talk when examined, yet the jury member will probably be unable to articulate how they arrive at their impression and may well be unaware of the cumulative effects of the procedures investigated by Atkinson and Drew. Conversation analytic research in courtrooms demonstrates how we might begin to investigate the kind of influences on juries which are so delicate that they cannot be grossly characterized (Drew, 1985a).

Atkinson and Drew's research also calls into question two commonplace guiding principles in court research: first that witnesses are generally passive and counsels generally active, and second, that the crucial issue is the truth or falsity of witness' testimony. As we have seen, witnesses, although highly constrained, are not necessarily passive victims of counsels, but capable of actively developing and packaging their own versions of events. Furthermore, although fact and fiction are vital matters for courts to establish, they may not be the most useful or the most vital categories for the researcher. The RUC constable's testimony, regardless of whether it will be seen as true or false, constructs a version of events. Even if false, it is an effective, persuasive defence. As we argued in Chapter Two, certain sorts of descriptions should not be ruled out of social psychological analysis because they appear to be factual descriptions of events. Factual descriptions are also constructions, they are also doing social psychological work and are equally worthy of our attention. To a large extent, when we study social influence, the truth or falsity of an account may be less relevant than the constructive procedures adopted in the courtroom.

Discourse and accounts

This chapter has described two contrasting approaches to accounts from social psychology and conversation analysis. The social psychological approach has concentrated to date on the development of typologies of accounts and the identification of relationships between different variables, such as the type of account, severity of transgression and status. The conversation analytic approach works from the assumption that phenomena like accounts will be best understood through looking at their positioning in sequences of discourse performing different kinds of act. Thus this approach views accounts as conversational events produced in the second part of an adjacency pair when a dispreferred response is being supplied, for instance, when an offer is rejected or an accusation challenged.

This research has clarified how accounts can be developed to deal with a number of different kinds of problems: turning down an offer without being offensive or challenging an accusation without generating strong disagreement. When understood as conventional procedures adopted for problems of this kind it is possible to make sense of both the broad categories of account giving and the fine details of individual accounts. Conversation analysis has also shown how we can move from everyday settings to more formal, institutional situations where interesting questions of control and power are raised.

The findings of this tradition raise apparently insurmountable difficulties for the experimental social psychological approach to accounts. Evidence concerning the important role of detailed linguistic features such as delay, stress and the selection of particular words casts doubt on research which is based on written vignettes and on experiments which generate accounts in the field using confederates. This is not to say that these problems could not in principle be surmounted, or that there is no value in experimental work on accounts; there may be some questions which are very difficult to answer without experimental techniques. However, the importance of some of these phenomena would not have become so clear without the systematic analysis of discourse conducted by conversation analysts coupled with a theoretical perspective which treats accounts in the context of language function.

More generally, in conversation analysis, we can see some of the broader theoretical aims described in Chapter Two fleshed out in a detailed, analytically based, research programme. The general concern with the action orientation of talk is now seen in terms of the detailed study of adjacency pairs (in effect, paired actions) and the way people mesh pairs together to perform further actions. Most importantly, conversation analysis emphasizes the vital nature of understanding each conversational turn in terms of the sequence in which it is embedded. The utility of sequential analysis should now be fully evident.

5

Speaking subjects

In the previous chapter we were concerned with discourse in relation to accounts of breakdowns or disturbing actions. We will now move on to the broader topic of discourse methods for characterizing people: the language of the self and 'subject'. This is a crucial area for social psychology given that the discipline usually takes the individual as its main unit of analysis, and defining the shape and nature of this individual is seen as involving some model or theory of the self.

The self has been a controversial area within social psychology. At one stage it seemed impossible to study scientifically something which has such confusing and diverse manifestations and which appears to be so private and hidden within the individual; this conflict was particularly centred on the disputes between humanist and behaviourist approaches (Matson, 1973; Wann, 1964). In recent years argument has continued to flourish but it has taken on a new form as social psychologists have come to question the terms of the debate itself and the very notion of the individual or the subject which is at the heart of psychology (Gergen and Davis, 1985; Harré, 1983; Henriques et al., 1984; Sampson, 1983; Shotter, 1984).

Our aim in this chapter is to describe some of the traditional models of the self developed in social psychology and then follow the new twists in the dispute, producing a critique of the principal assumptions underlying this traditional model building. We shall describe the challenges emerging from recent language-based or 'social constructivist' approaches which take a similar line to the discourse approach, and we will want to argue that, in the last analysis, any sociopsychological image of the self, in fact the very possibility of a self concept, is inextricably dependent on the linguistic practices used in everyday life to make sense of our own and others' actions.

Traditional images of the self

The key assumption behind all the traditional models we wish to describe is that the self is an entity and, like any other entity or natural physical object, it can be described definitively, once and for all. In other words, it is assumed that the self has one true nature or set of characteristics waiting to be discovered and once discovered a correct description of these characteristics will follow. Theorizing about the self is thus thought to be rather like theorizing about a chemical. Much of the structure of the chemical may be hidden and mysterious; different research groups may for a time offer competing descriptions, but given proper investigative methods, the true veridical description of the chemical will ultimately emerge.

This assumption is one a discourse approach will want to question but for the moment let us examine some of the competing theories which have been proposed and their different claims as to what counts as a proper description of this object – the self. Our review will build on an earlier discussion of this topic (Potter et al., 1984: ch. 8), and will focus on the metaphorical elements of these models rather than the technical details of the theories, seeing them as proposing a set of 'character types'.

Trait theory: the self as an 'honest soul'

Trait theory has been one of the most influential models in social psychology. This theory regards the self as a 'personality'. That is, it sees the person as consisting of measurable personality traits, abilities and attributes. Traits may be either superficial or deeply rooted, constitutionally inherent or the result of child rearing (Cattell, 1966; Eysenck, 1953). A person's behaviour or actions are thought to be largely determined by the combination of traits they possess. These traits will outweigh the influence of the immediate situation or the context surrounding the person. It is this image of the self which underlies the concept of the personality test or personality inventory with its aim of measuring individual differences in specific traits such as extraversion or introversion and recording the precise patterning and combination of traits within a particular individual.

As an example of this approach, consider the following person description offered by Eysenck and Eysenck (1964):

> The typical extravert is sociable, likes parties, has many friends, needs to have people to talk to, and does not like reading or studying by himself. He craves excitement, takes chances, often sticks his neck out, acts on the spur of the moment, and is generally an impulsive individual. He is fond of practical jokes, always has a ready answer, and generally likes change; he is care-free, easy-going, optimistic, and likes to 'laugh and be merry'. He prefers to keep moving and doing things, tends to be aggressive and lose his temper quickly; altogether his feelings are not under tight control, and he is not always a reliable person. (Eysenck and Eysenck, 1964: 8).

What kind of assumptions are being made here about the nature of people? Trait theory adopts what the literary critic Lionel Trilling (1974) has called the 'honest soul' approach to the self. People are viewed as if they are like the minor characters in a Victorian novel, the Doras, the Uriah Heeps, the Pickwicks, for instance, of Dickens' novels, as if they simply *are* their dispositions or the sum of their traits: honest, lazy, Machiavellian, earnest or whatever. These traits alone provide sufficient motive and explanation for their actions. Uriah Heep will continue to be underhand and obsequious whatever the situation as that is his disposition, just as Eysenck's extravert will continue to be the life and soul of the party.

In no sense could the honest soul or trait theory person be seen as acting out a part of 'managing' the impression given to others, they are entirely synonymous with their disposition and identify completely with it. The extravert is not putting on a facade, they cannot help but be extravert, it is their disposition. For this reason it would be meaningless to talk about this kind of self having an identity crisis (Rorty, 1976). Honest souls have only one identity, not many, and there is no distance or separation within the self to produce the possibility of this kind of self-conflict. It is not within the capacity of Eysenck's extravert, for instance, to wonder if they are being 'authentic' to their 'true' self, they always are that self. This speculation is just not possible if the person is conceptualized in this way. Trait theory people cannot be 'game players', they are 'honest' souls, conveying, in Trilling's terms, a 'sentiment of being', or an aura of solidity and unreflectiveness.

Critics of trait theory and those who wish to offer an alternative description of the self have noted the weaknesses and limitations of this conceptualization. Trait theory is highly asocial in its approach, it ignores the inconsistency in human behaviour (Mischel, 1968). Given enough personality test data, trait theorists can comment extensively and to a high level of sophistication on the traits individuals possess. However, in their own terms, this effort is wasted if, as it seems, these traits bear little relation to how people perform in non-test situations. The majority of people, for example, may come out as partly extravert and partly introvert on personality tests. Whether introversion or extraversion dominates depends on their perception of the situation. They cease to be predictable and trait-driven.

Furthermore, according to the opponents of trait theory, people are not just 'personalities', they are social creatures, they have different parts to play in society which require different manifestations of the self: mothers, daughters, doctors, style setters etc. This is the line that has been taken by a second very influential description of the self in social psychology, namely role theory. The social situation and a person's position within a society, not their character, is seen as channelling behaviour.

Role theory: the theatrical image of the self

Role theory perceives a tension between two 'facts': the fact of individual self-expression and the fact of society and social determinism. The concept of role is a means of reconciliation. Roles are defined as sets of activities, qualities and styles of behaviour that are associated with social positions (Dahrendorf, 1973, provides a classic description). Social positions exist independently of any particular individual; they are impersonal or supra-individual, and include, among others, occupational, religious, recreational and kin categories. Modern, complex, differentiated societies require the social positions of wives, husbands, criminals, priests, dentists, politicians, for instance. People who fill these social positions are expected to act in the appropriate way, they learn to play a role. Through being fixed in a certain social position in a structured society, a person acquires a self and a form of self-expression. Thus what determines a person's self and their personality is the social positions they occupy; dispositions are varied and socially manufactured.

According to role theorists, people conform to their roles not just because of obvious sanctions and rewards for doing so (e.g. prison sentences and higher salaries) but because of the more subtle mechanisms of socialization. Children learn to see themselves as others see them (Mead, 1934), the self is a 'looking glass self' (Cooley, 1902), it comes to reflect social expectations. Individuals learn to 'refer' to their social groups and through a process of 'social comparison' adjust their identities (Festinger, 1954). The girl and the boy learn their appropriate sex-role, for instance, and become feminine and masculine adults.

A very different kind of self-experience is obviously being posited here. People cease to become 'natural' characters, they become performers, social characters; the dramatic and the theatrical begin to provide more appropriate metaphors (Goffman, 1959). Like the actor on the stage, a person's actions are not expressive of a unique personality, but expressive of their role, and most individuals are interchangeable when it comes to role playing. As Gombrowicz notes:

> A human being does not externalize himself directly and immediately in conformity with his own nature; he invariably does so by way of some definite form; and that form, style, way of speaking and responding, does not derive solely from him, but are imposed on him from without – and the same man can express himself sometimes wisely, sometimes foolishly, bloodthirstily or angelically, maturely or immaturely, according to the form, the style presented to him by the outside world...(1979)

The role-player self thus has two characteristics denied the honest soul. First, a kind of social insincerity and, second, a multiple set of possibly discordant identities. The possibility of individual fragmentation is introduced, different roles may require different selves, the person is divided between many responses and may experience a conflict alien to the model of the person assumed by trait theory.

Insincerity arises from being aware of society. The honest soul is seen as unself-conscious in response and thus sincere to their disposition, whereas the role player is capable of putting on a facade, hiding behind a mask, and acting out a pre-ordained script. This aspect of self-experience, inherent in this image of the self, is very well expressed in some of the novelist David Lodge's characters.

> It is obvious, from his stiff, upright posture, and fulsome gratitude to the air stewardess serving him a glass of orange juice, that Philip Swallow, flying westward, is unaccustomed to air travel [ ] The sang froid of his fellow passengers is a constant source of wonderment to him, and he observes their deportment carefully. Flying for Philip Swallow is essentially a dramatic performance, and he approaches it like a game amateur actor determined to hold his own in the company of word-perfect professionals. To speak the truth, he approaches most of life's challenges in the same spirit. He is a mimetic man . . . (1978: 8–10)

Philip Swallow is not presented as possessing a personality in the way the trait theory person possesses his or her personality, he simply possesses the ability to put on the masks required of him, or reflect the expectations of his society. The attributes belong to the roles, although after life-long practice at playing the roles, they will become habitually assumed, and the individual will gain an equal predictability.

With role and trait theories therefore, we have two competing versions of what makes up the self and the individual and how they are best described. These two accounts are generally seen as mutually exclusive options in line with the model building assumption outlined earlier in which the self, like other objects, can only have one correct description. The final image of the self we shall consider adds yet a third, supposedly definitive, version of what the self is and thus how we experience ourselves.

Humanistic theories: the romantic image of the self

From a humanistic point of view, the classic role theory account of the self presents a morally offensive image of people. The role player is portrayed as a social dope, a victim of social circumstance. Dahrendorf argues, people know themselves and their friends as richer characters than this, people believe they have a sense of control and agency, a sense of creating new social forms as well as being created by them. The role player is perhaps but a pale imitation of human potentialities (Hamlyn, 1974).

Role theory places the self firmly within the public realm but inherent within its formulation is the possibility of a distinction between public and private selves. There is the social self described by role theory, but there is also a true or real background self which chooses to act out the roles and which monitors the success or failure of the performance. The humanist notes, there is room for a kind of double consciousness, just as the actor on the stage has a double consciousness. There is the role being acted out and there is the actor's real self, which guides the performance and, in some sense, remains removed or alienated from the part being played.

The humanistic tradition in psychology exploits this tension and potential self-estrangement (Perls, 1971; Maslow, 1968; Rogers, 1961). It has argued that both trait type theories and role theories wrongly represent human nature and that psychological research and therapy should focus on this authentic true self. An individual's life is seen as a process of searching to establish this true self, as a quest for self-fulfilment and self-actualization. The role player mentality and the sense of alienation which characterize modern life indicate that this quest has been interrupted and is incomplete.

The following extract from Fritz Perls nicely illustrates the assumptions at work here:

> In Gestalt therapy, we are working for something else. We are here to promote the growth process and develop the human potential. We do not talk of instant joy, instant sensory awareness, instant cure. The growth process is a process which takes time. In therapy we not only have to get through the role-playing. We also have to fill in the holes in the personality to make the person whole and complete again [ ] you have to invest in yourself and it takes time to grow. (1971)

There seem to be two, probably contradictory, images within this tradition. First, there is the concept of a pre-existent, authentic self which may be inhibited and thus require rediscovery, and, second, there is a self which is not pre-existent but needs to be willed into existence and self-consciously created from the wreckage of the cultural debris cluttering up the psyche. The latter self implies hard work, patient and careful self-analysis, exercising and trying out the new psychical elements which will make up the more fulfilled authentic self. While the first kind of self more frequently stresses spontaneity and simply being. It is assumed the conventions of social and public life form a veneer over an older, deeper, more basic self we all share in common; this veneer can be stripped away to reveal the healthy whole self underneath.

We have now considered three separate accounts of the self, presented as character types rather than empirically based theories. There are many other versions of the self available in psychology but in different ways trait theory, role theory and humanistic theories have been the most central to the development of the discipline. Before going on and examining the challenges to the general framework underlying these models, let us first consider in more detail the assumptions behind this kind of model building.

What is being assumed?

As we pointed out at the beginning, each of these models of the self claims to be the only valid self-portrait; either because it supposedly encapsulates some phenomenological or experiential truth (humanistic theory), is supported by psychometric research (trait theory), or appears to be the most sociologically coherent analytic tool for the social scientist (role theory). It is taken for granted that through patient investigation, whether it be the phenomenological stripping away of layers or the observation of large numbers of people, the true nature and substance of the self will be revealed.

This core assumption is a verson of the realist principle. McCabe's summary of the features of this principle for film and literary narrative discourses applies equally well to psychological discourse.

> The narrative discourse cannot be mistaken in its identifications because the narrative discourse is not present as discourse – as articulation. The unquestioned nature of the narrative discourse entails that the only problem reality poses is to go and look and see what *Things* there *are* [ ] The real is not articulated – it is. (1974: 12)

The psychological self-images we have been considering similarly do not call attention to themselves as constructions or discursive articulations but present themselves as representations of the *real* object.

Other assumptions are implicated here (Sampson, 1983). It is taken for granted that this self, the object to be discovered, is the *centre* of experience, an initiator of action, a coherent whole, separate from other distinct selves. These aspects are crucial to psychology's conception of the individual person and the human subject. They make it possible, for example, to contrast the *individual* with *society*, as natural pairs in a balanced dichotomy. The individual can be posed as the causal unit the researcher retreats to when explaining social phenomena, and represented as the possible origin point for society and, indeed, of any knowledge about the world (Henriques et al., 1984). It is presupposed that the self is a unitary entity, a relatively autonomous agent in the world and thus a source and explanation of the kind of phenomena which interest the psychologist. In fact this assumption comes to define what the psychologist should study and the prominence given to the laws of motivation, for instance, or the cognitive structure of the person. Even for the role theorist, the self is seen as bounded in this sense, and as the origin point of experience.

Towards a new conception of the subject

Attacks on these fundamental propositions have emerged from many different sources. They have recently been co-ordinated, however, by Kenneth Gergen (1985) under the general rubric of 'social constructivism', thus providing a summary of the main points of disagreement. In this section we will consider the critical points raised by Gergen and others and the growth in alternative language-based approaches to the self. It is worth noting in advance that, unlike some other developments reviewed in previous chapters, the movement to a discursive model of the self has been more affected by trends in semiology and post-structuralism than ethnomethodology, conversation analysis and the study of speech acts. For this reason this perspective is strong on theory and is more abstract and philosophically complex with few analyses of the nuts and bolts kind encountered in other chapters. In the final section of the chapter we will return to this sort of analysis but for the moment the less concrete will take precedence.

The main object of the critical movement has been to displace attention from the self-as-entity and focus it on the methods of constructing the self. That is, the question becomes not what is the true nature of the self, but how is the self talked about, how is it theorized in discourse? This is a move which is welcomed by the discourse analyst. It is suggested that methods of making sense are the key to any kind of explanation of the self, as people's sense of themselves is in fact a conglomerate of these methods, produced through talk and theorizing. There is not 'one' self waiting to be discovered or uncovered but a multitude of selves found in the different kinds of linguistic practices articulated now, in the past, historically and cross-culturally. 'Considered from this point of view', claims Harré, 'to be a self is not to be a certain kind of being but to be in possession of a certain kind of theory' (1985b: 262).

From this perspective, the trait theory, role theory and humanistic character types discussed in the last section become, not competing models, but different possible methods of making sense that someone might draw upon to describe themselves. These character types thus cease to be seen as mutually exclusive options; a person could, at one moment, depict themselves in trait terms, at another moment in role terms or even blend two or three of these types together in their self construction (Potter et al., 1984: 45–7). It is meaningless to ask which of these models is the correct description of the self, they are simply equivalent ways of making sense of the self with their own context, relative advantages and disadvantages.

There are several different strands combined in this constructive approach to the self which we need to tease out. A major strand is the argument that psychological models of the self are inevitably culturally and historically contingent, dependent on certain kinds of social practices. The assumptions on which modern Western psychology is based, the concept of the self as the centre of experience, for instance, which we discussed above, may be peculiar to this period of history and this type of society. What psychology discovers, therefore, may not be the timeless universal features of personhood. Psychology may simply elaborate instead upon the conventional ways people are described in this particular society. Psychologists may think in terms of traits, roles and autonomous selves because these are part of our culture's common sense about the self (Potter et al., 1984: ch. 8). If it is the case that psychological models of the self reflect not the true nature of the object, as supposed, but our social history, the realist principle would be undermined. The researcher should be encouraged to begin focusing on the multiplicity of self-constructions and their social and interpersonal functions.

Various careful analyses of indigenous psychologies or the psychological theories of non-Western people (Heelas and Lock, 1981), of the history of the self-concept in the West (Henriques et al, 1984; Lyons, 1978), and discussions of the overlaps in the images found in social science and in other arenas such as literature (Potter et al., 1984; Trilling, 1974; Wetherell, 1983, 1986) have given weight to this claim. We will shortly consider one type of non-Western indigenous psychology to demonstrate this strand of the argument and the divergencies possible in self-understanding.

The other major strand in this new approach to the self is to set up new prescriptions for future study. The social psychologist is now asked to study something different, not the person behaving in an 'environment', but the language practices and discourses prevalent in different contexts (Harré, 1983; Shotter, 1984). Gergen describes the background to the new research framework as follows:

> The language of person description (behavioral language) is not linked in any systematic way to spatiotemporal configurations of the body. Thus it appears the rules for 'what counts as what' are inherently ambiguous, continuously evolving, and free to vary with the predilections of those who use them [ ] Whether an act is defined as envy, flirtation, or anger floats on a sea of social interchange. Interpretation may be suggested, fastened upon, and abandoned as social relationships unfold across time. (1985: 6)

As we noted in the discussions of semiology in Chapter One and rules in Chapter Three, any human act does not determine the interpretations placed on it, varying interpretations and constructions of the action might emerge. Gergen argues that, if this is the case, then the task of the social psychologist is to study the variation of interpretation in descriptions of people. What is crucial is the discursive functions served by particular interpretations.

Gergen is perhaps overstressing the degree of open-endedness and flexibility in this process in order to emphasize the general point he wishes to make. As the examples from conversation analysis in Chapter Three demonstrate, there is considerable constraint and regularity in the procedures people use for articulating or making sense of an action, and successfully 'bringing off' their version of events in a persuasive manner. We would want to argue that not every interpretation or construction of the self will be acceptable in a specific situation. But the important point is that the social psychologist abandons the attempt to describe once and for all human acts and their meanings, subduing and struggling against indexicality, and instead attempts to describe the linguistic practices which produce an act as a certain type of event.

This type of research is not an idle or dilettante activity either. As many cultural analysts have demonstrated, it is a critical, political and potentially emancipatory activity. The methods of conceptualizing the self involved in different linguistic practices have vital consequences for the positioning of people in society; they are not neutral or without impact, they produce senses of the self which may be negative, destructive, oppressive, as well as senses which might change and liberate (Coward, 1984; Henriques et al., 1984; Parker, forthcoming; Williamson, 1978).

In the following sections we will enlarge on the two major strands of this new approach to the self summarized here, demonstrating through the work of particular theorists how the challenge against traditional models of the self has been mounted and, with more precision, what an alternative conception might involve. We will look first at the argument that conceptions of the self are culturally relative, and then at the claim that to research the self we need to study language.

Indigenous psychologies: the Maori self

While there may be some universals in how people across different cultures conceive of the self (Lock, 1981), so that, in fact, some basics of self-organization may be prerequisites for even a minimally organized society; it is clear cultures systematically differ in their theories of the person and self-practices. These differences are exceedingly difficult to analyse and decipher. It is a perilous activity comparing across cultures. But this research is fascinating because at its best it makes our own cultural practices appear strange and unnatural, as if they could be other than they are. This is perhaps the first step in successful discourse analysis, the suspension of belief in what one normally takes for granted, as we begin to think about how a practice is constructed and what it assumes rather than seeing it as a mere reflection of an unproblematic reality. The relativity of our own discourse of selves and people is made explicit when other cultures are studied.

One of the most interesting cultures that has been studied from this perspective is the Maori culture of *Aotearoa* or New Zealand. The account of the Maori self which follows is taken from descriptions given by Harré (1983) and Smith (1981) which in turn acknowledge the anthropological work conducted by Elsdon Best (1922).

According to Harré, Maori self-experience is rooted in a wider cosmology which enlivens the material world, so that 'each harmless and quiescent thing is charged: in our terms it has potential energy' (1983: 91). The person and the physical world are thus represented as a set of force fields, where the forces are interrelated with the activities of the gods or spiritual ancestors (*atua*) of a tribal group.

The social status and position given to any individual within the social group is dependent on their birth and genealogy, and a person becomes invested with a particular kind of power, *mana*, as a result of their birth circumstances. The positive successful achievements of a high-ranking person in war or intergroup negotiation is hence attributed to his strong *mana*, given by the gods, which is made manifest in actions. *Mana*, however, is a variable or inconstant force matching the contingencies and variability of everyday life. It could wane if ritual observances, particularly in relation to the spiritual ancestors, are not observed, and thus the previously successful chief could suddenly fail in battle as his power drains out of him because of some misdemeanour of which he may not even have been aware.

If one views the world in this kind of way, with the individual seen as the site of varied and variable external forces (and *mana* is only one of these possible forces which inhabit the individual), then different kinds of self-experience become possible. Specifically, individuals can cease to represent themselves as the centre and origin of their actions, a conception which has been taken to be vital to Western concepts of the self. The individual Maori does not *own* experiences such as the emotions of fear, anger, love, grief; rather they are visitations governed by the unseen world of powers and forces, just as an inanimate object, a stone or pebble, can be invested with magical taboo powers so that touching it places the offender in danger. As Smith points out,

> The Maori individual was an amalgam of various independent organs of experience, and it would appear from the description of these [ ] that to a significant extent these organs reacted to external stimuli independently of the 'self'. Thus Maori experience compared with our own was impersonal and objective. Because the 'self' was not in control of experience, a man's experience was not felt to be integral to him; it happened *in* him but not *of* him. A Maori individual was not so much the experiencer of his experience as the observer of it. (Smith, 1981: 152)

It is possible, given these descriptions, for the Westerner to begin to imagine a different kind of mental life, almost a different world of sensational experience, and through this imagining to begin to de-centre our own conventions for self-expression. As Smith is aware, however, there is the risk that we are still dealing in idealizations. A comparison of the conceptions of the self in two cultures requires a reification and homogenization of those conceptions in order to compare at all. We are also missing the Maori reading of our conventions to set beside our reading of theirs.

Ironically, very little is known about the ordinary construction of the self in our kinds of society. The Maori version contrasts with most aspects of idealized Western psychological models of the self but is it so alien to the way people in this society represent themselves in everyday conversation? People frequently talk about being taken over by emotions, about being the victim of their nerves; that is, as out of control of their experience. To properly discuss and compare Western images of the self with the Maori images in this way we first need to investigate our own indigenous psychologies with the care and attention anthropologists have paid to the foreign and the strange. But we know enough at this stage to support the claim that different cultures and historical periods produce different self-practices.

The grammatical and metaphorical self

As we noted, the second main strand in this new approach to the self is the emphasis placed on language as the medium for self-construction and thus for research on the self. Harré has described the human infant as an 'apprentice person' who has to acquire the 'linguistic resources for acts of self-description' (1985b: 259). The infant is in much the same position, therefore, as the social analyst of the self. In each case a body of knowledge needs to be acquired about how the self is conventionally articulated. What is originally gained unawares has to be 'self-consciously' retrieved anew and re-examined.

Language is the medium for this knowledge for both the child and the social scientist. As Harré says, the child is acquiring '*linguistic* resources'. Self-experience is formed as the child learns the grammar of our language and perfects communication. They also learn the conversationally acceptable ways of presenting oneself as a person. Credibility and the power to persuade others of what one wants them to accept only come through the use of some routes to self-expression, and what is credible and conventionally acceptable in one context may become unsatisfactory, ineffective communication in another. The pressure to be accountable and intelligible to others sustains and gives power to certain communal organization of self-experience (Gergen, 1987; Shotter, 1984).

One of the most familiar organizations in our grammar is the ability to split the person into subject and object. A person can refer to themselves as both I and me. According to Harré (1977c; see also Harré, forthcoming) this grammatical feature makes perfect sense of our willingness to subdivide ourselves and to describe the self as split when introspecting on self-experience; it thus explains one kind of self-construction. This feature of language makes sense, too, of some of the ways the self has been understood in social psychology.

We saw that a central feature of role theory formulations of the self is the possible division of people into public and private selves so that there is a social self, a *me*, and an *I* that is aware and can monitor this social self, evaluating it pretty much as one might comment on the actions of a friend. *I* can, in other words, see how this *me* appears to other people, without feeling *I* am completely identified with this particular *me*. *I* can always create other types of *me*. This is, of course, also the starting point for humanist theories and the search to define the authentic self from this plethora of divided selves.

Harré argues that it would be a mistake to take this commonplace way of thinking about the self at face value and, for instance, erect a philosophy or metaphysics of the self which might give a real-world ontological status to these I's and me's, seeing them as actual constituent entities. And it would be a mistake to follow the traditional psychological path and attribute a descriptive phenomenological significance to the possibilities of self-division, thus theorizing about the split ego or different layers of consciousness. The I and the me or the subdivided self, according to Harré, is simply a feature of grammar and the constraints and potentialities of self-description afforded by that grammar. It simply reflects one way we have for accounting for ourselves linguistically.

Harré offers some examples of how this presentational grammatical device works in practice, such as 'you are deceiving yourself', 'I made myself do it', 'I talked myself into it' (1977c: 330–4). In each of these examples the speaker makes use of the subject/object property of language to create two selves: a recalcitrant, dilatory, unwilling self and a powerful, controlling self. It is easy to see how this mundane linguistic practice could be confused with a genuine split into sub-agents in the head. It is also clear that this ability to divide the self in language is a very useful accounting strategy, through it one can disavow responsibility, manage accusations, claim credit and so on.

This, then is one approach advocated by the new conception of the self which is emerging. To look at how the self is constructed, the social scientist should research the grammatical matrix and everyday language usage. In addition, we should study metaphor and analogy, these too can cast light on why we understand ourselves as we do.

Shotter (1985), following Lakoff and Johnson (1980), has drawn attention to some of our guiding metaphors for the mind. We think of the mind, for example, as a container (things are 'held' in mind); as a machine (minds which fail to 'function' properly) and also spatially so that there are 'deep' levels of consciousness and 'higher' mental processes. Structural or architectural metaphors and stream or water images are among the most pervasive in literary and psychological discourse. Thus it is common to think of the mind as divided into regions or spaces, some of which may be 'partitioned' off so that the person can think of themselves, if necessary, as breaking down mental 'barriers' – a metaphor repeatedly employed by humanistic psychologists. There is also the furniture of the mind: the self may become cluttered up with old-fashioned and out-dated apparatus.

The image of the self as a stream of consciousness has a prestigious history in psychology. William James (reprinted, 1968) argued that the mind was composed of a flood, or successive series of thoughts and images. He came to this conclusion, he thought, as a result of careful introspection on self-experience but the origins may lie elsewhere, in a discursive system which offers exactly this kind of metaphorical shift.

The ideological self

One of the dangers of this kind of grammatical analysis is that the social dimensions of self-discourse can be neglected. Why, for instance, do some kinds of linguistic practices and some self-constructions flourish at particular historical periods and in certain societies, only to fall out of use in other periods? In concentrating on grammar we can forget that certain constructions of the self may survive because they serve important social functions or maintain a particular kind of society.

Warranting voice

Gergen (forthcoming) argues that the motive force behind the dominance of some self-constructions is people's desire for 'voice' or speaking rights, their wish to have their interpretation of events prevail against competing versions. The self is thus articulated in discourse in ways that will maximize one's warrant or claim to be heard. Some versions of the self will thus come to predominate in some contexts.

Gergen contrasts this kind of self-presentational impetus to self-construction with claims to voice which arise from the naked use of power, where might is used to force through a version of events, or an economic impetus, where the ability to construct in the most effective way possible is first dependent on having the money to do so (e.g. in advertising). He is suggesting that in everyday life with one's friends, family and colleagues voice is determined by how skilfully one can use warranting conventions. And a vital part of warranting one's actions, making them appear reasonable and justifiable, is being able to present different kinds of the self appropriately.

He also argues that this pressure explains the way the 'self' disciplines such as psychology and the philosophy of the mind have developed over time.

> In effect, as warrants are developed, disputed, and elaborated in defense, the result is a rich and variegated language of the self along with sets of supporting institutions and practices. What we take to be the dimensions of self in the present era may thus be viewed as the accumulated armamentarium of centuries of debate. They are symbolic resources, as it were, for making claims in a sea of competing world constructions. (forthcoming)

Thus psychologists and philosophers have reconstructed their theories of the self and introduced richer and more complex accounts prompted by their own need for successful self-presentation in the face of competition between philosophical schools and the desire to gain control and power.

We would want to take a somewhat less individualistic approach to the pressures favouring certain self-discourses over others. The urge to self-presentation seems too narrow a basis on which to build an analysis of variability and variation in broad social self-constructions.

Gergen's approach can be contrasted with a different tradition derived principally from some interpretations of the work of Foucault (1970, 1972, 1981), the earlier work of the Frankfurt School (cf. Sampson, 1983) and recent Marxist analyses of subjectivity, discourse and ideology (Althusser, 1971; Coward and Ellis, 1977). The main thrust of this work has been to demonstrate how the discursive articulation of certain kinds of selves or human subjects is intimately involved in the reproduction of certain kinds of society.

In this tradition, people become *fixed* in position through the range of linguistic practices available to them to make sense. The use of a particular discourse which contains a particular organization of the self not only allows one to warrant and justify one's actions in Gergen's sense, it also maintains power relations and patterns of domination and subordination. In constructing the self in one way, other constructions are excluded, hence, to use a common phrase found in this tradition, the creation of one kind of self or subjectivity in discourse also creates a particular kind of subjection. 'A subjectivity is produced in discourse as the self is subjected to discourse' (Parker, forthcoming).

Discourse and power

Several concrete analyses of the power relations involved in discursive self-presentations have been conducted on topics which should interest the social psychologist (e.g. Coward, 1984, and Hollway in Henriques et al., 1984, on constructions of femininity and masculinity; and Heath, 1982, on sexual relations). Rosalind Coward has demonstrated how discursive practices aimed specifically at women's selves construct a version of what should be pleasurable for women and thus encourages specific female desires. She examines the assembly of fashionable body images, ideal homes, the complex of encouragements and prohibitions organized around food and recipes in women's magazines and looks at how radio disc jockeys and popular music construct the people who are their audience. All of these realms are crucial for how women see themselves, women are positioned as consumers through the desires developed in this way, and although this discourse is pleasurable it is also oppressive.

> I see the representations of female pleasure and desire as *producing* and sustaining feminine positions. These positions are neither distant roles imposed on us from outside which it would be easy to kick off, nor are they the essential attributes of femininity. Feminine positions are produced as responses to the pleasures offered to us; our subjectivity and identity are formed in the definitions of desire which encircle us. (1984: 16)

The grammatical perspective on the self reminds us of the contingency of self-construction and its multifariousness while this kind of ideological analysis reminds us that it is not a game which is being played here. Research into discourse concerns crucial elements of people's lives, not only pleasure and desire but suffering and enslavement, and the possibilities for any kind of life in this society.

Discourse analysis at work on the self

Although, as we have seen, the new social constructivist approach to the subject has developed a sophisticated theoretical alternative to traditional self-concept research, there are few examples of detailed empirical analysis to back it up. We have a strong theoretical rationale for starting a programmatic study of self-discourse but the research itself has yet to be done in a systematic fashion.

In the last section of this chapter we will attempt to illustrate with some examples the kind of empirical programme required. In line with the analytic methods advocated so far we will stress function in particular. Not only do we need to be able to describe the content of representations of people in different contexts or the sheer range of self-images available in ordinary talk, but we also need to ask how these images are used and to what end, and thus what they achieve for the speaker immediately, interpersonally, and then in terms of wider social implications.

Self-construction and intergroup conflict

The examples we shall consider here concern the construction of selves that occurs when people attempt to make sense of intergroup conflict and in particular when they present one version of the conflict as factual. Our extracts will come from open-ended interviews conducted with New Zealanders concerning the question of sporting links with South Africa and more specifically the 1981 Springbok rugby tour of New Zealand (Wetherell and Potter, forthcoming b).

This tour was a highly controversial one in New Zealand. According to opinion polls it was not supported by the majority of the population, although there were a number of New Zealanders who felt very strongly the tour should go ahead, and it was strongly opposed by a large coalition of anti-apartheid campaigners who initiated protests and civil disturbance during this period. One of the scheduled matches had to be cancelled because of the degree of disturbance and every game involved a demonstration of some kind, culminating, in the final match of the tour, in what has been described as a riot. The conduct of the police during these protests was later called into question and became part of the debate surrounding the events of 1981 (Shears and Gidley, 1982).

Those we interviewed can be described as onlookers or spectators of this conflict, in the sense that none were involved in the protest movement, although all had generally strong views about the events surrounding the tour, both pro and anti. In the interview they were given the task of accounting for or explaining the conflict and violence to the interviewer and articulating their position. They did so, as we will try to demonstrate, by drawing on particular models of human nature in order to blame and accuse some parties while excusing and justifying the behaviour of others. Varying constructions of the self were brought into play in the process. These were generally third person models in the sense that other people rather than one's own self were being described. But from our discourse perspective, the same analytic principles apply, and discourse about others' selves is just as interesting as discourse about one's own self.

Violence, human nature and rational control of the self

Commonly three kinds of narrative characters were produced in accounts. One character was developed to explain the role of the police, and the two others to account for the actions of the protestors.

When asked if the police had been to blame for the violence of the tour, many of those interviewed responded in the following way:

1. With the police let's face it they're only people, they get angry you know and you quite often see them get carried away which is you know, how quite, um, how can I say, forgiveable. [ ] I would say it was a case of the police getting fed up cos they are just people after all, and I can quite imagine becoming heartily sick of the whole business and lashing out at someone. (Bradman: 15–16)

2. They might have made a few mistakes. But you know policemen are only ordinary people, they must have had a lot of provocation and I don't blame them if at the last they were a bit rough. (Owen: 16)

3. I think the police acted very well. They're only human, if they lashed out and cracked a skull occasionally, it was, hah, only a very human action I'm sure. (Bird: 11)

What is interesting about these accounts – and the many similar ones in our sample – is the concept of human nature, or ordinary human reactions they draw on. Human nature, the basic person, appears as flawed and brutish. Most of the time this uncivil nature is quiescent or restrained in some way, but given a sufficiently extreme situation or sufficient provocation it will appear. An aggressive response to provocation is depicted as natural or preprogrammed in human beings; presumably, the rational social agent has to learn at least a veneer of control, albeit an imperfect control, over this underlying aggressive potential. Of course, the police are supposed to maintain self-control, but these accounts stress that they too are at root 'only human'.

This character construction thus stresses the fallibility of human beings and the inevitable falling away from 'higher' standards. (A dominant metaphor is to speak of being 'carried' away or 'swept' along.) Its adoption in this context allows the police to be excused and their behaviour justified – the police cannot be blamed if everyone would have acted in this way (see Wetherell and Potter, forthcoming b).

A different kind of approach tended to be taken for the protestors. Very frequently protestors were divided into two types of people. This representation seemed to be shared by both those who supported and opposed their aims.

4. I think most, probably 90 percent of them, were there for the right reasons and the ones who got on television and hit the headlines were the 10 percent who wanted to beat up the police. (Maxwell: 10)

5. In my opinion a lot of the protestors that were there weren't genuine anti-apartheid, in fact if you asked them what apartheid meant they probably wouldn't be able to tell you. (Davison: 23)

6. I think that along with some very genuine protestors, there were some very non-genuine protestors, the people that are there just because there is a stirring going on. (Pond: 6)

Protestors as a class thus tend to be divided into those with genuine motives and those who are not genuine. This division solves a particular kind of accounting problem for those interviewed. Most wished to support the right to protest but also to condemn violent protest. The subdivision of protestors achieves this goal by separating what are two distinct principles into two types of people or narrative characters.

The concept of genuine and non-genuine motives is a fascinating one because of the model of the mind and rationality it presupposes. This becomes clearer if we look at further descriptions of the 'wrong element' or the non-genuine protestor.

> 7. I feel very strongly that it gave trouble-makers who weren't really interested in the basic morals of it an opportunity to get in and cause trouble, to beat up people, to smash up property. (Bird: 7)

> 8. There's always groups around the country, for instance, maybe a biker gang or something, who are anti-police, and it is a known fact that when the Springbok Tour happened, it was an excuse for them to be able to get into something and do something [ ] I reckon it was an outlet for all sorts of other groups as well who weren't really interested in the issue but just the fact of being able to be violent. (James: 20–1)

> 9. A lot of protestors weren't actually for the cause, they just went for the fun of the game. (Mills: 12)

What motivates this character is the pleasure of violence, the 'fun of the game'. It is accepted that the desire to cause trouble, to aggress against others is an understandable motive and sufficient explanation for behaviour in itself. This is subtly different from the way the police were depicted. Whereas the police were shown as having a natural violent *response* to provocation, they were seen to neither seek it out or enjoy it (cf. Extracts One to Three). It is this difference between the police character and the non-genuine protestor, of course, that allows the police to be excused and this group of protestors to be criticized. The same emphasis on violence at the 'base' of human nature is used but the police violence is understandable and indeed forgiveable, and the protestors' violence is worthy of the strongest condemnation.

Frequently this image of protestors becomes typified and reified into a social category, the 'stirrer' or 'trouble-maker', a category which is immediately recognizable to New Zealanders and prevalent in their discourse in all kinds of contexts. The 'stirrer' is an extremely useful accounting device. Political or other motivations behind violence can be dismissed or ignored since the 'stirrer' is fully explained by this kind of natural self which they possess, no other kind of account is needed.

Thinking in terms of wider ideological consequences, therefore, we can see how this technique for making sense of collective actions might protect and maintain a certain kind of status quo unchallenged. The violent protestor does not need to be taken seriously or speculated about any further. As they have no genuine motives and are completely defined by their understandable enjoyment of violence, energy need not be invested in listening to them. They are a *source* of violence; police violence is merely a *response* (cf. Reicher and Potter, 1985).

The other protestor character, the genuine protestor, who acts as a counterpoint to the non-genuine, has more of an honest soul appearance. For those who support the protest movement, the genuine tend to appear as admirable, committed, moral creatures, standing up for what they believe and compelled to protest by the gravity of the issue. For those espousing support for the tour, on the other hand, the genuine protestor appears as a more bumbling figure as below:

> 10. What angered me really was that a certain small group of New Zealanders, Minto, Awatere, who are communists I believe, led a lot of naive well-meaning New Zealanders who abhor apartheid and organized them, you know, to jump up and down and infringe the rights of other New Zealanders. (Pinter: 11)

> 11. It was mainly the extreme groups which took over, um and stirred people up and, ah, groups like that can, they can agitate normal people who really wouldn't probably even think much about it, and are doing things that they wouldn't normally do and they're usually the ones who get caught. (Wood: 9–10)

In these extracts the genuine protestor character is constructed, as it generally was by those who wished to support the tour, as a suggestible innocent, unaware of the implications of their actions, the well-meaning but essentially misguided humanitarian who is easily persuaded into supporting dubious causes.

This characterization like that of the 'stirrer' is a very effective accounting strategy. It articulates a self, a particular kind of personality or brand of honest soul, and the individual's actions are then explained by this self. The interviewee, hence, is rather like the trait theorist. People's behaviour is explained by their set of traits. What the discourse analyst sees is that in creating this character the psychologist and the New Zealander are not simply neutrally describing reality but constructing a version of events which has a particular practical consequence for the New Zealanders at least: discrediting this group of people.

One of the most interesting things about the characterizations we have described here is the sheer flexibility of the resource. A particular image of human nature is produced, for example. This image can be utilized either to blame or excuse, to praise or condemn. The object can be reconstructed in various ways to offer persuasive versions. For instance, in the extracts below we can see how the accounts can be reversed so that the police take on the attributes of the non-genuine protestor and the protestor the attributes of the police.

> 12. It seemed like he [reference to specific policeman] was almost enjoying the violence and that kind of gave me a revealing sort of side to it. (Rock: 14)

> 13. I wouldn't condone violence, but I can see how [ ] I can see how exasperated [the protestors] got. Um, obviously the lead, the leaders of the protest movements like HART and what have you didn't envisage that sort of confrontation at all. (Mills: 12)

Here it is the police who actively choose to indulge the human propensity for violence because they enjoy it and it is the protestors who lapse from civilized control and 'revert' in some way to natural human responses when provoked.

Overall, in this chapter we have tried to show how a discourse or language-based approach could revolutionize the study of the subject of psychology, the person, the self. We have presented the theoretical arguments which undermine the traditional approach to the self and in this last section we have presented a tentative analysis of some forms of discourse at work in a context where the presentation of other's selves is vital to the discrediting and increditing of the different groups involved in a conflict. Obviously these forms of discourse need to be explored much more thoroughly and indeed the analysis of self-discourse and person construction has only just begun in earnest, but enough has been achieved to show the functional emphasis of this analysis and what might be gained from continuing this enterprise.

6

Categories in discourse

Categorization is an important and pervasive part of people's discourse. In the course of conversation everyone populates their lives with friends, doctors, Americans, extraverts, immigrants and a thesauras of other categories of people. Pick up any newspaper and many of the stories will concern people who are described, evaluated and understood not in terms of any unique features of their biography but through their category membership: 'model reveals star's secret life', 'wife found murdered'.

Categorization is no less fundamental to the social scientist. Much of social psychology is concerned with the attributes of social groups – males, political extremists, working-class adolescents – and experimental or survey findings from representative samples of these people are recurrently extrapolated to other group members. That is, people are taken to be members of relatively enduring social categories, and *in virtue of their category membership* inferences are made from the attributes of individuals to the attributes of the rest of the category. Social categories are, in one way or another, the principal building blocks in many areas of social research.

As well as being a resource for both lay and scientific explanations of behaviour, social categories have increasingly become a topic of research in themselves. Social psychologists have focused on the *cognitive processes* underlying categorization and its *consequences*. What is the cognitive mechanism involved in categorization? How do people break up the social world into distinct groupings? And, given that a category has been applied, what effect will this have on people's perception or understanding? In this tradition, categorization is seen as a natural phenomenon rather like breathing; people automatically transform the polluting detritus of their over-complex physical and social reality into a simplified and readily assimilable form.

In contrast to this approach, workers in the more linguistically orientated traditions of ethnomethodology and discourse analysis have been interested in how categories are constituted in everyday discourse and the various functions they satisfy. Instead of seeing categorization as a natural phenomenon – something which just happens, automatically – it is regarded as a complex and subtle *social accomplishment*. In line with the central theme of this book, this work emphasizes the action orientation of categorizations in discourse. It asks how categories are flexibly articulated in the course of certain sorts of talk and writing to accomplish particular goals, such as blamings or justifications.

In this chapter we will overview the social psychological and discourse approaches in turn. We will stress in particular the implications of the discourse analyses for social psychological work on categorization, and suggest certain lessons for social research more generally.

Social psychology and social categories

Imagine looking at a television screen in an area of extremely poor reception. An image is there, but it is very difficult to decipher in the sea of dots. Someone familiar with the programme then points out that this is a talk show with two personalities in a studio set. You can now 'see' the image more clearly. Two vague shapes coalesce into people while the fuzziness around becomes the studio. The shapes have become both more integral and more distinct. The categories (people/studio set) clarify and simplify; certain regions are seen as more similar than before and certain contrasts are heightened. The traditional social psychological approach assumes that processes of *social* categorization are ultimately derived from perceptual mechanisms of this kind.

Categories and the physical world

A number of experiments have demonstrated effects of this type with non-social objects. In one classic study, for example, Tajfel and Wilkes (1963) showed people sets of lines with different labels on them and asked for an estimate of their length. All the lines differed, some were long and some short. The crucial finding was that if all the shorter lines were labelled A, and the longer ones B, the difference in length between the lines was exaggerated. At the same time there was a tendency for the lines carrying the same label to be seen as more similar. That is, if the lines could be viewed as members of *separate* categories – A and B – *differences* were accentuated and if they could be viewed as members of the *same* category *similarities* were accentuated.

It is claimed that this kind of categorization process is adaptive; it clarifies and systematizes the physical environment. With less confusing noise, and less complexity to handle, the argument runs, the person is better prepared for action (Tajfel, 1981, 1982; Tajfel and Forgas, 1981). These kinds of categorization processes have thus been more or less explicitly glossed in evolutionary terms. The image of the hunter on the savanna, simplifying and systematizing tasty zebras from the irrelevant grass and worrying leopards is difficult to resist. However, what happens when we make categorizations in the social arena?

Categories and the social world

One common answer to this question is: nothing changes. The effect of perceiving *people* in terms of categories is exactly the same as perceiving *objects* in this way. And indeed a body of research has demonstrated the same kind of effects. Wilder (1978), for example, showed some experimental participants a videotape of four people, one of whom was offering his opinions on various topics. In one version of the video the people were presented as a group (they sat at the same table and wore identifying tags), while in another version they were merely shown as unrelated individuals (other differences were, of course, held constant). The task of the participants was to judge how similar the opinions of the others were to the speaker. In line with the experimental hypothesis, Wilder found that seeing people as a group led to judgements of greater similarity between their views.

In another experiment, Allen and Wilder (1979) randomly split a number of boys into two groups and asked them about the opinions and preferences of the boys in their own and the other group. As expected, the boys perceived the opinions and preferences of members of their own group as similar to their own views but different to those of the other group. Moreover, the preferences and beliefs of the boys in the other group were seem as similar to one another. So, as in the Tajfel and Wilkes experiment on the length of lines, the opinions of people categorized together in Wilder's video, and the views of the boys in the same group were seen as more like each other. Similarly, the differences in perceived opinions between the two categories of boys were exaggerated and accentuated.

What has really excited social psychologists about this kind of research is the possibility of understanding and explaining racial stereotyping and hence discrimination. Could it be a natural consequence, as it were, of the way we have evolved to organize the world into categories? Could prejudice be the unfortunate outcome of the biases which emerge when the differences between categories are exaggerated and the differences within them downplayed?

A number of researchers (Hamilton, 1979; Taylor, 1981) have argued exactly that. As Wilder pithily writes, 'categorization, per se, propels the individual down the road to bias' (1986: 293). This is a depressing conclusion, and one that we will argue against later, for it suggests that bias and stereotyping are not social and psychological aberrations, induced perhaps by faulty child-rearing or distorting ideological processes, but an inevitable product of the way our cognitive system is organized, to respond to categories.

Categories and prototypes

Up to now we have described research on the perceptual *consequences* of categorization. However, there is another strand of work which is much more directly concerned with the mechanisms underlying this process: with how people 'think' in terms of categories, how, they assign a particular person to a specific category, for example. Social psychologists have again plundered the theoretical storehouse of cognitive psychology to deal with this problem.

The suggestion offered by Cantor and Mischel (1977, 1979) is that categories are cognitively organized around prototypes; a prototype being a typical or paradigm example. The theory of prototypes has, of course, been developed mainly in cognitive psychology by Eleanor Rosch and her associates (Rosch et al., 1976). Thus, moving out of the social arena for a moment, if we think of birds, the prototypical bird is something like a blackbird or sparrow. This is a classic and familiar example of the category 'bird' which shares most of its main features (has wings, flies, goes tweet and so on). At the same time we are aware that there are other birds such as ostriches and penguins which are very different from the prototype and may be treated as borderline cases; indeed, there may well be disagreement about whether they should be treated as full members of the category at all.

Using this notion, Cantor and Mischel offer a more precise statement of how members are assigned to categories. They suggest that the process is one of matching the potential member to the relevant prototype. Each person carries around a large set of preformed, mentally encoded prototypes; if the potential member shares enough features with one of these it will be included in the category. Thus, if we want to decide whether someone we meet should be categorized as an extravert we compare them to our model instance of extravert (loud voice, goes to lots of parties etc.). If they display enough of these features they will be so categorized.

It is important to note here that Cantor and Mischel are not proposing this process is like following a mechanical algorithm. It may well be that *no* one feature is essential for inclusion. They stress that social categories are not homogeneous entities where each member shares a specified set of features and no others; rather they are 'fuzzy sets' in which members have many things in common but also many differences.

A further feature of the theory of prototypes is the claim that categories will come in hierarchical clusters. To use Cantor and Mischel's example, we will not have one, unitary prototype of a 'cultured person'; rather this will be split up into lower level categories (e.g. 'patron of the arts') which can be subdivided even further ('donator to art museum' and so on – see Figure 6.1). Consistent prototypes will be drawn upon only at this more basic level of categorization; and hence it is here that stereotyping of category members will be most evident (Brewer et al., 1981).

FIGURE 6.1
The organization of sub-prototypes

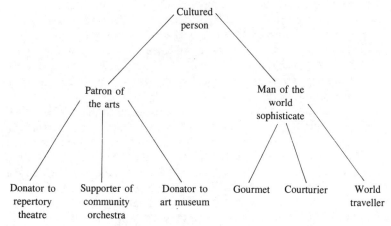

Source: Cantor and Mischel, 1979.

Problems with traditional categorization research

There is now a large and theoretically sophisticated body of research on the topic of categorization and its role in fostering stereotyping and intergroup discrimination (see Tajfel, 1981; Wilder, 1986, for reviews from different perspectives). Despite providing some important insights and findings it is prone to certain difficulties. We suggest these are a consequence of problematic base assumptions about the phenomenon of categorization and the failure to examine categorization as a social practice involving certain sorts of language use. Later in the chapter we will go on to examine some research which develops this alternative perspective. To begin with, though, let us enumerate these problem assumptions.

1. *Inevitability of biased categorization.* Social psychological research has come to view stereotyping as a consequence of purportedly basic and adaptive cognitive processes. People's very perception is seen to be based on categorizations which simplify, and thus result in distorted stereotypes.

2. *Categories have a fixed structure.* The theory of prototypes suggests that categories are fuzzy sets organized around prototypical instances. Categorical perception is dependent on a process of matching stimuli to prototypes, which are further organized in hierarchical structures.

3. *Categories are preformed and enduring.* People are viewed as carrying around a mentally encoded set of preformed and enduring prototypes of category members. These will be stable and will determine perception and understanding.

All these assumptions flow from the basic social cognition approach which attempts to explain social phenomena within the framework of cognitive psychology. It is cognitive processes and structures which are seen as the causal determinants here. The social phenomenon of stereotyping is caused by the way our cognitive systems operate on information, reducing and distorting in the light of the organized structures of prototypes.

If we take a discourse-orientated approach to categorization each of these assumptions becomes rather less convincing. We can contrast the cognitive perspective with the image of the person using their discourse to perform different kinds of acts which we have been developing throughout this book. From this perspective we predict that instead of being a 'victim' of mechanical categorization processes people will both draw flexibly on preformed categories and construct the sense of categories as they talk.

Categorization and particularization

In an important critique, Michael Billig (1985) had radically questioned the first of the assumptions identified above. He has argued against the idea that perception should be the primary metaphor for prejudiced judgement and that simplifying categorizations are necessarily adaptive.

He starts with a basic but telling point. The perceptual model leads us to overlook the fact that people are constantly prejudiced against groups whose members they have never met and hence we ignore the social convention component in prejudice. Furthermore, the stress on perception seems to make the expression of prejudice *in talk* a secondary or epiphenomenon. Given that many people spend considerable time propounding racist views in casual conversation about groups they may have rarely or never seen, this relegation seems entirely pointless. Like discourse analysts (see also van Dijk, 1985, and Reeves, 1983), Billig suggests that to understand prejudice more fully we need to bring talk or rhetoric back to centre stage, displacing perception.

In contrast to the claim that categorization is a natural and adaptive process, Billig suggests that both categorization and the *opposite* process of particularization (splitting categories in parts, or distinguishing specific instances from categories) are necessary for dealing with the world. The distorted emphasis on the process of categorization alone has led to what Billig describes as a 'bureaucratic model of thought':

> much of thinking is seen as a process of locking the unfamiliar into safe, familiar categories. . .the image of the person to emerge from this approach resembles that of a bureaucrat sensibly ordering the messy stimulus world. . .Just as a bureaucrat might defend office procedures, so these theorists [Hamilton, 1979; Snyder, 1981; Rothbart, 1981] talk of organization, order, management, efficiency, etc. (1985: 87–8)

What is lacking in discussions of social cognition is the ability to transcend the limits of familiar categories, to develop new procedures, and to reach out, through particularization, to the unique features of individual cases. These abilities are equally 'natural' to social life as those of grouping, classifying and categorizing.

Finally, Billig suggests that if we think about the reality of racist and stereotyped categorizations we can see the importance of both rigidity *and* flexibility in prejudiced judgement. For example, if a white British person is going to rigidly maintain that, say, West Indians are 'lazy and unmotivated' they will probably need to also constructively and flexibly manipulate their discourse to deal with any information threatening this generalization. Perhaps they will need to generate all sorts of subcategories of West Indians to neutralize potentially problematic examples of hard-working and motivated West Indian behaviour. That is, they may well rely on the very techniques of making exceptions and particularizing undervalued by the categorization approach to maintain their biased, prejudiced response. Billig proposes that instead of trying to understand prejudice in terms of the operation of the single process of categorization we should move to looking at how both categorization and particularization are managed wherever talk is manifested. Let us now go on to examine the research traditions which have followed this procedure.

Prototypes and variability

In a number of earlier chapters we demonstrated how discourse analysts use the detailed examination of variability in accounts as a basic research strategy. Different versions and forms of talk are the analyzable trace of the way language is used to bring about different ends. Varying accounts can be thought of as the residue of the social practices through which people organize their lives; practices ranging, as we have seen, from persuading others of the correctness of a large-scale scientific theory through to accounting for the refusal of a party invitation; from justifying racial inequality in a society to choosing a turn of phrase which starts to close down a telephone conversation.

At the same time, the embarrassing presence of radical and pervasive variability calls into question those theoretical perspectives – whether they focus on attitudes, rules, the self – which were meant to reveal an illuminating consistency in social life. To be of heuristic value, theories of this kind should be able to explain actual patterns of social behaviour, and allow us to predict patterns in the future. Failure in this central task is fatal.

Cantor and Mischel's theory of the operation of prototypes in the perception of category membership has similar general goals to the theories we criticized in earlier chapters. As we indicated, their model of prototypes suggests that people come to identify category members, and indeed grasp the meaning of categories via typical or paradigm examples which all properly socialized members of the group share. The category is 'anchored' to the prototype. If people's perception and understanding are determined by their prototypes in this way we should expect to find considerable consistency between descriptions of category members given by people from within the same subculture.

Prototypes of Maoris

We have looked at this issue of prototype variability in a study conducted with Ruth McFadyen (Wetherell et al., 1986) on middle-class, white, New Zealanders' discourse about Maoris, the indigenous people colonized by the British. In the course of semi-structured interviews, descriptions of Maoris came up repeatedly, in topics such as positive discrimination, land rights, and the South African rugby tour of 1981. If white New Zealanders do use stable prototypes of the category Maori there ought to be a high degree of consistency in the depiction of Maoris across different topics.

The problem for the theory of prototypes is that this consistency was not there, although the New Zealand situation resembles many other 'race relations' situations in Britain, America, Canada etc. and categorization theory is supposed to be particularly relevant to prejudice and stereotyping issues. Indeed, we did not need to look very far to find examples of highly variable discourse about this category of people. For example, we chose four interview transcripts at random and noted all adjectives the participants applied to Maoris. The entire list is reproduced in Figure 6.2. Out of a total of sixty-two adjectives, only three were the same: using the term 'friendly'. Of course, if we repeat this exercise with more transcripts we find some increase in overlapping terms – but we also find a concomitant increase in unique terms. It is clear that the variability is at least as striking as any consistency.

As we saw in Chapter Two, a common technique social psychologists have introduced to deal with variability of this kind is the use of some form of gross categorization. That is, the adoption of a categorization scheme which is broad and ambiguous enough to eliminate variability, or at least to cut it down. This kind of scheme could, for example, classify together apparently similar adjectives such as 'dirty' and 'scruffy'. The problem here, however, is that consistency becomes an achievement of the researcher rather than a feature of the discourse. For example, participants themselves may, on occasion, see important differences between the sense of 'dirty' and 'scruffy'; 'dirty' may be used to denote the distasteful and uncivilized, while 'scruffy' may refer to a laid back, streetwise

FIGURE 6.2
Four speakers' descriptions of Maoris

Speaker One
Independent
Responsibility in family gone
Mature
Worldly
Lost their culture
Stirring
Like to congregate
Lovely ethnic feeling for each other
Like driving
Like playing with machinery
Tend to go for jobs which are manual
Make good soldiers
Haven't got stickability
What you've got is theirs
They steal

Speaker Two
Passive
Not interested in language revival
Don't take advantage of education
Dirty
Scruffy
Evil-looking
Hot-heads
Isn't a leader

Speaker Three
Proud
Wonderful
Don't want to share their culture
Busy reestablishing themselves
Trendy
No motivation
Takes care of her children
Friendly relaxed manner

Music lovely
Use same sort of expression
Friendly

Speaker Four
Feel disadvantaged
Slow
Feel they have no self-esteem
Need to take a positive view of their life
Must look at selves and decide strengths
   and weaknesses
Feeling money will put disadvantages
   right
Feelings inside all wrong
Simply need not get together
Get cracking
All work together
Behaving in unacceptable way
Wider family is important to them
Balance good feelings: body, spirit, soul
Not observing own standards of hygiene
Not observing own cultural beliefs
Great difficulty opening up their hearts,
   telling how they feel
Demanding
Expecting
Need a bit more insight
Need more exercise and self control
Marvellous
Very good
Courteous
Smile
Welcome
Friendly
Happy

demeanor which could be essentially positive. These significant nuances would be lost if researchers simply aggregated terms. Classifications of this kind should not come from the researcher's commonsense semantics, but from a detailed analysis of participants' own use of discourse.

Even gross categorization of this kind would be unable to handle much of the variation found in this material. It is not easy to find sensible classifications which encompass contradictory adjectives such as 'they're proud' and 'they've lost their pride and dignity'; 'lazy race' and 'such hard-working people'; 'lack of greed' and 'quite selfish and greedy' (see Figure 6.3). For just about every statement made about Maoris an opposing or contradictory statement was also offered somewhere else in the material.

FIGURE 6.3
Inconsistencies between respondent's descriptions of Maoris

Lazy race	Such hard-working people
They're proud	Lost their pride and dignity
Proud of all their background	Humble
Want to split this society	Passive
They really know how to put a story across, to get the message across, are orators	They come across as clueless they don't know how to express their views
Great respect of older folks	Very good at taking advantage of their old
Less materialistic and more diverting in their culture	Quite selfish and greedy
Relaxed friendly manner	Ill at ease

Can prototype theory be sustained?

One way of responding to findings of this kind might be to suggest that different participants were drawing upon different prototypes. Variable accounts, then, would merely be a consequence of people's variable individual prototypes. However, the difficulty here is that variation was pervasive and extreme even within the talk of the same participants. One respondent, for instance, described Maoris as having 'an innate understanding of their land' and claimed shortly after that 'their land is just a bit of dirt to them'.

Another type of response to this inconsistency might be to argue that it is a consequence of the different *levels* of categorization operating (Brewer et al., 1981). In this view, contradictions are produced by people moving between different subprototypes of Maoris – Maori children, Maori parents, Maori leaders etc. Thus inconsistency only appears if the researcher assumes participants are working with the broad superordinate: Maori.

The first thing to note about this view is the danger of making the theory so flexible and post hoc that it can predict virtually anything. We reach the point where a prototype is posited to explain every single variation in accounts of Maoris, and the theory becomes empirically empty. However, even if we remain with the limited splitting into subtypes indicated above, the problem of variability returns to haunt the theory.

When our data were analysed in terms of the sorts of subtypes where prototype theorists might expect consistency we again found variability. In our respondents' discourse Maori parents, for example, are both 'very fond of their children' and they 'aren't interested in their kids'; Maori leaders are 'often too radical' and 'you don't see them agitating'.

Of course it might well be possible for a prototype theorist to do some judicious splitting into sub-subcategories, and to further emphasize individual differences, and thereby provide some sort of account of these data. But this is going to get very clumsy indeed. Our claim is that discourse analysts are able to provide a much more workable explanation of the variations which occur in participant's discourse. By highlighting the functions of talk we can explain why a category of people should be described in one way on one occasion and in a different way on another. Rather than demonstrate this in detail with the above data (see Wetherell et al., 1986, for examples) we will turn to ethnomethodologically inspired work on social categories, which was the first look at social categorization from this general perspective.

Motives and membership categories

Given that ethnomethodology's central concern is with the way people make sense of their world – their ordinary reasoning – and given that ethnomethodologists take a strongly functional view of talk, it is not surprising that they took an early interest in people's social categorizations. For these researchers, this was an area of discourse fundamentally involved in the way ordinary people make sense of social structure and provide coherence to their social worlds. At the same time, the ethnomethodological concern with the active *accomplishment* of social phenomena and interaction sensitized them to the possibility that categories might be more than simplifying perceptual sunglasses but deliberate constructions fitted for many tasks.

Harold Garfinkel himself took this approach in a detailed and fascinating case study of 'Agnes', a would be transsexual (Garfinkel. 1967). Garfinkel adopted the view that membership of the gender categories 'male' and 'female' is not merely a factual matter of biology but, in social psychological terms, negotiated *achievement*. The study documents the complex and subtle procedures Agnes had to learn so that she/he could successfully bring herself/himself off as a woman.

Harvey Sacks – whose work we introduced in Chapter Four – took the study of categories in another direction. He was particularly concerned with the kinds of inferences people make when category terms are used and, as a consequence of this, the ends categories work towards. In a paper edited from a lecture given in 1965 (Sacks, 1979) we can see just how radically his view of categories differed from the standard social psychological formulation.

Hotrodders and teenage drivers

Sacks starts with the question of why American kids generate so many new typologies of cars. Why, he asks, are the existing terms not good enough? Sacks notes how different category terms are enmeshed in, and can be used to exemplify, different world views. For a contemporary example we only have to think of 'gay' and 'faggot' as competing descriptive terms for 'homosexuals' (Watson and Weinberg, 1982). The example Sacks uses are the competing descriptions, 'teenage driver' and 'hotrodder' (remember, this is 1965). The former term is used by adults and reflects an adult view of teenagers who drive cars. The latter term, however, reflects an alternative, non-adult, world view; a world which revolves around customizing cars and racing them in the street, much to the displeasure of the police.

Sacks illustrates the way these competing descriptions are managed using a piece of recorded dialogue. To understand this exchange we need to know that a Bonneville is the sort of souped-up car driven by a 'hotrodder', while a Pontiac station wagon is an everyday, straight from Detroit, motor, the sort that might be driven by a 'teenager'. The categories of cars are linked to the categories of people. (The transcription is slighly simplified and edited from the original.)

1. *Ken*: In that Bonneville of mine, I could take that thing out, an' if I've gotta tie, and a sweater on, an' I look clean ninety nine percent of the time a guy could pull up to me, the same car, same colour, same year the whole bit, roar up on his pipes, and he's inna dirty grubby tee shirt, an' the guy [policeman] will pick the guy up in the dirty grubby tee shirt before he'll pick me up.
   (2.0)
   (   ):   hheh
   Ken: J'st just for   uh
   Al: (But) not many people get picked up in a Pontiac station wagon.

(Sacks, 1979: 7)

Ken is claiming that he can go out, smartly dressed, in what we learn from Al's interruption is his, in fact, non-customized Pontiac, get into drag races and then – because of his clothes and car – not get picked up by the police. Sacks suggests that Ken is seen to be trying to have his cake and eat it. He is claiming to be a hotrodder; while at the same time remaining loyal to the safe adult version of the world. Hence Al's sarcastic deflation:

why would the police pick someone up in a Pontiac like that? One reason for generating typologies of cars, then, is to mark alternative social categories. That is, the selection from the category of cars 'Bonneville'/'Pontiac' displays membership of the category 'hotrodder' versus 'teenager'. Al has picked Ken up on, in effect, an illegitimate claim to be a member of the category 'hotrodder'. What we are seeing here, according to Sacks, is the policing of a category and, ultimately, the preservation of an alternative version of the social world (see also Cuff and Hustler, 1982).

Membership categorization and ordinary reasoning

In his later work, Sacks (1972, 1974) went on to pay detailed attention to people's use of categories in their ordinary reasoning. On this topic, his best-known contribution concerned membership categories and categorization devices. Although this began with some of the most mundane features of our category discourse, its aim was to use these to illuminate the details and subtleties of complex social acts, such as blamings and mitigations.

A membership category is simply a commonsense equivalence class for the identification of people in talk, e.g. 'teenagers', 'Maoris'. A membership categorization device groups together membership categories. Thus 'family' is a membership categorization device (MCD) which groups together 'brother', 'mother', 'baby' and so on while the MCD 'gender' groups together the categories 'male' and 'female'.

It might seem that this is a rather clumsy way of referring to the fact, noted earlier in our discussion of prototypes, that categories may be ordered into hierarchies. However, the use of the term 'device' reflects the ethnomethodological emphasis on the *constructive* nature of talk; the collection of a set of categories together and the creation of an MCD are active accomplishments. Categories are not nested in a clear-cut, natural way like Russian dolls, for example, one inside another, but are grouped into collections by the use of potentially complex and contradictory sets of interpretative procedures. We shall return to these differences between ethnomethodological and social cognition approaches to categorization later.

Sacks suggests that there are certain basic practices which people draw on in their everyday discourse concerning categories. For example, there is a maxim of 'consistency' which states that if one category from a MCD has been used it may well be appropriate to use another from that MCD. For the hearer of the discourse this means that if two categorizations which could be from the same MCD (but are not necessarily so) are used, they will be heard as coming from the same MCD. For example, the categorization 'sister' could appear in the MCD 'family' and the MCD 'feminists'. How it will be interpreted will depend in part on, for instance, whether the category 'father' or the category 'activist' has already appeared in the discourse.

Sacks further points out that certain categories have what he calls 'duplicative organization'. What he means by this is that the category is not merely a boundary to an independent set of individuals; rather, the individuals may also be seen having some kind of interpersonal organization. We can contrast categories such as 'family' and 'gang' which are duplicatively organized and those such as 'redheads' or 'Scots' which may not be. The former may have 'in-group loyalty' and 'stick together' – the latter may not have these features (Watson, 1978). It is important to note that interpersonal features such as in-group loyalty are occasioned rather than necessary. That is, they are available to be established in the course of a particular account rather than intrinsically linked to the categories.

The overall point is that people draw upon knowledge of the organization of categories as a resource for producing economical and intelligible conversation. As well as relying on this kind of knowledge, Sacks notes that people also draw on conventional knowledge about the *activities* of members of categories. For example, one of the things we conventionally expect members of the category 'baby' to do is cry. Crying can thus be seen as an activity bound to the category 'baby'. Likewise, giving medical help and writing prescriptions are category-bound activities belonging to doctors. In fact, as Watson (1978) and Jayyusi (1984) have noted, it is not just activities which are conventionally bound to categories; a whole cluster of features may be expected of categories: the traits and preferences of the incumbents, where they live, what they look like, what they wear and so on.

The fact that membership categories can be conventionally tied to, or associated with, specific activities and other features, provides people with a powerful resource for making sense of their social worlds. In particular, it allows them to make inferences, or discursive connections to the category membership of the actors. And, conversely, given that they know only a person's category membership, they can make a good guess as to the kinds of things that person is likely to be doing. If someone is writing out a prescription we expect them to be a doctor; if there is crying we may look around for the baby. Put another way, if we hear a doctor crying or see a baby writing a prescription we will expect an account of the special circumstances which led to this aberrant behaviour.

Now of course, these features of categorization have also been identified by social psychologists. Tajfel (1981), for instance, talks about inductive category errors where people mistakenly work from some features of an individual, ignoring other features, in order to categorize them. Nevertheless a very different perspective underlies the similar points made by ethnomethodologists and social psychologists. This difference will become more and more obvious as we proceed to research examples.

The basic ethnomethodological insights have provided some powerful tools for revealing some of the details of social phenomena such as blamings, accusations, and mitigations (Drew, 1978; Jayyusi, 1984; Lee, 1984; Watson, 1978, 1983; Watson and Weinberg, 1982; Wowk, 1984). To illustrate how they can be used, we will take examples from studies by Rod Watson and Maria Wowk on the role of categorizations when blame is being allocated in a murder investigation.

Race, gender and blame

One of the attractions of studying murder confessions and police inter-rogations of suspects is that they bring issues of culpability and motive to the forefront of discourse. In general, suspects know that certain sorts of motivations may be seen as more culpable than others, and that a range of circumstances may make them appear less blameworthy and more under-standable. Thus when suspects construct descriptions of their crimes they do 'motive work' (Mills, 1940). That is, they construct a version of the crime and what led them to commit it in such a way that the act is mitigated or even justified (Scott and Lyman, 1968). In British and American legal systems punishment is not an automatic consequence of the sheer behaviour of killing someone; circumstances, beliefs and motives are all taken into account and punishment varied accordingly.

In this context, categorization is a resource which suspects frequently draw on to help produce the most appropriate motive account. Take the extract below, for example. Watson notes that there are at least three plausible motivations for the murder of a black female by the black male who is doing the speaking: financial, sexual and racial; and he suggests that this passage of talk works to preserve the racial motive and disclaim the financial one.

2. Then he turned off the ignition then the one in the back he said "alright who doing whoring around out here?" Then [the victim] said well if you want money, I don't have money so the [accomplice] in the back said we don't want your money [ ] and then he said "we disgusted him every time one of his *black sisters* goes to bed with *white men* and was going to put a stop to it." He asked [the victim] again why she went to bed with the *white men* and she told him she had three kids and he said [she] was a God damn liar and punched her in the face and about the body a couple of times. (Watson, 1983: 50, emphasis added)

In this part of the interview the suspect deploys two membership categorizations: 'black sister' and 'white men'. In terms of Sacks' consistency rule, we can clearly see the predicates 'black' and 'white' as from the MCD 'race'; however, it is not easy to view 'sister' and 'men' as from a single MCD. Watson suggests that this complex of categorizations, which both follows and flouts the consistency rule, is carefully constructed to produce a particular effect.

The category 'sister' is derived from the MCD 'family' which, as we noted above, is generally understood as duplicatively organized; it groups together categories of people who are then seen to have a variety of inter-personal bonds. The (black) suspect's categorization of the victim as a black sister thus stresses his co-incumbency of the category 'black' and trades on the affiliative, team-like properties of that co-incumbency. Watson's point is that the categorizations pull together the suspect and victim while contrasting the victim with those she purportedly goes to bed with ('white men' note, not 'white brothers'). This construction provides the motive. The impassioned murder of someone who has dragged her whole family – even if it is only a family in metaphorical terms – into the mire of disrepute is so much more understandable than the cold-blooded murder of a young woman where the only motive is the theft of a small quantity of money.

While in Watson's example the motive work is done more or less directly by the use of explicit categorizations, the categorization in the murder confession analysed by Maria Wowk must be inferred. The confession contains what Watson and Weinberg (1982) have described as a 'category puzzle'; a set of behaviours is described and the listener has the task of making sense of them. The problem they are faced with is: what kind of category member would act in this way? Here are some extracts from the confession.

3. *Suspect*. I got to the intersection (.2) of Brookland and Slade (1.0) when this girl walked up to me (.6) and propositioned me
(1.0)
Policeman. what did she exactly say to you Lewis?
Suspect. you look like a tough guy (1.2) y'look like the member of a gang (1.2) I told here I'm not a member of a gang (.) I'm an independent (.7) and she propositioned me again
[ ]
Policeman. what did she ask actually say to you
[ ]
Suspect. she asked me if I would like to get laid
[later in confession]
Suspect. urh (1.4) the girl got (.8) might say kind of (.2) pricky (1.0) and er::
[ ]
she propositioned me again (.6) and then she called me a prick hh (.) a no good sonofabitch (.) hhh and she threw what was left at (.2) the remainder (.) of the bottle of beer at me
[ ]
at that (1.2) I threw al (.) a right handed punch (.2) from the waist towards her shoulder...[goes on to describe killing] (Wowk, 1984: 80–1)

As we noted above, one powerful resource used in everyday reasoning is the idea of the category-boundedness of activity. People conventionally make inferences from categories to the activities of incumbents and, conversely, from activities to the category membership of actors. In this extract we are presented with both a category – 'a girl' – and activities – propositioning the suspect, calling him a 'prick' and a 'no good sonofabitch', throwing beer at him etc. The puzzle for the listeners is to provide a categorization which can account for these activities in a way that 'girl' fails to do.

Wowk suggests that, given the described activities, the conventional puzzle solution will be to further specify the category membership of the girl as a 'tramp', 'slut' or even 'hooker', all categories which have strongly derogatory implications. These provide a negative moral assessment in the way 'girl' does not. Yet, as they are not offered explicitly by the suspect, he can make a negative moral assessment of the victim available, while maintaining a position which allows him to deny that he views the victim as a slut. Nevertheless, reapportioning some of the blame in this way is exactly the upshot of the suspect's account.

In both of these analyses, then, we see a very different picture of the way categories operate from the one offered by social cognition researchers such as Wilder and Cantor. Rather than viewing the process of categorization as a defect in perception – albeit an adaptive one – these researchers have demonstrated how categorizations can be carefully inserted into discourse as part of the joint activities of blaming (the victims) and mitigation, and thus how categories can be read.

Categories, content and community

One of the features of the traditional social psychological approach to categorization is its tendency to treat categories as if they were distorting enclosures anchored to unitary consistent prototypes. Their damaging social consequences are said to arise from effects such as the over-inclusion of people into the category, and the possibly stereotyped nature of the prototype (Pettigrew et al., 1958; Tajfel, 1969).

The studies examined in the last section reveal a rather different set of categorization phenomena. They display categorizations used not so much for their 'boundary work', grouping and separating individuals, but for the category-based inferences made available. Watson demonstrated in Extract Two how the suspect's use of 'white men' and 'black sister' was not simply an exercise in inclusive grouping (although it inevitably achieved this) but the groundwork for an imputation of motive. Although, on the face of it, the idea of categories carrying a cluster of category-based attributes is similar to the notion of categories anchored to a prototype with a limited set of features, there is a crucial difference between these two models.

For the social cognition researcher the prototype determines perception through the operation of a feature matching process; if the stimulus shares the prerequisite number of features with the prototype it will be included in the category. For those who study the operation of categories in discourse, however, the cluster of category-based attributes is not viewed as a kind of mental picture influencing perception but as a potentially inconsistent cluster of expectations and associations drawn on in an *occasioned* manner. The point is that these expectations are selectively managed, in the context of passages of talk and writing, to present certain effects (Drew, 1978; Jayyusi, 1984). Thus some features may be made focal, others ignored, and yet others reconstructed. An understanding of the effectiveness of categorizations will thus depend on both elucidating the relevant cluster of attributes and the detail of their deployment in discourse. We will illustrate how this can be done by looking at a detailed study of how the categorization 'community' was used in accounts of a 'riot' (Potter and Reicher, 1987; see also Halliday and Potter, 1986; Reicher and Potter, 1985).

Uses of 'community'

In the spring of 1980 an event occurred in Bristol which came to be known as the 'St Paul's riot'. Fighting took place between police and youths on the streets of the St Paul's area of Bristol over a period of some hours. Several police vehicles and properties were destroyed, a number of police and civilians were injured – although none seriously – and the event dominated the next day's national news coverage and resulted in an emergency debate in Parliament. This seemed an ideal opportunity to look at the way social categories are used in the representation of conflict.

The study worked with an archive of documents: copies of reports and editorials from the local and national press, transcripts of television news and current affairs programmes, records of parliamentary proceedings, official reports and transcripts of interviews with people who were actively involved in the events.

Since much of the time the discourse of conflict was addressed to defining the nature of the protagonists, it was an especially rich context in which to study people's use of categorizations, and in particular their use of the categorization 'community'.

The analysis was initiated by selecting out from the archive all instances of the term 'community' and its synonyms, and went on to identify the different predicates used with the term, along with the varying ways it was adopted to refer to the protagonists in the events. It was immediately apparent that certain sorts of predicates were repeatedly used, in particular predicates describing a certain cohesive style of social relationship: 'closeness', 'integration' and 'friendliness', and those associated with certain metaphors: spatial ('close-knit'), organism ('growth') and agency (a community 'acts') – see Figure 6.4. Without exception, where the term 'community' was used with a strongly evaluative force it was positive: 'community' was seen as a good thing.

FIGURE 6.4

Predicates and metaphors used with 'community'

Sample predicates	Metaphors (where relevant)
Friendly	
Warm	
Happy	
Harmonious	
Close-knit	Spatial
Integrated	
Tight	
Grows	Organic
Evolves	
Matures	
Acts	Agency
Knows	
Feels	

Despite the broad agreement in the attribute cluster connected with the category 'community', considerable variability was evident in the application of the term. In some accounts, for example, the 'community' had been 'disrupted' or even 'finished' by the 'riot'; in others the 'riot' was merely a sign of the cohesiveness of the 'community'. In some accounts the police were depicted as part of the 'community'; in others the disturbance was a conflict between the 'community' and the police. Variability on this scale has now become a very familiar phenomenon. Yet it represents an enormous headache for any realist approach to participants' discourse, and particularly for those researchers bent on reconstructing exactly what went on, between whom, in the disturbance. It is for this reason that research generally uses procedures which render variability invisible. But, if we look to the action orientation of the accounts, differences become much more understandable.

One major difference in the data occurred between a broad group of accounts which depicted the events in St Paul's as a 'community relations'

problem and another group of accounts which treated them as a direct
conflict between the 'community' and the police. Contrast the following
passages which illustrate these two versions. The first is a statement by
the then Home Secretary, William Whitelaw, made in the parliamentary
debate which followed the disturbance; the second is from the beginning
of a report in the newspaper *Socialist Challenge*.

4. *Whitelaw.* As to what the Right Honourable Gentleman says about the
   community relations work of the police, it does so happen that a police officer
   in this particular area of Bristol, as I understand, has been very active indeed
   in the area of Community Council. He has been one of the most highly
   respected members of that council who have done a great deal of the sort
   of work that the Right Honourable Gentleman has in mind.

5. ON WEDNESDAY 2nd April, the mainly black population of St. Paul's,
   a Bristol inner-city district, responded to police harrassment by mounting
   a counter attack. The police are the most visible instrument of state repression
   of the black minority in Britain today. Almost exactly a year after the police
   riot in Southall, the black community of St. Paul's fought back against police
   brutality and won.

Extract Four was typical of one kind of interpretation of the disturbance.
Whitelaw was responding to a question about 'community policing'. He
formulated his reply in the rather broader terms of the 'community relations
work of the police' and claimed that this work already existed, citing an
active member of the 'Community Council'. The effect is to include
problems of policing under the topic of 'community relations' – which
he had earlier characterized as good – and to support this characterization
with strongly positive, but at the same time very vague, allusions to the
work of a 'community police officer'.

Throughout the parliamentary debate the 'riot' was described in this
manner as a problem of 'community relations' and the police were depicted
as part of the 'community'; thus preparing the way for a response to the
events which follows from the cluster of features bound to the category
'community'. If a '*community*' had been disturbed the problem will be
one of fractured interpersonal relationships and trust. Thus the proposed
response is directed at these points. It includes further representation of
police on community bodies as in Extract Four, the development of
personal relationships and trust between police and locals, and a construal
of the conflict in 'human terms'. In general, the use of 'community' in
this way leads inexorably to the introduction of 'community policing':
the perfect solution to 'community relations problems'.

Extract Five is very different. Instead of formulating the event as a riot
triggered by ailing 'community relations' it is depicted as an open conflict,
with the two sides explicitly characterized as the 'black community' and
the police. Furthermore, a clear-cut and straightforward causal story of

the conflict is offered: the 'black community' was responding to 'harassment' and 'brutality', so the conflict is a *natural* part of an ongoing *intergroup* struggle.

In accounts of this kind, the cluster of category-bound attributes and the positive force of 'community' contribute three consequences. First, the police are implicitly blamed; for 'communities' are not reasonable targets for police attack (unlike, say, 'thugs' or 'crazed rioters' – see Trew, 1979a). Second, actions against the police are legitimated. As 'communities' have the category-bound attribute of harmonious personal relationships, if they become involved in violence it will most likely be seen as externally caused and justifiable. Third, any potential dismissal of people fighting with police as marginal or pathological is undermined; depicting them as 'the community' they are made central and indeed representative of the area. Versions of this kind lead to a distinct, alternative set of solutions. Instead of 'community policing' being the answer the curbing of a repressive and racist police force is proposed.

Categories and the construction of discourse

Earlier in the chapter we identified three kinds of assumptions which are perenially made in traditional social psychological work on categories and which become questionable when a discourse-orientated perspective is adopted. These were that categories are preformed and enduring, they have a fixed structure and inevitably lead to biased perception. Having explored some of the research on categories in discourse we are now in a position to see the problems with these assumptions more clearly.

The idea that categories are enduring, preformed entities is hard to maintain in the light of widespread variation in the content of category accounts (as well as papers cited above, see Gilbert and Mulkay, 1984: ch. 5; Yearley, 1984b). This variation and the active reconstruction of categories cannot be easily reconciled with the popular cognitive models in this area, especially Eleanor Rosch's theory of prototypes, but is perfectly compatible with discourse theory which sees variation as thrown up in the wake of action.

Likewise, the concept of categories structured as fuzzy sets anchored to prototypes and organized in hierarchies differs markedly from the notion of structure revealed in discourse analyses. As we saw in the previous section, the relatively static exemplar or prototype is replaced with the idea of a cluster of potentially inconsistent features and expectations. It would be wrong to think of these expectations as constituting a clear-cut, prestructured, enduring list. Nor should our talk of the 'function' of category accounts be taken to mean that categorizations *in themselves* notably lead to certain consequences. The relevance and detailed nature of the expectations associated with a category is worked up in passages of discourse. This is not to say that prior expectations and understanding are not important; rather that these are drawn on as a resource from which the detailed sense and implication of the category account is manufactured. We will elaborate on this idea in Chapter Seven when we introduce the notion of linguistic repertoires.

The suggestion that categories have a fundamental role in biasing perception is replaced, in the discourse analytic work, with the idea of categories being actively constructed and drawn on for many *different* actions: bias and tolerance effects included. It may well be that categorizations are often associated with phenomena such as over-inclusion and simplification; however, research on categories in discourse has shown that categorization is very far from the mechanical cognitive process implied by traditional work. Many different studies have shown that categories are selected and formulated in such a way that their specific features help accomplish certain goals. This accomplishment does not depend merely on the homogenizing properties of categorization, their ability to group a set of stimuli, but on features specific to the category. For example, we saw how accounts could use descriptions of actions bound to the category 'tramp' in the course of a blaming, or features bound to the category 'community' to provide certain actions with legitimacy.

One of the benefits of the discourse approach to categorization is that it has directed attention away from the cognitive processes assumed to be operating under people's skulls and on towards the detail of how categories are actually used. The study of categories unfolds into the general study of the organization of discourse and its consequences (Billig, 1985, 1987). It is not surprising that categories are so important, because they are the nouns from which we construct versions of the collectivities in which we live. In a sense, they are the building blocks of our many versions of the social world; however, once we look closely at the blocks we see that they themselves are not solid and defined, but have to be moulded in discourse for use in different accounts.

end

7

From representations to repertoires

One of the main aims of social psychology is the identification of broad patterns in human behaviour. Social psychologists have not just been interested in individual actions, but in the way these actions are fitted into episodes, systems or sequences (Clarke, 1983; von Cranach and Harré 1982; Forgas, 1979). Recently, one particular theory with this kind of integrative goal has attracted an enormous amount of interest in social psychology – Moscovici's (1976, 1981, 1982, 1984a) theory of social representations. Social representations are seen as mental schemata or images which people use to make sense of the world and to communicate with each other. It has been suggested that this concept offers a new frame-work for understanding the organization of attitudes, beliefs and attributions and will be able to provide a principled criterion for distinguishing the members of different social groups.

Because the theory of social representations has been so important to the new styles of research emerging in European social psychology and because, in certain respects, it covers the same kind of ground as discourse analysis, we will examine it in detail in this chapter. This will give us an opportunity to demonstrate how discourse analysis can fulfil the need for more integrative perspectives, developing broader units than those traditionally used by linguists (phoneme, word, sentence) and conversational analysts (turn, adjacency pair, closing) to make sense of social life.

One unit which has been explored in a number of discourse studies is the interpretative repertoire (Gilbert and Mulkay, 1984; Potter and Mulkay, 1982, 1985; Wetherell, 1986). The interpretative repertoire is basically a lexicon or register of terms and metaphors drawn upon to characterize and evaluate actions and events. For example, the categorization 'community', at which we looked in Chapter Six, is achieved by the use of a cluster of terms and metaphors which are selectively put forward to provide evaluative versions of the events taking place in a 'riot'. In this sense, we can identify a small-scale interpretative repertoire: the community repertoire (Potter and Reicher, 1987).

This chapter will, thus, contrast social representations and interpretative repertoires. We will first overview the theory of social representations, and point to a number of problems with both its coherence (McKinlay and Potter, forthcoming) and the way its principal concepts have been applied in research (Litton and Potter, 1985; Potter and Litton, 1985). The rest of the chapter will then introduce a body of research using the notion of interpretative repertoire which, although more modest in its goals, has, we feel, a number of advantages in comparison with Moscovici's approach. We hope to be able to demonstrate these advantages.

The theory of social representations

Social representations is not an easy theory to describe. Moscovici's writings are fragmented and sometimes contradictory (McKinlay and Potter, forthcoming) and researchers have tended to interpret the theory in widely divergent ways (Parker, forthcoming). It has been used to examine a range of social phenomena: for example, alliances in a student protest movement (Di Giacomo, 1980), explanations of road accidents (Barjonet, 1980), the design of experiments (Farr, 1984), and in two of the most developed projects, people's representations of psychoanalysis (Moscovici, 1976) and health and illness (Herzlich, 1973). In the following exposition we will stay as close as possible to Moscovici's various theoretical statements (1981, 1982, 1984a, 1985).

Representation and object

Social representations are mental entities. They are made up of both abstract and concrete elements (concepts and images, respectively). In each representation these elements have a specific structure. For most representations the concrete elements or images are the most important; in these cases the representation will be built around what Moscovici calls a 'figurative nucleus'. Social representations provide, quite literally, the means for people to understand and evaluate their worlds. For Moscovici, *all* thought and understanding is based on their working.

For example, in traditional public opinion polling people are often asked questions about, among other things, political parties. People give their opinion about the party; so we have, on the one hand, the party and, on the other, the psychological entity: the opinion. In contrast to this, social representations theory proposes a rather more complicated threefold model. First, there is the political party; second, there is the person's social *representation* of that party; third, there is the person's opinion, which is derived from the representation.

The person's representation of the British Conservative Party might be made up of specific abstract elements, e.g. 'a previously humanitarian grouping that has become authoritarian and racist', and concrete elements, an image, for instance, of a broad grouping of 'moderates' who have been 'penetrated' by a powerful group of 'extremists' from the 'far right'. This version of the party is clearly not a mere neutral description, but one which provides a negative evaluation. If this person was asked by a pollster which way they might vote in a general election they might say they used to vote Conservative but no longer. Moscovici's important point is that to understand *why* the person has offered this particular opinion we need to understand the person's social representations (concepts and images) of political parties (as well as their associated representations of the democratic process, the workings of the economy and so on).

Social representations are also assumed to underpin attributions or the causal explanations people give for events. We can see why if we carry on with the political party example. If the person with the representation of the Conservative described above is asked to explain why the party supported a particular piece of racist immigration legislation his or her explanation may centre on the malign influence of penetration from the far right; racist legislation is not an expected and intrinsic part of Conservative behaviour, for this person it is introduced from the outside. Yet another person, with a different representation of the party, may well attribute the legislation to the Party itself, acting naturally and normally, in terms of its usual ideology. The representation thus provides a model of the causal processes speakers might use in explanations.

Why social?

From the foregoing it might seem that the social in social representations is merely redundant baggage, and that representations are individual phenomena – we each carry around our own unique versions of the world, including representations of political parties and so on. In this view, the theory could just become part of individual cognitive psychology incidentally used to explain and understand social phenomena. However, Moscovici is keen to deflect this interpretation. For him, social representations are irreducibly social in at least three senses.

First, social representations are intrinsically linked to communication processes, and in particular to people's unstructured everyday talk: their gossip, chat, pub arguments and family discussions. As Moscovici puts it, 'representations are the outcome of an unceasing babble and a permanent dialogue between individuals' (1985: 95). So social representations are social in the sense that they *originate* in the course of social interaction.

Second, they are social because they provide an *agreed code* for communication. That is, to the extent that people share representations, they will be able to understand what other people are talking about and will have fluid and intelligible conversations. The agreed representations provide a stable, external version of the world which can form a topic for conversation. On the other hand, disagreement in representations will lead to conflict, dispute and misunderstanding; the conversationalists will by stymied in their attempt to communicate.

The third sense in which representations are social is their provision of a theoretically coherent way of distinguishing between social groups. Because social representations supply a conventional code for communication, and because they are the central dynamic for understanding, all who share a representation will *agree* in their understanding and evaluation of an aspect of the world. The representation will thus be a crucial unifying and homogenizing force. In Moscovici's theory, then, what makes a group a group is exactly the sharing of representations among members; the edges of representations will mark the edges of groups.

In terms of our example, the representation of the Conservative Party as penetrated by right-wing extremists will not be an individual construction but the outcome of many conversations about the Party, ideas disseminated through the media and so on. As the representation is generated and becomes more established it will become easier and easier to talk about the Party in these terms, and indeed, to presuppose this representation as unavowedly literal and factual. The people who share this representation are, in an important sense, a social group: they will understand, evaluate and ultimately act in the same way.

Construction, anchoring and objectification

Social representations are said to have a crucial *constructive* effect. They do not merely *mediate* between objects and beliefs. When a group makes sense of its world, that world will be constructed by, and in terms of, social representations. Experience of political parties, say, is constrained by social representations. If the leader of the Conservatives acts in a certain way the meaning of her actions will be constructed by people's representations of the Party and politics in general.

Moscovici also proposes a mechanism for people's methods of coping with new and unfamiliar experiences. Familiar experience can, of course, be simply dealt with in terms of a person's existing storehouse of social representations. The unfamiliar is more problematic. Moscovici suggests that novel or strange objects are dealt with in two stages, known as 'anchoring' and 'objectification'.

In the first stage – anchoring – the novel object is assigned to one of the categories of thought, or elements, in an existing representation. This process is very similar to the way prototype theorists view the assignation of stimuli to categories (see Chapter Six). The novel case is related to typical or paradigm cases, and this allows the unfamiliar to be understood in terms of the more familiar. In the second stage – objectification – the novel object is transformed into a concrete, pictorial element of the representation to which it is anchored, and this new version of the representation is diffused, in the course of conversation, throughout the social group. Thus what was novel and disrupting now becomes, for that group, part of their concrete reality.

To go back to our person with the social representation of the Conservative Party, if that person encounters a new political party of the right (he or she reads about it in *The Times* and chats to friends about it) he or she may anchor it to his or her representation of the Conservatives. The rationale might be that it shares a stress on private ownership, law and order, and the beneficial effects of market forces, other elements in the representation of Conservatives. Once anchored in this way, the process of repeated communication with other group members generates a concrete image of the new party, drawing on features of the representation of Conservatives. Thus, it will be placed on a left-right continuum in relation to other parties, an image of its leaders and supporters will be formed and so on.

Problems with social representations

This theory has probably generated such enthusiasm among social psychologists partly because of its promise to throw light on to the constructive (Berger and Luckmann, 1966) aspects of social life, partly too because of the claim to provide an integrated frame for understanding attitudes, attributions and beliefs, and partly because it provides a rationale for a specifically social psychological level of analysis. It seems to offer an antidote to the increasingly common cognitive reductionism in the discipline; or the move to explain our collective social lives as a consequence of the operation of the mental entities and processes of individuals. All the same, there are a number of difficulties which suggest that it may disappoint the enthusiast and resist easy practical application. We will concentrate on three: the relation between groups and representations, the nature of consensus assumed by the theory, and the roles of language and cognition.

Groups and representations

In this theory social groups are constituted by their shared social representations; the consensual adoption of representations 'establishes a group identity' (Moscovici and Hewstone, 1983: 116). Although theoretically coherent, this premise raises immediate practical difficulties when carrying out research (Potter and Litton, 1985). Empirical studies of social representations typically start with apparently well-defined and homogeneous social groups and attempt to explicate their representations. The first problem is that this *presupposes* the correctness of the notion that representations delimit groups. There is a vicious circle of identifying representations through groups, and assuming groups define representations.

A second problem here is that researchers cannot easily identify psychologically salient social groups independently of participants' representations of those groups. This leads to damaging inconsistencies. On the one hand, group categories will be treated as naturally occurring phenomena which can be used as a clear base for research conclusions. On the other hand, group categories can themselves be understood as social representations constructed in the course of participants' communication. For instance, we might be interested in a particular protest movement which we see as split between hard-line militants and moderates and we may wish to interview both militants and moderates in order to discover the representations which distinguish them. But, in taking militants and moderates as natural groupings, we have already accepted one version or representation of the protest movement which happens to draw on the militant/moderate categorization; there may well be other representations which do not make this distinction but create some other kind of 'natural' groupings. These representations might not only give different labels to the factions in the movement (e.g. right-wingers and radicals for moderates and militants) but may well see the movement as divided into different kinds of groups altogether. There is no way of talking about the groups concerned independently of social representations, yet Moscovici wants to argue that group membership determines those social representations.

In ethnomethodological terms, we are back with the topic/resource problem described in Chapter One – the object which is the topic of analysis is also an analytic resource (Zimmerman and Pollner, 1971). As social psychologists we have our own representations of the world and we use these as a resource in our analysis, but our research topic is the nature of representations themselves. The methods we adopt to make the research possible are the very thing we should be studying. This would not matter if the categorizations of participants and researchers were neutral, factual, descriptive acts. But, as we saw in the last chapter, this is not the case.

Finally, difficulties arise because of the ambiguous empirical status of social representations. If they are going to be related to social groups there must be some clear-cut, repeatable way of pointing to representations and discriminating one from another. Yet Moscovici does not provide an analytic technique for performing this vital preliminary. The problem here is that it involves some well-defined notion of consensus and we will see in the next section that this is no simple matter.

Consensus in representations

The premise that representations are consensually shared across a number
of people is a central feature of Moscovici's theory. This claim seems
relatively precise and unambiguous until we try to use it in practice.
When we looked in detail at the way three different empirical studies of
representations operationalized consensus or agreement among a sample
(Potter and Litton, 1985), we found that they tended to draw upon analytic
procedures which simply *presupposed* consensus and smoothed over
internal diversity. Some of these studies used numerical averaging techniques which, *in their very nature*, homogenize participants' responses.
Di Giacomo (1980), for example, studying students' representations of
a protest movement with a word association technique, simply presented
average scores for these associations across the sample. These scores seem
to demonstrate that the students share an undifferentiated representation
but an average may disguise considerable variation among a sample. A
set of ten scores with an average of ten sounds a lot more similar that
five scores of zero and five scores of twenty (cf. Hewstone et al., 1982).
We need to know the details of the spread and use of a representation,
whether some people apply it on many different occasions with a broad
interpretation, or some on a more restricted basis. Other studies on social
representations (e.g. Herzlich, 1973) have presented only representative
instances of accounts and similarly seem to make no attempt to look for
the kinds of variation which might cast doubt on their consensual status.

It is perhaps not surprising social representations researchers work in
this way because, as it stands, the notion of consensus or the degree of
agreement among people is a very difficult thing to define. For example,
in a study conducted with Ian Litton (Litton and Potter, 1985) we tried
to identify consensual representations in a set of accounts of the St Paul's
street disturbances introduced in Chapter Six. What representations of the
'riot' will people commenting on the event (journalists, residents, police,
spectators) share in common? We found that it was essential to make a
variety of distinctions before our study of consensus could even get off
the ground. In particular, we had to distinguish between what we shall
call 'use' and 'mention' and between 'theory' and 'practice'.

A representation which is *used* is one drawn on in an explanation of
events; for example 'the riot was caused by poor housing'. In contrast,
a representation which is *mentioned* is not used to explain events but merely
to refer to an *available* explanation: for example 'the left-wing press have
claimed the riot was caused by bad housing, but. . .'. Use and mention
are often combined in the same account, with a single 'correct' explanation
being promoted in contrast to an alternative 'mistaken' explanation (this
is just what would be expected in the light of Billig's, 1987, stress that
discourse is, in an important sense, argumentative).

With regard to the explanations which are used, rather than merely mentioned, it is possible to make a further distinction between use in *theory* – in a range of broad generalized formulations – and use in a range of more specific or *practical* situations. For example, we can distinguish explanations which refer abstractedly to the frequent part the police force plays in general in amplifying the severity of riots from the explanation given by a *specific* policeman defending his role in the St Paul's 'riot'. There is no hard and fast distinction here – it is merely meant to indicate the possibility of more or less theoretical and more or less practical accounts. The crucial point for Moscovici is that consensus or agreement among a sample of people could be assessed at either of these three levels. We could count all the instances of mention, use in theory or use in practice. Serious confusions are generated if these different levels are simply collapsed together as they usually are. After all, mention can be the polar opposite of use. The importance of distinctions of this kind becomes recognized when we begin a careful analysis of participants' discourse.

Representations: cognitive or linguistic?

A further problem with operationalizing social representations for research practice is *at what level* the operationalization should take place. As we have seen, Moscovici describes representations as mental entities made up of both abstract and concrete elements, that is, both concepts and images. He seems to locate representations as cognitive units. However, for research purposes we are inevitably faced with discourse, whether it be participants' responses to structured procedures like scales or questionnaires, or their accounts elicited in open-ended interviews. This issue is one we have come up against time and time again in this book. Given the essentially performative and indexical nature of language use how can researchers construe it as a neutral record of secondary phenomena, in this case cognitive or mental states?

More generally, the cognitive assumptions underlying the theory are highly problematic. Moscovici's account of the dual processes of anchoring and objectification for dealing with unfamiliar objects, is little more than an exercise in speculative cognitive psychology. Given the metaphorical language in which it is couched, it is not at all clear how claims about the process could be tested; for example, how would researchers know if they had found an instance of anchoring? And are we really to assume that, most of the time, people are understanding, say, the political process in terms of *visual images*? Do blind people have a radically different notion of political parties and the economy?

There are important contradictions in the way these cognitive processes are described (McKinlay and Potter, forthcoming). Moscovici states that *all* cognition, all mental experience, is based on representations. But if our perception of the world is entirely circumscribed by our representations of the world, how can we even recognize new or unfamiliar social objects? How can the process of anchoring begin at all? Moscovici is vague on this point. Some of these problems might be resolvable, but it is questionable whether a social psychological theory with such a heavy emphasis on the essentially social should saddle itself with such a weight of unformulated cognitive baggage.

Interpretative repertoires

We will spend the rest of this chapter introducing the notion of an interpretative repertoire. This concept does some of the same sort of explanatory work as social representations. That is, it attempts to look systematically at the organization of phenomena which social psychologists have traditionally understood in terms of attitudes, beliefs and attributions. However, this notion has the advantage of having been developed in analytic practice. It is not handicapped by presupposing a one-to-one concordance with group boundaries, and it does not deploy the type of speculative cognitive psychology which underlies social representations theory. We will illustrate the nature and functioning of interpretative repertoires using one of the most developed areas of research in discourse analysis, namely the study of scientific discourse.

One example of this kind of research was discussed in Chapter Three. In this chapter we will concentrate on an extended series of studies of biochemistry conducted by Michael Mulkay and Nigel Gilbert (Gilbert and Mulkay, 1984). The central aim of this work was to reveal the interpretative procedures used by scientists and the relationship between the construction of discourse and the particular ends to which it is put (Potter and Mulkay, 1985). Mulkay and Gilbert describe how scientists' accounts are put together to portray their actions and beliefs in contextually appropriate ways.

Mapping the language of chemiosmosis

The starting place for their research was a group of biochemists working in the UK and USA on the transmission of protons across the cell wall, and on the involvement of these protons in the formation of the complex molecule adenosine triphosphate (ATP). In the next paragraph, we present a thumbnail sketch of this work. It is not necessary, however, for the reader to understand the details of the science in order to grasp Gilbert and Mulkay's conclusions regarding interpretative repertoires.

ATP is the basic chemical used to store energy in cells. Research into ATP has been dominated by two contrasting theories. One group suggested that ATP is generated in a chain of reactions using a high energy chemical intermediary. The other group – championed by a biochemist Gilbert and Mulkay call Spencer – maintained that a chemiosmotic mechanism acting at the cell wall was responsible for the transfer of protons. Ultimately the chemical intermediary proved elusive, the chemiosmotic theory became widely accepted, and Spencer was awarded the Nobel prize (although this is not to say that the alternative theory does not still have vociferous advocates). We are dealing, therefore, with an active, high-prestige area of the natural sciences.

Gilbert and Mulkay jointly conducted extended, open-ended interviews with thirty-four of the most productive researchers in this field. These interviews were fully transcribed. They also amassed an archive of research papers, monographs, letters and other documents. Several different sources of discourse thus formed the data base for their analyses.

Contexts of discourse

One of the first steps in this research was to compare the detailed content of the accounts scientists gave in their publications with the accounts they gave in interviews (Gilbert and Mulkay, 1980, 1984). Gilbert and Mulkay designated these two situations in which scientists generated discourse the 'formal' and 'informal' contexts, respectively.

The comparison concentrated on the introduction and method sections of articles, examining the way the *same* actions and beliefs were depicted in articles and then in interviews. The differences between the two were striking. For example, the introduction to an article might describe it as presenting a point of methodology; while in an interview the author of the article might describe the same research as really militantly in *support* of a particular, controversial theory; or, the introduction to a paper might state that *results suggest* a new model; and yet in an interview the scientist might describe the process as exactly the reverse of this: that is, claiming that the *model suggested* the results.

The following two extracts – the first from the introduction to a paper, the second from the author's account of the same research – illustrate the sort of differences Mulkay and Gilbert found.

1. A long held assumption concerning oxidative phosphorylation has been that the energy available from oxidative-reduction reactions is used to drive the formation of [ ] ATP. Contrary to this view, recent results from several laboratories suggest that energy is used primarily to promote the binding of ADP and phosphate in a catalytically competent mode (1) and to facilitate

the release of bound ATP (2, 3). In this model, bound ATP forms at the catalytic site from bound ADP and phosphate with little change in free energy. (Gilbert and Mulkay, 1984: 41)

2. He came running into the seminar, pulled me out along with one of his other post-docs and took us to the back of the room and explained this idea that he had...He was very excited. He was really high. He said, 'What if I told you that it didn't take any energy to make ATP at the catalytic site, it took energy to kick it off the catalytic site?' It took him about 30 seconds. But I was particularly predisposed to this idea. Everything I'd been thinking, 12, 14, 16 different pieces of information in the literature that could not be explained, and then all of a sudden the simple explanation became clear...And so we sat down and designed some experiments to prove, test this. [ ] It took him about 30 seconds to sell it to me. It was really like a bolt. I felt, 'Oh my God, this must be right! Look at all the things it explains.' (Gilbert and Mulkay, 1984: 47)

In the formal paper experimental results *suggest* a model – in the interview the central idea of the model becomes a *dramatic revelation*. Moreover, the results described as doing the *suggesting* in the paper are described in the interview being *produced from* the intuitively formulated model. Other differences are also apparent, particularly the impersonal science reporting style of the journal article and the depiction of scientific actions and judgements, if they appear at all, as constrained by data, experiments and, ultimately, the demands of the natural world.

Gilbert and Mulkay observed similar variations when looking at the method sections of articles. Despite the exact and exhaustive aura of method sections in science journals, and despite the idea that they are supposed to give sufficient detail to allow any competent scientist to replicate the research procedures, a very different view was frequently found in informal talk. This presented method sections as vague outlines which scientists only interpret with the aid of their considerable craft skills. This view is illustrated in the following extract.

3. You get a feel for what you need. I can tell you a story about this. I went to the workshop once to get something made. There was no way they could do anything for me for a week or a month. They were making something for Dr X. I said, 'What are you making for Dr X?' 'Dr X requires his water bath to operate at 36.5 C and *nothing else*.' I said, 'That's ridiculous.' And I consulted with Dr X and he produced this paper showing that in this experimental protocol, they'd worked at 36.5 C. It didn't matter a damn really, whether it was 35 or 40 C, as long as you stayed roughly where you were. Dr X was not an experimenter and no longer does any. If you are an experimenter you know what is important and what is not important. (Gilbert and Mulkay, 1984: 53)

These examples are just some of a range of differences which Gilbert and Mulkay identified. Overall, they argued for the existence of two broad interpretative repertoires to describe these differences. For reasons which will become clear, one was labelled the 'empiricist repertoire' and the other 'contingent repertoire'.

Interpretative repertoires are recurrently used systems of terms used for characterizing and evaluating actions, events and other phenomena. A repertoire, like the empiricist and contingent repertoires, is constituted through a limited range of terms used in particular stylistic and grammatical constructions. Often a repertoire will be organized around specific metaphors and figures of speech (tropes); we saw this, for example, with the community repertoire described in the last chapter.

The empiricist repertoire predominated in the context of formal research papers. In this discourse the experimental data were given both chrono-logical and logical authority. That is, the data were construed as coming first and forming the foundation for theory. The author's involvements and commitments were almost never explicitly mentioned. Laboratory work was characterized in a highly conventional manner, as following from impersonal rules which were universally effective. The discourse had a neutral style which seldom referred to the judgements of the author. And when the scientist did apppear he or she was presented as forced to undertake actions by the demands of natural phenomena or the constraints of invariant rules. The basic principle of the empiricist repertoire was, therefore, that actions and beliefs are a neutral medium through which empirical phenomena make themselves felt.

In informal interviews, when scientists were talking to a social researcher, the empiricist repertoire also featured. But, in these situations the contin-gent repertoire was also prevalent. This portrayed actions and beliefs as heavily dependent on speculative insights, prior intellectual commitments, personal characteristics, unspecifiable craft skills, social ties and group memberships. A much wider range of lexical, grammatical and stylistic resources was used in this repertoire. The general connection between scientists' actions and beliefs and the realm of biochemical phenomena was much less clear-cut.

The basic principle of the contingent repertoire was that professional actions and beliefs are crucially influenced by factors outside the realm of empirical phenomena. That is, actions and beliefs are not forced by empirical realities but are a contingent product of manifold extra-neous influences. The nature of the two repertoires is summarized in Figure 7.1.

It is not, however, sufficient for analysis to simply identify these different forms of language in the abstract. We need to know, first, the uses and functions of different repertoires, and second, the problems thrown up by their existence. One important function Mulkay and Gilbert identified was accounting for error.

FIGURE 7.1

Scientists' two interpretative repertoires

(1) **The Empiricist Repertoire**

Experimental data is given logical and chronological priority

The author's personal and social commitments are not mentioned

Laboratory work is conventional and follows from impersonal rules

Basic principle: Actions and beliefs are a neutral medium through which
empirical phenomena make themselves felt

(2) **The Contingent Repertoire**

Action and belief are depicted as dependent on speculative insight, prior
commitment, personal characteristics, social ties

The connection between action and belief and the phenomena under study
is less clear-cut

Basic principle: Scientists' professional actions and beliefs are importantly
influenced by factors outside the realm of physical phenomena

Accounting for error

Mulkay and Gilbert note that there was a basic asymmetry in the way
scientists account for true belief and their accounts for error (Gilbert
and Mulkay, 1984; Mulkay and Gilbert, 1982a). Each scientist partici-
pating in the research took his or her own scientific beliefs as basic and
unproblematic. Indeed, this assumption could be posited as the fundamental
principle of scientists' discourse. We are not, of course, claiming that the
scientist's belief is a static inner object of reference – each researcher
modified and reformulated his or her view in a flexible and contextualized
manner. The point is that *whatever* the version the scientist currently
espoused it was taken as primary. Scientists warranted their beliefs through
reference to the constraining role of experimental evidence and the correct
application of procedural rules, that is, warranting via the empiricist
repertoire (Gilbert and Mulkay, 1982; Mulkay and Gilbert, 1983, 1985;
Potter, 1984).

Scientists have a problem, however, when they account for mistaken
beliefs: how can they make sense of the many errors committed by other
scientists? If scientific views are prompted just by the experimental
evidence – as the empiricist repertoire has it – why do some scientists'
get it wrong? This problem was handled with the contingent repertoire.
The clear-cut connection between empirical phenomena and the beliefs
and actions of scientists was undermined and reference made to a variety
of personal and social factors influencing belief. At its simplest, other
scientists make mistakes because some social factor comes between them
and the facts.

Take the following pair of error accounts for example.

4. I had no axe to grind. It's an advantage not being able to contribute in the theoretical sense. I mean, you don't feel that you have time and publications and reputation based on previous contributions and it's very easy to go the way the evidence seems to point. It leads to more flexibility. People like Gowan and Fennell especially and Milner, certainly had many publications and they discussed one theory as they went along and they had a lot invested in that field and I think they were psychologically a little bit reluctant to follow the lead of – utterly new, strange and different coming from somebody else completely. Certainly that remains the case with Pugh. (Gilbert and Mulkay, 1984: 64–5)

5. *This* is the effect of removing membrane potential. Now we ask what happens if we *now* prevent [ ] a hydrogen ion accumulation inside, when we don't think we can have any membrane potential. Now you will have, you will have people, particularly people at [a particular university], who will give you absolute hell about those experiments. But the people at [that university] are wrong. The people at [that university] are wrong because they are too damned dogmatic. They think this an insuperable barrier to the chemiosmotic theory or at least it is beyond the range that's acceptable to the chemiosmotic theory. And that's no way to do science. The facts are pretty clear experimentally and these people are sort of misquoting the fact. (Gilbert and Mulkay, 1984: 65)

In each of these accounts, the speaker's own view – the correct view! – is connected directly to the experimental evidence. That is, their theoretical position is pictured, through the empiricist repertoire, as arising directly from the natural world as revealed by experiment. In Extract Four, the scientist claims that as he does not have an axe to grind it is easy for him to follow the direction pointed to by the evidence. Likewise, in Extract Five, the scientist describes the facts as being clear experimentally, despite the fact that other scientists cannot recognize them.

In contrast to this, the speakers characterize erroneous belief – the views of scientists they disagree with! – using the contingent repertoire. False claims are represented as a consequence of flawed personalities or distorting group allegiances. In Extract Four, certain scientists are said to have too much interest in a theory, so they are unable to give it up when contradictory findings appear. In Extract Five, reference is made to the personality of scientists at one institution, who are too dogmatic to see the value of a new theory.

The contents of the contingent repertoire are much more varied than the empiricist repertoire. For instance, factors adduced to explain scientific error include: failure to understand, prejudice, commitment to one's own theories, reluctance to make the effort, complexity of the theory, dislike of the new theory, extreme naivety, narrow disciplinary perspective, threat to status, insufficient experimental skill, false intuition, subjective bias, accepting the views of an authoritative figure, being out of touch with reality, personal rivalry, emotional involvement, general cussedness, being too busy, living in a country where theory is not popular, stupidity, pig-headedness, being American and therefore thinking in a woolly fashion! Each of these factors was used at some point to explain why *other people* got it wrong (Gilbert and Mulkay, 1984).

The 'that's how it is' response

One possible response to this set of accounts is to simply accept them as a document of how it is in the field of chemiosmosis, to say 'that's how it is' in the field and take them at face value. But there are a number of features which rule out this path of action. First, the accounts of *different* scientists are often highly inconsistent. For example, one scientist may describe a theory as so *complicated* that it is very difficult to grasp, while another scientist describes the main virtue of the theory as its *simplicity*. Second, Mulkay and Gilbert repeatedly found that the error accounts of the *same* scientist were highly inconsistent. There was an enormous flexibility in the way these scientists constructed their discourse in order to claim the high ground of 'truth' so vital for their self-presentation.

An even more startling conclusion emerged. If the accounts of these researchers were combined, virtually everyone in the network had their work explained away by at least one other scientist. Between them the scientists provided a contingent account of the entire scientific field in which every contributor was either scientifically incompetent or crucially affected by non-scientific factors. Again, this seems like a very good reason for not taking their discourse as a model of what is the case in biochemistry.

Looking back to Chapter Three where we described how scientists presented the operation of rules for theory choice, we can now see that the pattern of accounts found there conformed to the broader pattern for error accounting. Scientists in that case presented the operation of rules with respect to their *own* theories in a clear-cut determinist fashion: the rule constrained the action of choice. An empiricist account of rule operation dominated. But, when describing the rule use of other scientists who they felt were mistaken, rules became a flexible strategic resource open to many interpretations. A contingent account of rule operation became pre-eminent. Our knowledge of interpretative repertoires helps us understand the fine grain as well as the global pattern (McKinlay and Potter, 1987; Yearley, 1985).

Mulkay and Gilbert's general finding, then, was that the researchers they interviewed used an asymmetrical pattern of accounting for 'correct' and 'false' belief. This pattern of accounting solved an interpretative dilemma, reconciling the basic idea of the empiricist repertoire – facts arise naturally from experimental findings – with the observation that other scientists regularly seem to get them wrong. The contingent repertoire introduced a package of non-scientific resources for explaining these errors and, as a consequence, allowed each scientist to maintain a coherent version of their social world which featured their own beliefs as the unthreatened truth.

The truth will out device

So far, we have indicated in general terms the nature of the empiricist and contingent repertoires, and documented one important use of the contingent repertoire. The notion of repertoires has enabled us to distinguish contrasting sets of terms used in different ways. These differences should, however, also be salient to the participants. Do the scientists act as though the repertoires were contradictory? If scientists simply blend the two repertoires together without perceiving any problem then the claim to have discovered two contradictory interpretative systems would seem rather flimsy.

One way of checking whether analytic discoveries have reality for the participants is to see if they themselves orientate to them (Atkinson and Heritage, 1984; Levinson, 1983). We use the term 'orientate' rather than, say, 'notice' or 'understand' very deliberately, because we are not concerned whether participants are *consciously aware* of these organizations, just whether they are a genuine feature of their interpretative practices.

Gilbert and Mulkay's contingent and empiricist repertoires are two highly contrasting ways of making sense of scientific actions and beliefs. On the whole these repertoires were kept separate in time and space. The contingent repertoire was rarely used in formal papers and although both were drawn on in interviews, most of the time they appeared in different passages of talk or, as in error accounting, were applied to very different topics. However, there were occasions in interviews when the two repertoires appeared together and were applied to the same class of events. If a genuine dimension of the scientists' interpretative apparatus has been captured these cases ought to cause problems requiring discursive solutions. This is exactly what Gilbert and Mulkay found.

In the following passage the speaker uses both the contingent and empiricist repertoire in giving a general account of the field.

> 6. *Interviewer.* I think that's all. Perhaps we could ask one further question. Are there any things which you think are important about this field, but which we haven't touched on?
> *Scientist.* Yes, you haven't touched on personalities *very* much. Spencer and so on. I'm not sure I want to talk about them. But I think they *have* contributed.
> *Interviewer.* Would you say something general without naming names?
> *Scientist.* The thing of which I'm well aware is that the attitude that Mulhern

took to anything Burridge published, which was of severe, critical, bitter opposition. He didn't like him. His bitterness has disadvantaged he, Mulhern enormously. Because it meant that other people distrusted his judgment. And there have been occasions when people have said 'Oh, him' instead of 'oh, that'. Sometimes people have been out to prove that somebody else is wrong, rather than [unclear]. But I think that inevitably things were seen in that way. I've seen other fields where things have been much more bitter. But science generally does progress very well and objectively, despite the subjective element. I think there *is* a subjective element.

Interviewer. Do you have any idea how this personal element gets eliminated?

Scientist. Only because a sufficient number of experimenters try to make the position clear. If other people are interested enough, if it's important enough, then the work will be done again or, more likely, its ramifications will be pursued. Predictions will be followed up, more experiments done, and in the fullness of time a much clearer position will become apparent. Just as happened with the chemiosmotic theory. And then, any personal rivalry will be seen for what it was, in relation to the facts, as they become more fully established.

Interviewer. So the experimental evidence...

Scientist. At the end of the day solves everything [general laughter].

Interviewer. Overwhelms these private antagonisms.

Scientist. That's right. (Gilbert and Mulkay, 1984: 96)

It is worth exploring this exchange step by step. At the start of the extract the interview is drawing to a close. The two social researchers and the scientist (it is very useful to interview in pairs when concerned with technical material of this kind, Mulkay, 1974) have been talking for over two-and-a-half hours and the interviewer asks the stock closing question: what has *not* been covered? The scientist rather hesitantly brings up the issue of personalities and the interviewer, sensing something of interest, probes.

At this point, despite being asked to speak in general terms, the scientist describes the antagonism displayed by a particular scientist, Mulhern. He then goes on to characterize events in the whole field in these sorts of terms; that is, he gives a contingent account of the development of the field.

The interviewer then asks the scientist to explain how this personal element might be eliminated. How is it that science can be both riven with personal disputes and prejudices and yet 'progress very well and objectively'? In analytic terms, how can the contradictory empiricist and contingent versions of the field be sensibly articulated in the same passage of talk. It is at this point that the scientist draws on a particular interpretative technique: what Mulkay and Gilbert have called the 'truth will out device' or TWOD. He suggests that work which, presumably, has been initially rejected will be re-evaluated in the future. More experiments will be completed and '*in the fullness of time the position will become clear; the facts will become fully established; the experimental evidence will solve everything*'.

This extract demonstrates how a speaker can use the TWOD, a very common rhetorical device, to deal with a particular interpretative problem. Up until the start of Extract Six the scientist had made extensive use of the empiricist repertoire. In this extract he tentatively starts to introduce notions from the contingent repertoire. The problem is that his own scientific actions begin to seem arbitrary and pointless. Why continue researching if beliefs are only accepted because of personalities and power? However, the looming contradiction can be dealt with by producing a *temporal* separation of elements. There may be contingent factors operating at the present but in the future empiricist factors will come to dominate. The structure of the TWOD, which was recurrent in the interviews, emphasizes that in due course, in the fullness of time, the facts will become fully established: the truth will out.

For the scientist, this device is important not because it reconciles potential contradictions between versions, but because it re-establishes the importance of the empiricist repertoire. As we indicated when describing accounting for error, this is the dominant repertoire. Scientists make the basic presupposition that their own actions and beliefs are determined in an empiricist manner by experimental facts. The TWOD allows this version to be maintained while at the same time giving the speaker leeway to apply the contingent repertoire to a wide range of persons, events and even whole scientific fields.

For the analyst, this device is important because it corroborates the argument that the discourse of these scientists is organized into two broad interpretative repertoires. Interpretative repertoires are used to solve problems, but they also generate difficulties of their own (Levinson, 1983). In this case it was expected that difficulties would arise when the repertoires were used together, and that is what was found. If these difficulties had not emerged Mulkay and Gilbert would have had rather less confidence in their basic analytic claims.

Once interpretative repertoires have been identified in this way analysts can make sense of diverse areas of social life. Repertoires have been used in a number of studies to systematically understand scientists' accounts of theory choice (Gilbert and Mulkay, 1982; Mulkay and Gilbert, 1983, 1985; Potter, 1984); their versions of the application of scientific knowledge (Potter, 1982; Potter and Mulkay, 1982), their readings of scientific texts (Potter, 1987), their accounts of the role of models (McKinlay and Potter, 1987), the construction of argumentative letters (Mulkay, 1985); and the construction of scientific jokes (Mulkay and Gilbert, 1982a).

Language, representation and repertoire

Having overviewed some of the research conducted with linguistic repertoires we are now in a position to spell out, in a bit more detail, the advantages of this analytic notion compared with social representations.

In the first place, repertoires are not construed as entities *intrinsically* linked to social groups, so research has not been hampered by the need to engage in the often problematic exercise of identifying natural group boundaries. In the work on biochemistry, for example, it was found that *all* the biochemists drew regularly on both interpretative repertoires when constructing their accounts. These repertoires have been found in the discourse of other scientists, and it has even been suggested that analogous interpretative procedures are used in the legal profession (Yearley, 1985). Rather than make the somewhat unlikely assumption that *all* these people – biochemists, social scientists, and lawyers – are members of the same social group, it is much more fruitful to accept that repertoires are available to people with many different group memberships, and patterns of accounting may not be the neatest way of dividing up society, or confirming conventional group categorizations.

A more serious problem with any proposed relation between groups and repertoires is the sort of realistic, decontextualized notion of group membership necessarily assumed. As Chapter Six demonstrated, group or category membership is an occasioned phenomena, an achievement. This is not to say people are always free to change membership and categorization in any way they desire, much of the time membership is an occasioned product of other people, or of broader institutional arrangements (one only has to think of the complex apparatus used in South Africa to police membership status). Yet studies such as Garfinkel's (1967) show the constructed nature of even apparently obvious natural categories like gender (see also Potter et al., 1984: ch. 1; Wetherell, 1986). Mulkay and Gilbert's research, apart from the aspect we have considered, also displays how biochemists produce highly varying group divisions in their field when engaged in different interpretative tasks (Gilbert and Mulkay, 1984: ch. 6). The general point, of course, is that in discourse analysis, groups and the way they are constructed in the course of accounts, have become an important topic of research in themselves.

A second major difference with social representations theory is that there is no attempt in discourse analysis to find consensus in the use of repertoires in the sense that some people are found to *always* use a certain repertoire, and certain people another. Interpretative repertoires are used to perform different sorts of accounting tasks. Because people go through life faced with an ever-changing kaleidoscope of situations, they will need to draw upon very different repertoires to suit the needs at hand. From this theoretical perspective what is predicted is exactly variability rather than consensus. Consistency is important in discourse analysis, it is useful to identify the occasions where some people draw on one repertoire and some another, but analysts do not assume that on other occasions these people would necessarily produce the same repertoires.

The third major difference between the two perspectives concerns the place made for cognitive phenomena in people's explanations. Discourse analysis has eschewed any form of cognitive reductionism, any explanation which treats linguistic behaviour as a product of mental entities or processes, whether it is based around social representations or some other cognitive furniture such as attitudes, beliefs, goals or wants. The concern is firmly with *language use*: the way accounts are constructed and different functions. We are not denying the importance and interest of cognitive science and the insights it has to offer; the point is that analysis and explanation can be carried out at a social psychological level which is coherently separable from the cognitive. The irony, of course, is that a coherently social, social psychology is exactly one of the espoused goals of social representations theory. However, it is discourse analysis which offers a systematically *non-cognitive* social psychology as an alternative to the increasingly pervasive cognitive variety.

Finally, we should stress that there are no grandiose claims accompanying the notion of interpretative repertoires. Moscovici's intention was to produce a *theory* of social representations. We are not arguing that this theory should be replaced with a *theory* of interpretative repertoires. The concept of repertoire is but one component in a systematic approach to the study of discourse. It cannot be isolated from other kinds of discursive phenomena. In addition, it is a preliminary step, further analyses are bound to refine this analytic unit. It may appear awfully gross in several years time, and it may well be replaced by a hierarchical understanding of narrow to broad regularities in the content of discourse. We won't say that one day 'the truth will out', only that, in this case, 'time may tell'.

end

8

How to analyse discourse

In most textbooks and monographs the methodology chapter comes near the front, for the perfectly sensible reason that it helps to know how experiments are conducted, surveys carried out and so on, before looking at findings in detail. There are very good reasons for following the reverse procedure when introducing discourse analysis. Unlike experimental methodologies which have become conventionalized and formalized over the years, allowing an almost recipe-style format, discourse analysis is just emerging, developing and changing. We have tried to present several specimen analyses and theoretical origins in previous chapters before attempting to abstract general methodological principles in this penultimate chapter. Traditional social psychological textbooks also take a relatively cavalier attitude to the issues raised by the philosophy of science. For them, methodology rarely raises troubling questions. For us, however, things are not so cut and dried. We will begin our systematic overview of discourse analysis methodology with a consideration of some points raised by the philosophy, history and sociology of science.

Philosophy, sociology and methodology

As the 1980s progress, it has become more and more difficult to turn a blind eye to the radical changes occurring in our understanding of the way science operates. We have to thank philosophers, historians and sociologists of science for this new view, or, more precisely, this new collage of views which has crystallized in the last few decades. Mention of just three areas of change gives a reminder of the veritable revolution evident in our conception of science.

The traditional, and fundamental, distinction between observations, or data statements, and theoretical statements has been thrown into doubt by people such as Hesse (1974), Kuhn (1962) and Popper (1959). It is now taken for granted that any observation of the physical or social world is imbued with theoretical interpretation. It has been demonstrated that even the simplest scientific description is dependent on a whole variety of theoretical assumptions. Without the distinction between fact and theory or observation and conceptual framework the simple-minded positivist view of science developing as a steady accumulation of simple 'unvarnished facts' ceases to be tenable (Feyerabend, 1975).

The premise that certain crucial experiments can be identified which overturn one theory and show the correctness of another has equally been shown to be largely mythical (Lakatos, 1970). Historical work has suggested that crucial experiments are not a factor in the actual choice between competing theories, rather they are performed or at least recognized as 'crucial' *after* the choice, to provide illustration and legitimation (Kuhn, 1977).

Similarly the image of experimental replication as a hard criterion for the adequacy of findings has taken a severe knock recently as a result of sociological investigations by Collins and others into the actual process of replication (Collins, 1974, 1985; Mulkay, 1986). Collins has shown that decisions about the successful replication of an experiment are inextricably bound up with the question of what counts as a competent experiment in the first place and, further, the exact nature of the phenomemon of interest. Replications do not simply fail or succeed, they are highly negotiable events.

There are many ways of interpreting the practical upshot of this new perspective on science. Some philosophers have argued, for example, that falsification is the only clear-cut criterion for developing knowledge (Popper, 1963), others that the only proper way to assess scientific development is to compare entire research programmes (Lakatos, 1970), and some have claimed that now 'anything goes': the more plurality in theory and method the better (Feyerabend, 1975). Sociologists of science have tended to argue that the problem is not one of generating better philosophical or practical criteria for the progression of knowledge but our hopelesly idealized view of the scientific enterprise, the quality of the knowledge it produces, and its role in transforming our lives (Barnes, 1982; Collins, 1985; Latour and Woolgar, 1979; Law and Lodge, 1984; Mulkay, 1979b; Yearley, 1984a).

Psychologists have been particularly prone to the trap of comparing their discipline to mythical versions of the natural sciences. They have tended to see the natural sciences as data driven, guided by experiment and almost exclusively concerned with the production of general laws (Harré, 1986b; Sloman, 1976). It is probably as a consequence of such misperception that the theoretician and the non-experimental are still regarded with suspicion in psychology. There is a dearth of full-time theorists. The fact is, of course, that this occupation is seen as absolutely essential in natural sciences such as physics. However, the message we wish to get across in this work is that developing an adequate theoretical understanding or interpretation is at least as important as perfecting a cast iron methodology, and theories can be assessed using a set of empirical techniques, experiments being only one example.

Ten stages in the analysis of discourse

For convenience and clarity we will split the process of discourse analysis into ten stages. In practice, of course, these stages are not clear sequential steps but phases which merge together in an order which may vary considerably. However, we hope the didactic advantage will outweigh any potential confusions. Throughout our exposition we will use illustrations from conversation analysis and Mulkay and Gilbert's study of biochemists' discourse, as these indicate a range of different issues and practical considerations.

Stage one: research questions

It should be perfectly clear by now that the questions asked by discourse analysts can be many and varied. We can investigate micro-conversations between two people, say, husband and wife, patient and doctor, teacher and pupil and the discourse produced by public figures aimed at an audience of millions. We can focus on the detail of an exchange and then hypothesize about its functional effects as it becomes part of collective social interaction. In this new and fast-growing field the surface of possibilities has hardly been scratched. Yet there is one coherent theme or restriction linking these possibilities together. Participants' discourse or social texts are approached in *their own right* and not as a secondary route to things 'beyond' the text like attitudes, events or cognitive processes. Discourse is treated as a potent, action-orientated medium, not a transparent information channel.

Crucial questions for traditional social psychological research thus cease to be relevant. For example, we are not asking whether a sample of people are revealing their 'genuine' attitudes to ethnic minorities, or whether fans' descriptions of what happens on the soccer terraces are 'accurate'. The concern is exclusively with talk and writing itself and how it can be read, not with descriptive acuity. By restricting the questions asked in this way, discourse analysts are liberated from many pseudo-issues which have been a recurring headache for traditional researchers. This does not mean that we are indulging in easy escapism, postponing the 'big' questions or ruling them out of court. As must be apparent from previous chapters, discourse analysis adopts a radically new approach to the formulation of these issues and we will return to this point in the final chapter.

The research questions discourse analysts do focus on are broadly related, as we have seen, to construction and function: how is discourse put together, and what is gained by this construction. For example, the research on scientists' discourse looked at how accounts were constructed using the empiricist and contingent repertoires, and the function these accounts served in presenting scientists' own views as constrained by the facts and making others' errors understandable. Conversation analysts have examined how coherent sequential discourse is constructed with the aid of a limited set of turn-taking rules, and also how participants perform particular acts within the constraints of this rule system. To summarize – our research questions give priority to discourse, in any form, and ask about its construction in relation to its function.

Stage two: sample selection

Although many considerations in sampling remain unchanged whatever the area of social research, there are always some differences in emphasis. The first point, where discourse analysis diverges most radically from the traditional view involves the basic question of sample size.

Discourse analysis, at least at present, is an extremely labour-intensive approach. There is no discourse equivalent to feeding results into a computer and then making sense of a limited pattern of significant and insignificant differences. Even after the demanding process of transcription and preliminary coding is complete, the researcher is inevitably required to read and reread large bodies of transcript and documents. There is a danger here of getting bogged down in too much data and not being able to let the linguistic detail emerge from the mountains of text. If one is interested in discursive forms, ten interviews might provide as much valid information as several hundred responses to a structured opinion poll. Because one is interested in language use rather than the people generating the language and because a large number of linguistic patterns are likely to emerge from a few people, small samples or a few interviews are generally quite adequate for investigating an interesting and practically important range of phenomena. For discourse analysts the success of a study is *not* in the least dependent on sample size. It is *not* the case that a larger sample necessarily indicates a more painstaking or worthwhile piece of research. Indeed, more interviews can often simply add to the labour involved without adding anything to the analysis.

The crucial determinant of sample size, however, must be, here as elsewhere, the specific research question. A number of classic studies have concentrated on a *single* text, with the goal of showing how a certain effect can be achieved (e.g. Eglin, 1979; Gusfield, 1976; Potter et al., 1984; Smith, 1978; Woolgar, 1980). In these cases the value or generalizability of results depends on the reader assessing the importance and interest of the effect described and deciding whether it has vital consequences for the area of social life in which it emerges and possibly for other diverse areas. One can analyse, too, in a fine-grain way, one-off representative instances of what are unmistakably commonplace phenomena. At the other extreme, researchers have conducted interviews across an extensive sample, because the commonplace or important patterns are not recognizable in advance and recurrently used systems of terms need to be elucidated (Gilbert and Mulkay, 1984; Wetherell and Potter, forthcoming a).

In many cases, practice will be governed by what is available: if you have access to an extensive archive of transcribed telephone conversations, or to a collection of media reports of riots, then that is the analytic starting point. Generally there is no 'natural' boundary line to be drawn in these cases, or no point at which sampling can be said to be complete. It is simply a case of giving a clear and detailed description of the nature of the material one is analysing and its origins. 'Important' texts, like Nobel prize speeches or Minister's official reports can be interesting; but mundane conversation is equally so, and is perhaps always the analytic first base (Heritage, 1984; Sacks, 1972).

Stage three: collection of records and documents

It should be evident that discourse analysts work very frequently with *records* and *documents* of interaction, as opposed to material garnered from the researcher's own dealings with participants. Traditionally, one of the most important advantages of collecting naturalistic records and documents is the almost complete absence of researcher influence on the data (Webb et al., 1966). Transcripts of everyday conversations, news reports, scientific papers, letters, official documents, are features of the social fabric that the researcher has had no part in producing. From the discourse analysis point of view in particular, this material is helpful because it allows the researcher to capture the widest possible variation in accounts. For example, a person may offer a specific, limited version of their world in an interview compared to their writings or their un-structured conversation with their peers (Gilbert, 1980). By collecting documents from many sources, recording interactions, and then combining this with more directive interviewing, it is possible to build up a much fuller idea of the way participants' linguistic practices are organized compared to one source alone.

Yet another advantage accruing from records of interaction is that people undermine each others' versions in these documents in a way which is illuminating and probably beyond the bounds of the researcher's com-petence, not to mention the morality and ethics guiding research. In effect, you can use people's own ability to artfully (and very helpfully) poke holes in each others' positions to reveal their constructed nature. The most obvious material of this kind is ordinary conversation, and, as we have seen, there is a large and growing literature about the analysis of this form of discourse (Atkinson and Heritage, 1984; Levinson, 1983). However, we have also looked at scientists' conference disputes (Chapter Three), letters to newspapers (see Mulkay, 1986, on letters generally) and Parliamentary debates recorded in *Hansard*. This latter source of data not only has the advantage of recording MPs and ministers constructing their own versions of the social world and undermining opponents, but is an ideologically powerful form of spoken material which comes ready transcribed, saving considerable work (see also Reeves, 1983; for a useful exploration of the possibilities and problems of documentary research see Plummer, 1983).

It is at this stage in many research projects that two types of problem come to the fore: one practical and one ethical. The practical one concerns taperecording. If you are handling natural conversational material you will need a recording of sufficient quality to enable transcription and bear repeated listening. Fortunately, modern taperecorder technology has provided machines which are pocket-sized, run off batteries, have internal microphones, and are sensitive enough for a high quality recording of, say, a group of people having a discussion in a medium-sized room. The pragmatics of taperecording are usefully discussed by Stubbs (1983) and Labov (1972b). The ethical problems are much less tractable. The conundrum concerns the dubious morality of taking surreptitious recordings weighed against the potential disadvantages of participants' knowledge that recording is occurring. There are various approaches to this problem, all of which have merits and demerits (see Stubbs, 1983). Obviously, before using any letters or private documents, conference and workshop transcripts etc., full permission should be obtained from all the participants.

Stage four: interviews

Although naturalistic records, documents and transcripts of conversations have a number of advantages, interviews have the virtue of allowing the researcher room for active intervention. In particular, they enable the researcher to deliberately question an entire sample of people on the *same* issues, giving greater comparability in responses, and increased simplicity in initial coding.

Interviews, however, are a very different tool for discourse analysts than for orthodox social researchers (Brenner, 1985; Cannell and Kahn, 1968). The goal of traditional interviews is to obtain or measure consistency in participants' responses; consistency is valued so highly because it is taken as evidence of a corresponding set of actions or beliefs. If the interview talk is consistent, the argument goes, it must reflect a consistent reality beyond; consistent discourse demonstrates the interviewer has found some genuine phenomena and not biased or distorted responses. Consistency *is* important for the discourse analyst as well, but not in this sense, only to the extent that the researcher wishes to identify regular patterns in language use.

Given the theoretical primacy of the talk itself in the discourse mode of research and the focus on how talk is constructed and what it achieves rather than whether it is an accurate description of the participant's internal state, consistency is often less useful and desirable for analysis than variation in interviews. Consistency suggests that participants are drawing on a limited number of compatible discourses or interpretative repertoires when answering questions. Analyses which identify only the consistent responses are thus sometimes uninformative because they tell us little about the full range of accounting resources people use when constructing the meaning of their social world and do not so clearly reveal the function of participants' constructions.

How, then, does the researcher go about generating an interview which allows rather than restricts the diversity of participants' accounting practices? The first answer to this question is that you cannot, in fact, usually stop this diversity appearing, except perhaps by confining respondents to simple yes and nos – and even here it will seep out. As we argued in Chapter Two, a close look at a verbatim transcript of virtually any interview reveals a degree of variation in responses normally only repressed by some sort of precoding or by burying under gross categorization.

The second answer to this point is to make the interview a much more interventionist and confrontative arena than is normal, dropping the formal procedures which act as a device to restrict variation in traditional interviews (Potter and Mulkay, 1985). This does not mean the interview should be turned into some sort of dispute. We are suggesting that the researcher should try to generate interpretative contexts in the interview in such a way that the connections between the interviewee's accounting practices and variations in functional context become clear. One of the ways this can be done is to tackle the same issue more than once in an interview, in the course of a number of different general topics.

For example, we asked those interviewed in our New Zealand studies questions relating to equality of rights in relation to three different topics: the Springbok tour, Maori land disputes and explanations of unemployment. The different kinds of answers given allowed us to illuminate the more general features of interpretations of equal rights. Another method is to adopt follow-up questions to responses which pose alternative or problematic views or facts for the interviewee. If the interview is seen as a forum in which the respondent regurgitates preformed and largely static opinions this approach will seem strange; but if it is viewed as an active site where the respondent's interpretative resources are explored and engaged to the full this will seem perfectly natural.

It is important when conducting interviews of this kind to construct a detailed schedule which sets out the questions to be asked, and specifies the probes and follow-up questions which should be produced if particular responses are offered. This guides the interviewer through the questions, makes sure the same question is asked of each respondent, and records any information which may be of use to the interviewer. Bringing off an interview which systematically covers a range of topics, yet is open-ended enough to allow the respondent to elaborate on their views in a relatively naturalistic conversational exchange, is a craft skill that takes some developing. It will always be something of a compromise. It pays to conduct and transcribe some pilot interviews before the research proper so that the adequacy of the schedule can be assessed, and any necessary modifications made to question wording and overall organization.

Finally, it is important to stress that since the interview is no longer considered a research instrument for accurately revealing an unbiased set of opinions, but seen as a conversational encounter, the researcher's questions become just as much a topic of analysis as the interviewee's answers. These questions set some of the functional context for the answers and they must be included. In practice this means that the linguistic nuance of the question is as important as the linguistic nuance of the answers. The *whole* interview must be transcribed, rather than just the interviewee's part. Unlike traditional interviews, the researcher's questions are seen as active and constructive and not passive and neutral.

To summarize – interviews in discourse analysis differ from conventional interviews in three ways. First, variation in response is as important as consistency. Second, techniques which allow diversity rather than those which eliminate it are emphasized, resulting in more informal conversational exchanges and, third, interviewers are seen as active participants rather than like speaking questionnaires.

Stage five: transcription

When working with either records of interaction or interviews it will be necessary to make transcriptions from audiotape. Both the importance and difficulty of this task are often underestimated. A good transcript is essential for a form of analysis which involves repeated readings of sections of data, and the process of transcription itself can be helpful in forcing the transcriber to closely read a body of discourse. However, even the most basic transcription is extremely time consuming, and is a skill that requires practice to perfect. The idea that transcription is 'simply putting the words down on paper' is very far from reality. Transcription is a constructive and conventional activity. The transcriber is struggling to make clear decisions about what exactly is said, and then to represent those words in a conventional orthographic system (Stubbs, 1983).

The time taken for transcription varies with the transcription system adopted. If you are working with high quality recordings of small numbers of people engaged in relatively formal conversations like interviews, and your system pays little attention to pause-length, hesitations, overlaps and intonation, the ratio of tape time to transcription time is about one to ten. That is, one hour of tape will take ten hours to transcribe. This includes the time taken to audio-type a first hearing, using a foot-pedal to stop and start the tape, into a word processing system, check a draft printout against the tape, and then put in corrections. If you wish to include phenomena such as timed pauses and overlaps in your transcription scheme it will take much longer. For the full 'Jefferson style' transcription used by conversation analysts (Atkinson and Heritage, 1984; and see Appendix One) the tape time to transcription time ratio is probably increased to more than one to twenty.

The question of exactly how detailed the transcription should be is a thorny one. There is certainly a variety of work attesting to the significance of intonational features of discourse (e.g. Brazil, 1981; Jefferson, 1985; Kreckel, 1981, 1982). However, for many sorts of research questions, the fine details of timing and intonation are not crucial, and indeed they can interfere with the readability of the transcript, particularly when dealing with extended sequences and for people unused to the system. Moreover, for a project working with, say, ten interviews, an hour in length, the Jefferson system is likely to turn three weeks of hard slog into six or more weeks. So it is important to think very carefully about what information is required from the transcript, and at what level the analysis will proceed. One advantge of transcribing on to a word processor is that it allows editing in more detailed information from the tape if it is found to be relevant.

A final pragmatic point concerns the way transcript is presented on the paper. Transcript is a very expensive and vital commodity – a researcher may well read some sheets fifty or sixty times. Thus it is important to print it out as clearly as possible: using a readable type face, a new ribbon, double spacing it on the page, and using short lines. Cutting corners in any of these areas is false economy.

Intermission

At this point the researcher usually sits back in contentment and surveys a whole set of cardboard boxes with bits of paper in them. Some contain documents of various kinds, others are full of transcript and cassette tapes. There are literally hundreds of thousands of words waiting to be transformed into exciting research findings, and with this thought contentment can easily be transformed into total immobility and panic. Where should one start? We find it reassuring to begin with some coding.

Stage six: coding

The first thing to note regarding coding is that it is quite distinct from doing analysis itself. The goal is not to find results but to squeeze an unwieldy body of discourse into manageable chunks. It is an analytic preliminary preparing the way for a much more intensive study of the material culled through the selective coding process.

The categories used in coding are obviously crucially related to the research questions of interest. Sometimes they can be fairly straight-forward. For example, when researching scientists' criteria for theory choice (Potter, 1984 – see Chapter Three), the first step was simply to select out from a body of transcribed conference interaction all references to criteria, however oblique, and the selection of theories. When looking at the topic of community (see Chapter Six), all occasions where this category was used were selected during the initial coding. At other times the phenomenon of interest may not become clear until some analysis has taken place and a number of attempts at theoretical interpretation of the data. In these cases the process will be a cyclical one of moving between analysis and coding. For example, in our study of New Zealanders' accounts of racial inequality our understanding of what should be coded out of the transcripts changed repeatedly as our analysis became more sophisticated (Wetherell and Potter, forthcoming a). Once the topic of analysis was clarified, however, the return to the data and preliminary coding became less problematic.

It is important to stress that as coding has the pragmatic rather than analytic goal of collecting together instances for examination it should be done as *inclusively* as possible. In this sense it is quite different from standard techniques of content analysis where, for all intents and purposes, coding data into categories and looking at the frequency of occurrence is simply equivalent to the analysis (Berelson, 1971; Holsti, 1968; Mostyn, 1985). At this stage in the research we are in the business of producing a body of instances, not trying to set limits to that body. Thus all borderline cases, and instances which seem initially only vaguely related, should be included. All pages of transcript coded as containing relevant instances are then photocopied and placed in a file of their own. This file serves eventually as the basis for detailed analysis. If a number of codings are done simultaneously and, given the time it takes to read through a large body of text, this is worth doing; it may well be that the same page of transcript will appear in a number of different categories, and hence a number of data files. At the end of this process we are ready to move into the most interesting stage: analysis proper.

Stage seven: analysis

Analysis of discourse is like riding a bicycle compared to conducting experiments or analysing survey data which resemble baking cakes from a recipe. There is no mechanical procedure for producing findings from an archive of transcript. There is no obvious parallel to the well-controlled experimental design and test of statistical significance. In fact the results of studies of discourse are warranted, and critically examined, in a way that is novel to psychology. We will explore techniques of validation in the next section; for the moment we will concentrate on how to get analysis off the ground.

Just as with bike riding, it is not easy to convey the analytic process in abstract. Words fail us at this point, it is not a case of stating, first you do this and then you do that. The skills required are developed as one tries to make sense of transcript and identify the organizational features of documents. Nevertheless, there is a basic lesson that is inescapable: analysis involves a lot of careful reading and rereading. Often it is only after long hours struggling with the data and many false starts that a systematic patterning emerges. False starts occur as patterns appear, excitement grows, only to find that the pattern postulated leaves too much unaccounted, or results in an equally large file of exceptions.

Academic training teaches people to read for gist – which is precisely the wrong spirit for discourse analysis. If you read an article or book the usual goal is to produce a simple, unitary summary, and to ignore the nuance, contradictions and areas of vagueness. However, the discourse analyst is concerned with the detail of passages of discourse, however fragmented and contradictory, and with what is actuallly said or written, not some general idea that seems to be intended. In ethnomethodological terms, we are so used to 'repairing the indexicality' (Garfinkel, 1967) of talk, and reconstructing it in ways that make sense for us, that it is very difficult to throw off this habit. Thus, part of the process is inevitably a critical interrogation of our own presuppositions and our unexamined techniques of sense making (Ashmore, 1985; Potter, forthcoming). The analyst constantly asks: why am I reading this passage in this way? What features produce this reading?

Analysis is made up principally of two closely related phases. First, there is the search for pattern in the data. This pattern will be in the form of both variability: *differences* in either the content or form of accounts, and consistency: the identification of features *shared* by accounts. Second, there is the concern with function and consequence. The basic theoretical thrust of discourse analysis is the argument that people's talk fulfils many functions and has varying effects. The second phase of analysis consists of forming hypotheses about these functions and effects and searching for the linguistic evidence.

We can see how this operates by looking once more at Mulkay and Gilbert's research on the biochemists (Chapter Seven). In their search for pattern Mulkay and Gilbert started with accounts of the *same* actions, events or beliefs produced in different circumstances. In this situation consistency would be expected, if one was working with a realist view of talk, and any variation between accounts is thus extremely revealing. As we saw, this approach did demonstrate radical and pervasive variability on many levels as well as a great deal of consistency. But consistency was not due to accounts describing a consistent world; it arose because different types of accounts were restricted to different kinds of contexts.

Mulkay and Gilbert suggested that the consistent pattern resulted from scientists constructing their discourse in terms of two contrasting interpretative repertoires. They went on to hypothesize about the function of these two different repertoires: for example, the empiricist repertoire seemed to be an extremely effective resource for justifying one's own scientific belief, because it tied that belief directly to the facts making personality, social and economic interests irrelevant. The contingent repertoire embodied an alternative set of resources and was a persuasive means of accounting for others' errors and the failure of the scientific community to endorse one's own beliefs.

The strength of Mulkay and Gilbert's analysis lies in the fact that it explained both the broad organization and much of the moment-to-moment detail. The hypothesized functions provided an explanation for the pattern evident in the discourse. This explanation was analytically more coherent than the alternative possibility that accounts were patterned in this way because the scientific world simply is like this.

It should be clear, then, that there is no analytic method, at least as this term is understood elsewhere in social psychology. Rather, there is a broad theoretical framework, which focuses attention on the constructive and functional dimensions of discourse, coupled with the reader's skill in identifying significant patterns of consistency and variation. This does not mean that the reader has to take the conclusions of this kind of analysis on trust, however, because there are several stages of validation; some are an extension of the analysis, others intrinsic to the presentation of findings.

Stage eight: validation

There are several analytic techniques which can be used to validate the findings of this kind of research. The four main ones are: (a) coherence, (b) participants' orientation, (c) new problems, and (d) fruitfulness. We will take them in turn.

(a) Coherence

A set of analytic claims should give coherence to a body of discourse. Analysis should let us see how the discourse fits together and how discursive structure produces effects and functions. If there are loose ends, features of the discourse evident in the data base which do not fit the explanation, we are less likely to regard the analysis as complete and trustworthy. If the explanation covers both the broad pattern, and accounts for many of the micro-sequences, then we will take it more seriously.

Apparent exceptions to the analytic scheme are particularly relevant to the assessment of coherence. This topic was discussed in Chapter Three where we introduced the notion of confirmation through exception. If a regular pattern of accounting is discovered, which we hypothesize is designed for a special goal, then we must look for and examine exceptions to this pattern. Cases that lie outside the explanatory framework of a theory are almost always more informative than those that lie within, and often dredge up important problems. If there is clearly some special feature of the exceptions which marks them off from the standard examples and thereby determines their status as exceptions, the explanatory scope of our scheme is confirmed. If there are no special features which plausibly explain difference, the exclusive nature of our scheme must be questioned.

(b) Participants' orientation

The kinds of phenomena which interest discourse analysts have genuine consequences for people's social lives. We are not interested in the dictionary definitions of words, or abstract notions of meaning, but in distinctions participants actually make in their interactions and which have important implications for their practice. When looking at variability and consistency, it is not sufficient to say that *as analysts* we can see that these statements are consistent and these dissonant; the important thing is the orientation of the participants, what *they* see as consistent and different.

There are a number of ways of checking this orientation. In conversation analysis the researcher is helped by the fact that conversations are organized on a turn by turn basis, where each turn orientates to the previous one. So although a turn of talk may, for example, take the standard syntactic form of a question, if the recipient treats it as an accusation the analyst is also justified in interpreting it this way. If the participants view the turn as an accusation this overrides the theoretical consideration of what a question ought to look like. Atkinson and Drew's study of courtroom exchanges described in Chapter Four illustrates the utility of this approach.

In Mulkay and Gilbert's study of biochemists' discourse one of the central claims was that scientists constructed their discourse largely from two incompatible interpretative repertoires. To warrant this claim Mulkay and Gilbert not only demonstrated that the repertoires *appeared* incompatible to the analyst, they also showed that this incompatibility was recognized by the scientists themselves. On the one hand, their discourse was organized in such a way that the two repertoires were kept separate. On the other, when the repertoires were produced on the same occasion special difficulties were created for the scientists which had to be resolved by the use of a particular interpretative device: the TWOD. If the participants had not experienced these predicted difficulties, that is, if they had not orientated to the suggested inconsistencies, then we would be very suspicious about the validity of the findings.

(c) New problems
One of the primary goals of discourse analysis is to clarify the linguistic resources used to make certain things happen. However, these resources will not only *solve* problems, but will also create new problems of their own. If we think of a car engine, it converts chemical energy into mechanical propulsion reasonably effectively, but in doing so it generates heat. Thus the car needs a cooling system to mop up the excess heat and keep the engine working smoothly. The existence of new problems, and solutions, provides further confirmation that linguistic resources are being used as hypothesized.

If we look back to the TWOD again, we can see it as an example of this process. The two interpretative repertoires used by the scientists are very serviceable for certain tasks; however, they create problems of their own, particularly when used together. The TWOD deals with the contradictions which arise and its existence provides further confirmation of the basic analytic suggestions. The extremely powerful turn-taking system posited by conversation analysts (Sacks et al., 1974) provides another example. The system is extremely effective for producing coherent sequential discourse, but it creates a problem of how to end conversations; after all, if the system was too effective people could starve to death. What is needed is an additional system which enables people to close conversations down (Schegloff and Sacks, 1973). The existence of this secondary system acts as a validity check on the existence of the primary system (Levinson, 1983).

(d) Fruitfulness
The fourth criterion of validity, and in many ways the most powerful, is fruitfulness. This refers to the scope of an analytic scheme to make sense of new kinds of discourse and to generate novel explanations. This is, of course, a general criterion of validity for scientific explanations and theories; if they can be used to generate fresh solutions to the problems in a field of research then we accord them more respect.

Both the sequential model at the heart of conversation analysis and the notion of repertoires deployed in work on scientists' discourse have been highly fruitful in this sense. For example, the sequential model has taught us a great deal about the fundamental problem of accounting for indirect speech acts, such as the use of questions like 'have you got a Mars bar?' to make requests (Levinson, 1983; Merritt, 1976). As we have indicated, the notion of repertoires has helped delineate many varied aspects of scientists' discourse, including unexpected discoveries like the structure of scientific jokes (Gilbert and Mulkay, 1984; Mulkay and Gilbert, 1982a).

These four techniques for validating the findings of discourse analysis allow for a stringent examination of any claims. It is often suggested that non-experimental work or qualitative research is less rigorous than the standard alternative. Textbooks, for example, often promote an image of this kind of work as the arena for hypothesis generation, with the rigorous work of testing and evaluation done through experiment. Yet there is no need for this to be so; research of the kind discussed in this book has undergone a searching and critical examination, on a variety of levels, to assess its adequacy. This is not to say that the criteria described here are absolutely watertight or infallible. However, the philosophy and sociology of science described at the beginning of this chapter tell us that infallible criteria exist only in the land of positivist mythology: there are no crucial experiments, knock down refutations or definitive replications in the real world of science.

Stage nine: the report

In work of this kind the final report is a lot more than a presentation of the research findings, it constitutes part of the confirmation and validation procedures itself. The goal is to present analysis and conclusions in such a way that the reader is able to assess the researcher's interpretations. Thus a representative set of examples from the area of interest must be included along with a detailed interpretation which links analytic claims to specific parts or aspects of the extracts. In this way, the entire reasoning process from discursive data to conclusions is documented in some detail and each reader is given the possibility of evaluating the different stages of the process, and hence agreeing with the conclusions or finding grounds for disagreement. In this sense discourse analysis could be said to be more rigorous than experimental reports as it is often impossible to independently check the analysis in these cases.

In practice this means that the analytic section of a discourse article will be considerably longer than the corresponding section of more traditional empirical reports (an issue which journal editors will need to consider if they are not to discriminate against the publication of this research). A sizeable portion of the article will be taken up with extracts from transcript or documents and the rest will be detailed interpretations which pick out patterns and organization in the materials. The way discourse is used in this kind of analysis contrasts with superficially similar work in social psychology and interpretative sociology in which extracts are presented to illustrate a causal story or model derived from participant observation (Collins, 1983) or reconstructed from accounts in the manner of ethogenic analysis (Harré, 1979). In discourse analysis the extracts are *not* characterizations or illustrations of the data, they are examples of the data itself. Or, in ethnomethodological terms, they are the topic itself, not a resource from which the topic is rebuilt.

Discourse analysis reports will thus also contrast with traditional content analysis reports (Holsti, 1968). Although content analysis was developed for use with documents and open-ended materials, its theoretical assumptions, and assumptions about coding, are very different. It uses discourse as a convenient dependent variable which records causal processes revealed by the numerical assessment of occurrences within categories. We have already noted that one difference between this approach and discourse analysis lies in the lack of a theory of language as an active, performative realm (see Chapter Two). A second contrast in terms of coding is worth reiterating here.

Essentially, content analysis trains coders to reliably place passages or parts of discourse into particular categories. For example, Tetlock (1984) has coded politicians' speeches into different categories of 'integrative complexity' and then related these codings to other variables, such as political allegiance (do right-wingers, for example, make simpler political speeches than left-wingers?). The reliability of the coding is checked by measures of inter-rater reliability, which are basically correlations between the categorizations of different coders.

The problem here, as we have noted, is that although a high inter-rater reliability tells us that coders are agreeing we do not know the exact basis of this agreement (Abraham, 1984). All we know is that coders are using much the same interpretative procedure. The readers of the final report are presented with a definition of the category, and even one or two example categorizations, but virtually none of the interpretative work on which the research is based appears in the text. All we see is a numerical summary. This makes sense given the theoretical assumptions of content analysers, but is less than adequate if we theorize language itself as the topic of interest. Hence discourse analytic papers bring to the fore those aspects which traditional content analytic studies leave the reader to take on trust. Namely, the detail of interpretation of a text. If a discourse analysis report sometimes *looks* less rigorous than a report of content analysis research this is probably more to do with the rhetorical effectiveness of tables of numbers than any lack of stringency.

In terms of the practice of discourse analysis, the discipline of making interpretations fully explicit for final reports often reveals difficulties and raises questions not apparent at earlier stages. On some occasions a discursive organization which seemed clear-cut breaks down and leads the researcher back to the coding, or even to the 'raw' documents and transcripts. A useful lesson can be learned here: the process of writing helps clarify analytic issues and thus it is often better to do a rough draft of the analysis and discussion quite early on than leave the report as a separate postscript to the research. More generally, this reminds us that these stages are a conceptual scheme rather than a rigid temporal narrative. Discourse analysis involves fluid movement between the different stages, with coding, analysis, validation and writing each leading back to earlier phases and ultimately to the talk and writing which were the original point of departure.

Stage ten: application

The final stage in the process is one often ignored in social research – application. Indeed, the whole issue of application is vexing. There is little understanding of how it occurs and the knowledge we do possess is fragmented and contradictory, with many studies finding it difficult to identify any clear-cut applications of social science research (Kallen et al., 1982; Potter, 1982; Weiss and Bucuvalas, 1980). Interestingly, the position is similar in the *natural* sciences. Recent findings in the sociology of science have undermined our twentieth-century notion of technology – non-stick frying pans, bridges, atom bombs, micro-computers – arising naturally and straightforwardly from advances in pure science (Layton, 1977; Sherwin and Isenson, 1967), so perhaps social scientists should not feel their position is unique. Nevertheless, we feel that researchers should pay considerably more attention to the practical use of their work over and above the amassing of research findings and the furtherance of careers (Stringer, 1982). The image of a benign body of practitioners waiting to read the journals of pure scientists and put research findings into practice is heartwarming but unrealistic.

This is a particularly interesting issue for discourse analysis because of the criticism sometimes voiced that it is 'just looking at words – not real things'. It is implied that a discipline concerned with language and its function will perhaps be of abstract interest but no practical use. It is important to remember that virtually the entirety of anyone's understanding of the social world is mediated by discourse in the form of conversations, newspapers, novels, TV stories and so on.

For example, none of us has actually 'seen' the National Health Service – it is not the kind of entity that could be seen: it is geographically highly disparate and largely abstract. Yet we have conversations about 'it', read newspaper articles about 'it', and express opinions about 'its' future. One of the positive fruits of discourse analysis is to promote an informed critical attitude to discourse of this kind; to be more aware of its constructive nature and the close connection between the way textual versions of the world are put together and specific policies and evaluations are pushed.

There are various models for the application of discourse analysis. One possibility is popularization, giving the knowledge away as freely as possible (Miller, 1980). An example of this kind would be Atkinson's (1984a) work on how conversation analysis has helped demonstrate the techniques used by political orators to elicit responses from an audience. He suggests that an audience better educated about the workings of various rhetorical devices may respond to speeches in a more sophisticated and critical manner. To promote this end he produced a popularizing book as well as being involved in a widely discussed television programme (in which a 'naive orator' was shown generating rapturous applause at a party political conference after being trained to use the devices).

A second possibility is to open up a dialogue with the people who have been researched. An example of this kind would be Mulkay's (1986) study in which a scientist is actively and critically involved in the process of analysing scientists' discourse. It is too early to say whether these models, or some other, perhaps involving the educational system, will be the most fruitful. The main point is that application is very much on the agenda and should not be relegated to an optional extra.

Conclusions

It is important to re-emphasize that there is no *method* to discourse analysis in the way we traditionally think of an experimental method or content analysis method. What we have is a broad theoretical framework concerning the nature of discourse and its role in social life, along with a set of suggestions about how discourse can best be studied and how others can be convinced findings are genuine. The ten stages we have outlined are intended as a springboard rather than a template.

Just like the biochemistry discussed in the previous chapter, discourse analysis is heavily dependent on craft skills and tacit knowledge (Collins, 1974; Polanyi, 1958; Ravetz, 1971). People who run social psychology experiments will of course know that these too are complex social accomplishments which take considerable skill and organization to work effectively. In describing discourse analysis, it is particularly difficult to convey the sorts of frustrations and breakthroughs the researcher experiences when engaging with discursive data. Profound changes in understanding take place in the course of repeated readings. The initial reaction is often that it all makes perfect, consistent sense, and that there is no phenomenon to be researched. However, in the later stages of analysis the same discourse can seem so fragmented and contradictory that it is difficult to see how it could ever be taken as sensible in the first place.

Discourse analysis has radical implications for our understanding and interpretation of findings derived from traditional methods. As we have emphasized in a number of chapters, if we take a functional view of talk and writing we cannot simply put that view to one side when we deal with the talk participants produce in experiments or the written answers people give to survey questions. The functional perspective demands that we think about what people are doing in their experimental 'responses' and what performative effects follow from survey answers.

It is important to stress finally that we are not making a general case that experiments or surveys are intrinsically flawed and should be abandoned by social researchers, or even that they might not have an important role to play in the study of discourse. At this point in time the very phenomena of interest to discourse analysts are still being defined and understood, and much of the most exciting research has come from naturalistic studies of texts or conversations. It may be that in the future experiments will come to the fore, but at the present the sheer lack of basic knowledge of the factors governing language use, coupled with the extreme delicacy of the processes of interest, makes it very difficult to design well-controlled experiments. We would not, however, wish to advocate hegemony for discourse analysis in social psychology, or rule out any future overlaps with other established methodologies.

9

Controversial topics and future directions

This book has described a distinctive and novel social psychological approach to language. In the final chapter we would like to consider three controversial issues touched upon at various points in the book but which now need to be drawn together and re-emphasized. These are the problematic relationship between language and mental states, the connection between language and the world 'out there', and the issue of reflexivity. In the rest of the chapter we will look at some future directions for discourse analysis and its developing relationship with traditional social psychology.

Discourse and the world 'under the skull'

Open souls telling more than they know

If we wanted to pick out two of the most diametrically opposed positions on the status of people's talk, Harré's early work with Secord (1972) and Nisbett and Wilson's (1977) research would be good candidates. Harré and Secord propounded the 'open souls' doctrine which, at its most basic, responds to the question 'why did these people do that?' with the answer 'why not ask them?' (Harré and Secord, 1972: 101–23). Of course, as our discussion of ethogenics in Chapter Three demonstrated, Harré's position is much more subtle than this formulation of the open souls doctrine suggests. Harré and Secord are not claiming people have perfect insight into their own motives, or that telling researchers about those motives is an uncomplicated matter, but they are suggesting that the appropriate analysis of accounts will reveal to the researcher the nature of the social competence responsible for generating both accounts and actions (Harré, 1977b). The basic aim of the research is to move from an analysis of language to an understanding of an internal, causal, mechanism – the person's social competence.

In contrast, Nisbett and Wilson (1977) propose that people's 'verbal reports' about the causes of their actions are highly inaccurate. When people give verbal reports, they argue, much of the time they are 'telling more than they can know'. Nisbett and Wilson discuss a series of studies which seemed to show that people's explanations of why they liked a stimulus, for example, or why they changed their mind on an issue, were simply mistaken. They go on to make the alternative suggestion that people's accounts are not in any way accurate reports of mental events and processes. Instead explanatory accounts offer conventionally derived beliefs about behaviour ('I came to a stop because the light started to change'), or are ad hoc and possibly mistaken causal hypotheses which make sense of the behaviour ('I liked the party because of the people').

There are various positions on the nature of this disagreement between Nisbett and Wilson and those who favour the open-souls approach (Bainbridge, 1985; Ickes et al., 1986). Some argue that this is, in fact, a pseudo-conflict, because Nisbett and Wilson confuse what is essentially a conceptual theoretical issue about how a social science should be conducted with an empirical point (Gergen, 1982; Sabini and Silver, 1981; Shotter, 1981). In general, mainstream social psychology splits down the middle on this issue. Many studies implicitly adopt the open-souls approach and see no difficulty in taking a verbal or written utterance as a clear reflection of a cognitive or mental state. Large amounts of attitude research, for example, falls into this category, as does the study of social representa- tions, aspects of research on the self, person perception and so on. In many other cases, however, the social psychologist becomes suspicious of the veracity of people's descriptions of their internal states. As we saw in Chapter Two, some attitude theorists such as Fishbein and Azjen (1975) argue that people can misrepresent their basic underlying attitude as a result of normative pressures. There is considerable tension in social pyschology between the principle that people can be trusted to describe their internal states and the principle that the researcher must remain vigilant and sensitive to the possibilities of conscious or unconscious fraud. This issue, however, is rarely discussed systematically and is generally left to the commonsense of the researcher.

Discourse analysis takes a rather different position when faced with this problem of the relationship between utterances and mental states. We argue that the researcher should bracket off the whole issue of the *quality* of accounts as *accurate* or *inaccurate descriptions* of mental states. The problem is being construed at entirely the wrong level. Our focus is exclusively on discourse itself: how it is constructed, its functions, and the consequences which arise from different discursive organization. In this sense, discourse analysis is a radically non-cognitive form of social psychology.

It is important to be clear about this point. Discourse analysts are not suggesting that the phenomena traditionally thought of as mental should be excluded from analysis because they are in some way private, mysterious, unknowable. As we saw in Chapter Five, the *language* of the self and mental life is a public one which is available for analysis (Coulter, 1979a). In practice, much of the phenomenon of the mind is intersubjectively constituted as the person speaks, writes, reminisces, talks to others and so on. But because discourse analysts do not accord a different status to the 'inner' and the 'outer', or to the 'mental' and the 'non-mental', the question of how, precisely, a person's description of their mental state represents or matches that mental state becomes irrelevant. The descriptive accuracy of discourse and its adequacy as a map or chart of private, subjective, mental experience is the non-issue from our perspective.

Beyond intra-psychic explanations

It may seem odd to be promoting a non-cognitive social psychology when the vast majority of current research is attempting to give intra-psychic explanations of social behaviour. However, as we have seen, there are both theoretical and methodological advantages to this orientation. In the course of this book we have looked critically at a number of fundamentally intra-psychic explanations which draw on notions of attitudes, rules, the self, categories and representations and which try to move from language to the mental state. In each case we have described an alternative approach which concentrates on description and explanation in terms of discursive organizations instead of moving, in Garfinkel's (1967) phrase, under the skull.

There is a powerful tradition of non-cognitive thought in linguistic philosophy and ethnomethodology which has been concerned particularly with our vocabulary of mentalistic terms: words like belief and memory which, at first sight, appear to be references to mental states and entities. Gilbert Ryle (1949) and Ludwig Wittgenstein (1953, for a more elaborate account see *Remarks on the Philosophy of Psychology*, 1980) have been central in propounding this approach in philosophy, while Jeff Coulter (1979a, 1983, 1985), Rom Harré in his more recent writings (1983), and John Sabini and Maury Silver (1982) have, in different ways, done much to develop the implications for social research.

The central plank of this position is the argument that much of our vocabulary of mentalistic terms has no 'inner' referent at all; instead of being merely descriptions of mental states these words are *themselves* an autonomous part of particular social practices. Take the term 'understanding' as an example. When first thinking about this word, we are probably tempted to view it as a description of some private or inner experience. However, when we look closely at the way this word is actually used this view seems less convincing. Ryle has pointed out that this term if often used to mark a claim to success, the sort of situation where one might say 'I have been working at the problem and I think I understand it now'. However, merely having a moment of insight or a feeling of having cracked the problem is not sufficient. If the person with the feeling of comprehension tries to apply their ideas and finds they do not work, they will know that they were mistaken in the belief that they understood.

Furthermore, if *other people* assess the understanding gained, they may decide that the person only *thinks* they understand – they do not *really* understand. The general point is that although cognitive processes are clearly going on, and people without a brain certainly do not understand, this is not a sufficient condition for understanding. Understanding is assessed by *public criteria* and *practical tests*. The term understanding is properly used when these criteria can be, or have been, satisfied, not merely when people have a certain experience. Similar arguments have been used with a variety of other terms, such as 'knowledge' (Harré, 1983), 'memory' (Coulter, 1979a, 1983; Harré, 1983), 'belief' (Coulter, 1979b), 'intention' (Anscombe, 1957), 'envy', 'anger' (Sabini and Silver, 1982) and 'motives' (Mills, 1940; Peters, 1959; Sharrock and Watson, 1984 – and see Chapter Four).

For the most part, this argument in linguistic philosophy and ethno-methodology can be smoothly integrated with discourse analysis as it has been outlined in this book. In suggesting the relationship between language and mental states is a non-issue, we are agreeing with this tradition which treats descriptions of mental states as discursive social practices. There are, however, two drawbacks that might arise. The first stems from the danger of getting involved in fruitless debates about the reality or non-reality of mental entities, which can easily end in the kind of linguistic imperialism which denies all significance to cognitive processes. The second problem is that it is easy to move from this position to making the assumption that other sorts of discourse are straightforwardly referential. One of the main arguments of the discourse analysis described in this book is that *all* language can be analysed in terms of construction and function, not merely the language of self-reference. As we have seen, descriptions of scenes and events are as much an arena for presenting motives, giving disclaimers, and justifying actions, as accounts using the mentalistic terminology of desires and beliefs.

Discourse and the world 'out there'

People sometimes assume discourse analysis denies the existence of a world 'out there'. 'Why this concentration on language', they ask, 'when people out there are giving birth, making money and being murdered by oppressive regimes? Why don't you study these real processes and not just language which is a second-hand superficial medium?' This contrast between the real material world and language opens a veritable snake-pit of philosophical and political issues but it is important to briefly review why discourse analysts argue one should focus on language construction and function in this context.

Bottles, ships and hidden construction

To begin with we need to look at how this issue is formulated. A dichotomy is created between 'real' events and linguistic representations of those events. This formulation, like the dichotomies between mental/non-mental or subjective/objective, is not, of course, a neutral or natural division. It is a philosophical construction with a long history in Western societies and by agreeing to discuss in these terms one is fated to end up hung on one of the contradictory poles. Why do we talk about a world 'out there' in the first place? Is this world in some way independent of human affairs, a realm removed from human constructive activities?

Collins (1985) has provided a rather nice analogy in relation to his research on scientists which captures some of the constraints this kind of thinking generates. Social researchers and people in general populate their worlds with many different kinds of basic objects: societies, selves, biologies, physical phenomena, material realities and so on. Following Collins' analogy these objects are like ships in bottles. Their presence is unquestioned and miraculous. The ship is in the bottle, it looks like it must always have been there, it is impossible to think how it could be otherwise, the finished product is all that is visible. Those who marvel at ships in bottles, of course, have never observed the elaborate and detailed process of construction, as the ship is re-created with small pulleys, matchsticks and so on. The process of manufacture is left obscure. In the same way discourse analysts argue that the constructive process used to furnish the world 'out there' and the dichotomies which result remain obscure. The world and its objects appear ready completed. There seems no alternative but to accept it as it appears. Discourse analysis aims to explicate the constructive activity involved in the creation of a 'world out there' and for this reason is reluctant to take any dichotomy for granted, without researching why problems should be formulated in this way.

Factual accounts as topic

There are two problems which immediately arise when the question of discourse and 'the world out there' is posed. First of all, as we have noted, the form of the question implies access to some clear-cut, non-discursive realm which discourse 'relates to'. However, any formulation of the nature of that realm will inevitably be framed in discourse and, as we have shown repeatedly throughout this book, you do not need to study many of these formulations to find significant variation between them. So, in practice, when addressing this issue, the nature of the world out there is either stipulated by analytic fiat, some versions are reified and some ironized, which is clearly unsatisfactory, or the focus should shift to the question of how the versions themselves are managed (Cuff, 1980).

The second problem with discussions of 'discourse and the world' is the implication that the resolution will necessarily be a philosophical matter. Discourse analysts have preferred a different route. They have focused attention on situations where issues of 'fact' or 'perception' come to the fore, such as the discourse of science or the courts (cf. Pollner, 1974, 1975; Smith, 1978). Discourse analysts ask questions such as: what procedures are used to authorize factual accounts? How are factual accounts produced to perform a specific act? How is the effect of 'mere description' generated in discourse? For example, in Chapter Four, we discussed how defendants in court constructed factual accounts in such a way that they provided mitigation for potentially culpable behaviour. In general, this path seems a more fruitful one than being caught within a certain formulation of language and the world.

Discourse and reflexivity

Reflexivity is another issue that has increasingly come to the fore in discourse analysis. We met one sense of this term in Chapter One in our discussion of Wieder's work. Reflexivity in this sense refers to the fact that talk has the property of being both *about* actions, events and situations, and at the same time *part of* those things. However, there is a second, more general, sense of this notion which draws attention to the point that the findings of discourse analysis apply equally to the social texts produced by discourse analysts as to anyone else. Put another way, if the upshot of research of this kind is to question the simple realist model of the operation of discourse, and suggest that 'realism' is, at least partly, a rhetorical effect constructed through the careful choice of particular linguistic forms, then what are we to make of the discourse in which this claim is itself couched? How should we deal with the fact that our accounts of how people's language use is constructed are themselves constructions?

Most of the time this problem does not actively trouble discourse analysts as they practise their craft. It is possible to acknowledge that one's own language is constructing a version of the world, while proceeding with analysing texts and their implications for people's social and political lives. In this respect, discourse analysts are simply more honest than other researchers, recognizing their own work is not immune from the social psychological processes being studied. Most of the time, therefore, the most practical way of dealing with this issue is simply to get on with it, and not to get either paralyzed by or caught up in the infinite regresses possible. However, there are other intriguing responses to reflexivity.

Reflexivity as a topic and a strategy

One approach has been to take social research, and its discourse, as a topic of study in its own right. We have already described some research of this kind. For example, in Chapter Three psychologists' justificatory accounts of their theory choices were examined, In another example, Stringer looked at how factual discourse was used as an unexplicated resource in a sociopsychological analysis (Janis, 1972) of the 'Bay of Pigs' incident from the early months of the Kennedy presidency (Potter et al., 1984: 100–15). Stringer's account shows that Janis's group dynamics explanation tended to use his source texts (particularly Schlesinger's book about the presidency, *A Thousand Days*) as neutral historical documents, and failed to acknowledge the strategic purposes these texts might have been fulfilling, in particular their role in justifying Schlesinger's own actions. For other work of this kind see Bazerman (1984) and Gusfield (1976).

The problem with approaching the issue in this way is that the constant emphasis on *other people's* texts can blunt the radical implications of reflexivity. The point is that *all texts*, even the one we are writing and you are reading at this very moment, are subject to the same processes and have the same constructed, action-oriented aspects. Taking reflexivity merely as a topic defers attention from the most focal, present text. To overcome this problem, some researchers have wanted to draw attention more directly and forcefully to the construction of *their own* texts by departing from the standard conventions of academic writing and exploring 'new literary forms' (see Woolgar, forthcoming).

The point of these 'new literary forms' is not to document or describe problems of reflexivity but to give a practical demonstration of their effect (Woolgar, 1982). The goal is to remind the reader that the text is not a mere record of events, a collation of facts, but is a complex, multifaceted social achievement (Stringer, 1985). One way the conventional and constructed nature of the analyst's text can be pushed to the foreground is to present the analysis using a very different set of conventions. For example, Mulkay (1984b, 1985) has used a dramatic, theatrical play format to illustrate the multiple versions of the idea of replication drawn on by scientists and social researchers when legitimating their activities. Others have used the literary form of the lecture and encyclopedia (Ashmore, 1985), parody and dialogue (Mulkay, 1985).

Another method of illustrating problems of reflexivity in practice has been to construct analyses with a self-referential quality. These studies examine *at the same time* the topic and their own investigation of that topic. Typically, this operates by utilizing two, or more, parallel discourses, one of which is concerned with the subject of the research while the second tackles the construction of that subject in the first discourse. For example,

Wynne (forthcoming) has examined accounts of the onset of multiple sclerosis and her own discursive formulation of those accounts in a parallel text (see also Ashmore, 1985; Mulkay, 1985). Reflexivity in these cases is a means of exploring and illustrating rhetorical construction through analysing one's own analysis, and is an exciting development which challenges the literary skills of the social scientist.

The development of discourse analysis

The theoretical coherence of discourse analysis

It will be apparent that in the course of this book we have discussed research derived from a number of rather different theoretical perspectives. We have treated this work as a whole because it shares several basic assumptions about participants' discourse. In particular, all the research we have covered is concerned in one way or another with the action orientation of discourse. It takes discourse as a research topic in its own right rather than treating it as a transparent medium through which the 'real facts' of attitudes, events or behaviours can be recovered. Moreover, it takes a social perspective which focuses on the role of discourse in interaction and sense making rather than being concerned with, for example, abstract questions of semantics, text coherence or aesthetics.

Nevertheless, there are still important issues of theoretical disagreement between the different perspectives discussed here. One issue which particularly distinguishes those adopting a conversation analysis approach centres on the question of sequence. Conversation analysts, such as Sacks, have argued that a sequential analysis is fundamental for explicating the sense of utterances for participants (see Chapter Four). A full analysis of a particular speaker's turn of talk will, in this view, depend on an explication of the sequences of turns in which the particular turn is embedded; only through this procedure will its nature and consequences be adequately understood.

Those taking a more semiological perspective emphasize the importance of a *combination* of sequential considerations and considerations of replacement. That is, they argue that the researcher needs to understand both the discourse which is *actually* produced, and the discourse which *could* have been produced, but was not on this occasion (Culler, 1976; Fiske and Hartley, 1978; Hartley, 1982; Hodge and Tripp, 1986). From this perspective, to get the necessary analytic grasp on an account talking of a 'disturbance', say, we need to know the sequence in which that particular account was embedded, and the fact that alternative accounts talked of a 'riot' rather than a 'disturbance' (Potter and Reicher, 1987).

Despite these differences and possible disagreements, we have chosen to present this research in a way that draws attention to similarities and shows the potential for integrated work. In our view the areas of agreement are sufficient to warrant this integrated approach, and we hope each of the individual perspectives and research traditions will benefit from more cross fertilization than has occurred until now. As we pointed out at the very beginning of the book, a lot of research has been conducted in relatively isolated groupings within different disciplines, yet there are many parallels in the questions asked and the sorts of techniques used to answer them.

Discourse analysis and traditional social psychology

There are potentially three kinds of interaction which could occur between discourse analysis and what we have referred to as traditional social psychology or the vast majority of research which is concerned with cognitive process and the explanation of social behaviour. The first kind of interaction is, basically, no interaction at all. Much of the time, discourse analysis simply asks a different set of questions using a different kind of method. Insofar as this is the case, it occupies the role of a new, but distinct, facet of the many which make up social psychology.

The second kind of interaction which could develop would allow discourse analysis to act as a resource for more traditional work. One of its main inputs here would lie in improving our understanding of the sort of discourse which is the bedrock of traditional social psychological methods. As so much of social psychology is based more or less directly on participants' discourse in one form or other, a clearer picture of its organization and working should aid the construction of better methodological techniques and the interpretation of 'verbal responses'.

As we noted in Chapter Two, there is already a large literature on issues of response bias, experimenter effects, demand characteristics and so on. It is well-known that participants' discourse varies according to subtle cues in the wording or sequencing of questions and in experimental protocols. Research on language function could fit these phenomena into a broader theoretical framework, and ultimately may be able to make detailed predictions as to the sorts of wordings which will produce certain effects; what kinds of question wording, for example, will lead to answers stressing social desirability and what constructions might lead to answers stressing social differentiation?

The third kind of interaction would build on the tension between the theories and findings of the two areas. Tension and conflict are, of course, an essential and creative part of scientific development. We stressed this kind of interaction in Chapters Two to Seven where we tried to demonstrate how sets of findings from areas of traditional social psychology could be better understood with perspectives from discourse analysis. Initially, one of the important advantages of discourse analysis may well be to raise difficulties with currently accepted models and theories. Eventually, however, the debate is likely to work in both directions, with traditional researchers attempting to explain discursive organizations as the upshot of the workings of cognitive processes.

Discourse analysis should also be highly pertinent when questions of generalization and application become dominant. In most cases, when the results of experimental work are checked in naturalistic situations, people's utterances or writings are all that is available to the analyst. A proper evaluation of experimental results thus depends, perhaps ironically, on analysis of discourse. At some point event the most rigorously controlled behavioural experiments will need to be backed up with techniques capable of dealing with the kinds of naturalistic records examined in this book.

Similarly with application, as Tajfel (1972) pointed out, to properly apply a social psychological theory it is necessary to develop a detailed analysis of the social context in which the application is to take place. The variables modelled in a theory are only defined in an abstract, operational fashion, and may be manifested in a variety of different ways when applied, depending on specific features of the social context. Put simply, what counts as, say, helpfulness in one context may become something very different in another (Van der Vlist, 1982). Yet, as with evaluation, the detailed analysis of the social context, very largely, reduces to an analysis of participants' discourse. However precise and clear-cut the theory, if it is to be properly applied in a practical context, the researcher or practitioner must deal with naturally occurring discourse with all the complexities that it involves.

Future directions

Someone is supposed to have asked Humphrey Lyttleton, the great jazz musician, where jazz was going, and he replied 'If I knew where jazz was going I would be there already!' Identifying future directions for discourse analysis is somewhat similar. As the work develops it throws up its own brand of problems and suggests exciting and interesting new avenues of research. Nevertheless, it is possible to discern three areas in which there is increasing interest.

The first is in the painstaking examination of complex, worked-over, written texts. There are an increasing number of studies which are concerned with the role of these kinds of texts (children's stories, journalism, democratic texts, other political texts etc.) as potent constructions of social life which, through the achievement of particular versions of the world, encourage evaluations and actions from readers (Adams, 1986; Chua, 1979; Eglin, 1979; Kress, 1983, 1985; Kress and Hodge, 1979; Kress and

Trew, 1978; McHoul, 1982; Smith, 1974, 1978, 1982, 1984; Woolgar, 1980; Yearley, 1981). The classic work of this kind comes, however, not from social research but from literary theory, namely Barthes' (1974) analysis of the sense-making processes at work in a short story by Balzac. In general, there is a great deal of scope in this field for constructive interchange between social researchers and literary theorists (Culler, 1983; Harari, 1979; Rorty, 1978; Suleiman and Crosman, 1980).

The second likely area of expansion is the study of what has classically been known as rhetoric (Billig, 1987), the use of discourse to persuasive effect. This topic has always been important, and is one where the concerns of discourse analysis coincide with those of political scientists (Edelman, 1977; Shapiro, 1981, 1983; Shapiro and Banham, 1983). This field has recently received a powerful impetus as a result of research applying the techniques and theories of conversation analysis to recordings of the interaction between political orators and audiences (Atkinson, 1983, 1984a, 1984b, 1985; Grady and Potter, 1985; Heritage and Greatbatch, 1986). There is room here for an approach to the perennial social psychological issue of persuasion in terms of the *process* of interaction between producer and recipient, and the detailed linguistic format of the persuasive text.

The third area of expansion encourages discourse analysts to address concerns in the arena of ideology. Thompson (1984) has pointed out three central ways in which discourse contributes significant ideological consequences. It can be used in the presentation of situations of domination and exploitation as legitimate and proper, to mask the existence of these situations, and to reify current social relationships as natural or, indeed, essential. This is an enormously complicated area which raises many considerations outside the detailed analysis of texts. However, a number of studies have tried to tackle questions of discourse with ideological import, for example, in the political representations of the 'the Orient' and middle-eastern politics (Said, 1978, 1981), in the organization of accounts of employment opportunities (Wetherell et al., 1987), and the justification of racial disadvantage (Trew, 1979; Wetherell and Potter, forthcoming a).

One of the advantages of discourse analysis is that the data are everywhere – in conversations, on television, in the newspapers, on advertising hoardings – and the resources needed to start work are minimal. If we have indicated the interest and value of the systematic analysis of accounts of all kinds this book will have succeeded in its aim. The most exciting developments, as always, lie in the future.

Appendix: transcription notation

The form of notation used throughout this book was developed by Gail Jefferson. A more complete description is found in Atkinson and Heritage (1984).

Extended square brackets mark overlap between utterances, e.g.:

A: Right ⌜ so you
B: ⌞ I'm not sure

An equals sign at the end of a speaker's utterance and at the start of the next utterance indicates the absence of a discernable gap, e.g.:

A: Anyway Brian=
B: =Okay, okay

Numbers in brackets indicate pauses timed to the nearest tenth of a second. A full stop in brackets indicates a pause which is noticeable but too short to measure, e.g.:

A: I went (3.6) a lot further (.) than I intended

One or more colons indicate an extension of the preceding vowel sound, e.g.:

A: Yea::h, I see::

Underlining indicates that words are uttered with added emphasis; words in capitals are uttered louder than the surrounding talk, e.g.:

A: It's not right, not right AT ALL

A full stop before a word or sound indicates an audible intake of breath, e.g.:

A: I think .hh I need more

Round brackets indicate that material in the brackets is either inaudible or there is doubt about its accuracy, e.g.:

A: I (couldn't tell you) that

Square brackets indicate that some transcript has been deliberately omitted. Material in square brackets is clarificatory information, e.g.:

A: Brian [the speaker's brother] said [ ] it's okay

References

Abraham, C. (1984) 'Problems in Categorizing Content: A Discussion of the Limits of Content Analysis'. Paper presented at the British Psychological Society, London Conference, December.

Adams, J. (1986) *The Conspiracy of the Text: The Place of Narrative in the Development of Thought*. London: Routledge and Kegan Paul.

Allen, V. L. and D. A. Wilder (1979) 'Group Categorization and Attribution of Belief Similarity', *Small Group Behaviour*, 10: 73–80.

Allport, G. W. (1935) 'Attitudes', in C. Murchison (ed.), *Handbook of Social Psychology* Vol. 2. Worcester, Mass.: Clark University Press.

Althusser, L. (1971) *For Marx*. London: Allen Lane.

Anscombe, G. E. M. (1957) *Intention*. Oxford: Blackwell.

Argyris, C. (1975) 'Dangers in Applying Results from Experimental Social Psychology', *American Psychologist*, 30: 469–85.

Ashmore, M. (1985) 'A Question of Reflexivity: Wrighting Sociology of Scientific Knowledge'. Unpublished D. Phil Thesis: University of York.

Atkinson, J. M. (1983) 'Two Devices for Generating Audience Approval: A Comparative Analysis of Public Discourse and Texts', in K. Ehlich and H. van Riemsdijk (eds), *Connectedness in Sentence, Discourse and Text*. Tilburg: Tilburg Papers in Linguistics.

Atkinson, J. M. (1984a) *Our Master's Voices: The Language and Body Language of Politics*. London: Methuen.

Atkinson, J. M. (1984b) 'Public Speaking and Audience Responses: Some Techniques for Inviting Applause', in J. M. Atkinson and J. C. Heritage (eds), *Structures of Social Action: Studies In Conversation Analysis*. Cambridge: Cambridge University Press.

Atkinson, J. M. (1985) 'Refusing Invited Applause: Preliminary Observations from a Case Study of Charismatic Oratory', in T. A. van Dijk (ed.), *A Handbook of Discourse Analysis* Vol. 3. New York: Academic Press.

Atkinson, J. M. and P. Drew (1979) *Order in Court: The Organization of Verbal Interaction in Judicial Settings*. London: Macmillan.

Atkinson J. M. and J. C. Heritage (eds) (1984) *Structures of Social Action: Studies in Conversation Analysis*. Cambridge: Cambridge University Press.

Atkinson, P. (1985) 'Talk and Identity: Some Convergences in Micro-Sociology', in H. J. Helle and S. N. Eisenstadt (eds), *Micro-Sociological Theory*. London and Beverly Hills, California: Sage.

Austin, J. (1961) 'A Plea for Excuses', in J. D. Urmson and G. Warnock (eds), *Philosophical Papers*. Oxford: Clarendon Press.

Austin, J. (1962) *How To Do Things With Words*. London: Oxford University Press.

Bainbridge, L. (1985) 'Inferring from Verbal Reports to Cognitive Processes', in M. Brenner, J. Brown and D. Canter (eds), *The Research Interview: Uses and Approaches*. London: Academic Press.

Bar-Hillel, Y. (1954) 'Indexical Expressions', *Mind*, 63: 359–79.

Barjonet, P. E. (1980) 'L'influence sociale et des representations des causes de l'accident de la route', *Le Travail Humain*, 43: 243–53.

Barnes, B. (1982) *T. S. Kuhn and Social Science*. London: Macmillan.

Barnes, B. and J. Law (1976) 'Whatever Should be Done with Indexical Expressions?, *Theory and Society*, 3: 223–37.

Barthes, R. (1964) *Elements of Semiology*. New York: Hill and Wang.

Barthes, R. (1972) *Mythologies*. London: Paladin.

Barthes, R. (1974) *S/Z*. London: Cape.

Barthes, R. (1985) *The Fashion System*. London: Cape.

Baumeister, R. F. (1982) 'A Self-Presentational View of Social Phenomena', *Psychological Bulletin*, 91: 3–26.

Bazerman, C. (1984) 'Modern Evolution of the Experimental Physics Report', *Social Studies of Science*, 14: 163–96.

Beattie, G. W. (1983) *Talk: Analysis of Speech and Non-Verbal Behaviour in Conversation*. Milton Keynes: Open University Press.

Becker, H. S. (1963) *Outsiders: Studies in the Sociology of Deviance*. New York: The Free Press.

Berelson, B. (1971) *Content Analysis in Communication Research*. New York: The Free Press.

Berger, P. L. and T. Luckmann (1966) *The Social Construction of Reality*. Harmondsworth: Penguin.

Best, E. (1922) *Spiritual and Mental Concepts of the Maori*. Wellington, New Zealand: Dominion Museum Bulletin No. 2.

Billig, M. (1985) 'Prejudice, Categorization and Particularization: From a Perceptual to a Rhetorical Approach', *European Journal of Social Psychology*, 15: 79–103.

Billig, M. (1987) *Arguing and Thinking: A Rhetorical Approach to Social Psychology*. Cambridge: Cambridge University Press.

Bogdan, R. and S. J. Taylor, (1975) *Introduction to Qualitative Research Methods*. New York: Wiley.

Bourhis, R. Y. and H. Giles (1977) 'The Language of Intergroup Distinctiveness', in H. Giles (ed.), *Language, Ethnicity and Intergroup Relations*. London: Academic Press.

Bower, G. H. and R. K. Cirilo (1985) 'Cognitive Psychology and Text Processing', in T. A. van Dijk (ed.), *Handbook of Discourse Analysis* Vol. 1. London: Academic Press.

Brannigan, A. (1981) *The Social Basis of Scientific Discoveries*. Cambridge: Cambridge University Press.

Brazil, D. (1981) 'The Place of Intonation in a Discourse Model', in M. Coulthard and M. Montgomery (eds), *Studies in Discourse Analysis*. London: Routledge and Kegan Paul.

Brenner, M. (1985) 'Survey Interviewing', in M. Brenner, J. Brown and D. Canter (eds), *The Research Interview: Uses and Approaches*. London: Academic Press.

Brewer, M. B., V. Dull and L. Lui (1981) 'Perception of the Elderly: Stereotypes as Prototypes', *Journal of Personality and Social Psychology*, 41: 656–70.

Broadbent, G., R. Bunt and C. Jencks (eds) (1980) *Signs, Symbols and Architecture*. New York: Wiley.

Brown, D. and S. Levinson (1978) 'Universals in Language Use: Politeness Phenomena', in E. Goody (ed.), *Questions and Politeness: Strategies in Social Interaction*. Cambridge: Cambridge University Press.

Brown, G. and G. Yule (1983) *Discourse Analysis*. Cambridge: Cambridge University Press.

Brunswik, E. (1955) 'Representative Design and Probabilistic Theory in a Functional Psychology', *Psychological Review*, 62: 193–217.

Button, G. and N. Casey (1984) 'Generating Topic: The Use of Topic Initial Elicitors', in J. M. Atkinson and J. Heritage (eds), *Structures of Social Action: Studies in Conversation Analysis*. Cambridge: Cambridge University Press.

Cannell, C. F. and R. L. Kahn (1968) 'Interviewing', in G. Lindzey and E. Aronson (eds), *The Handbook of Social Psychology* (2nd Edition) Vol. 2. Reading, Mass: Addison-Wesley.

Cantor, N. and W. Mischel (1977) 'Traits as Prototypes: Effects on Recognition Memory', In L. Berkowitz (ed.), *Advances in Experimental Social Psychology* Vol. 9. London: Academic Press.

Cantor, N. and W. Mischel (1979) 'Prototypes in Person Perception', in L. Berkowitz (ed.), *Advances in Experimental Social Psychology* Vol. 12. London: Academic Press.

Cattell, R. B. (1966) *The Scientific Analysis of Personality.* Chicago: Aldine.

Chalmers, A. (1980) *What is This Thing Called Science?* Milton Keynes: Open University Press.

Chomsky, N. (1965) *Aspects of a Theory of Syntax.* The Hague: Mouton.

Chomsky, N. (1966) *Cartesian Linguistics: A Chapter in the History of Rationalist Thought.* New York: Harper and Row.

Chua, B. H. (1979) 'Democracy as a Textual Accomplishment', *The Sociological Quarterly,* 20: 541–9.

Cicourel, A. V. (1974) *Theory and Method in a Study of Argentine Fertility.* New York: Wiley.

Clarke, D. (1983) *Language and Action: A Structural Model of Behaviour.* Oxford: Pergamon.

Collett, P. (1977) 'Rule as a Scientific Concept', in P. Collett (ed.), *Social Rules and Social Behaviour.* Oxford: Blackwell.

Collins, H. M. (1974) 'The TEA Set: Tacit Knowledge and Scientific Networks', *Science Studies,* 4: 165–86.

Collins, H. M. (1983) 'The Meaning of Lies: Accounts of Action and Participatory Research', in G. N. Gilbert and P. Abell (eds), *Accounts and Action.* Aldershot: Gower.

Collins, H. M. (1985) *Changing Order: Replication and Induction in Scientific Practice.* London and Beverly Hills, California: Sage.

Cooley, C. H. (1902) *Human Nature and the Social Order.* New York: Scribner's.

Coulter, J. (1979a) *The Social Construction of Mind.* London: Macmillan.

Coulter, J. (1979b) 'Beliefs and Practical Understanding', in G. Psathas (ed.), *Everyday Language; Studies in Ethnomethodology.* New York: Irvington.

Coulter, J. (1983) *Rethinking Cognitive Theory.* London: Macmillan.

Coulter, J. (1985) 'Two Concepts of the Mental', in K. J. Gergen and K. E. Davis (eds), *The Social Construction of the Person.* New York: Springer-Verlag.

Coulthard, M. (1977) *An Introduction to Discourse Analysis.* London: Longman.

Coward, R. (1984) *Female Desire.* London: Paladin.

Coward, R. and J. Ellis (1977) *Language and Materialism: Developments in Semiology and the Theory of the Subject.* London: Routledge and Kegan Paul.

Von Cranach, M. and R. Harré (eds) (1982) *The Analysis of Action.* London: Academic Press.

Crane, D. (1980) 'An Exploratory Study of Kuhnian Paradigms in High Energy Physics', *Social Studies of Science,* 10: 23–54.

Cuff, E. C. (1980) 'Some Issues in Studying the Problem of Versions in Everyday Situations', *Occasional Paper No. 3.* Department of Sociology, University of Manchester.

Cuff, E. C. and D. E. Hustler (1982) 'Stories and Story-Time in an Infant Classroom: Some Features of Language in Social Interaction', *Semiotica,* 42: 119–45.

Culler, J. (1975) *Structuralist Poetics.* London: Routledge and Kegan Paul.

Culler, J. (1976) *Saussure.* London: Fontana.

Culler, J. (1983) *On Deconstruction.* London: Routledge and Kegan Paul.

Dahrendorf, R. (1973) *Homo Sociologicus.* London: Routledge and Kegan Paul.

Davidson, J. (1984) 'Subsequent Versions of Invitations, Offers, Requests and Proposals Dealing with Potential or Actual Rejection', in J. M. Atkinson and J. Heritage (eds), *Structures of Social Action: Studies in Conversation Analysis.* Cambridge: Cambridge University Press.

Denzin, N. K. (1978) *The Research Act* (2nd edition). Chicago: Aldine.

van Dijk, T. A. (1984) *Prejudice in Discourse: An Analysis of Ethnic Prejudices In Cognition and Conversation.* Amsterdam: John Benjamins.

van Dijk, T. A. (ed.) (1985) *Handbook of Discourse Analysis* Vols 1–4. London: Academic Press.

van Dijk, T. A. and W. Kintch (1983) *Strategies of Discourse Comprehension.* London: Academic Press.

Drew, P. (1978) 'Accusations: The Occasioned Use of 'Religious Geography' in Describing Events', *Sociology*, 12: 1–22.

Drew, P. (1984) 'Speakers' Reportings in Invitation Sequences', in J. M. Atkinson and J. Heritage (eds), *Structures of Social Action: Studies in Conversation Analysis.* Cambridge: Cambridge University Press.

Drew, P. (1985a) 'Analyzing the Use of Language in Courtroom Interaction', in T. A. van Dijk (ed.), *Handbook of Discourse Analysis* Vol. 3. London: Academic Press.

Drew, P. (1985b) 'Some Properties of Competing Descriptions of Events'. Paper presented at the British Psychological Society Social Psychology Section Conference, Cambridge, September.

Drew, P. (1986) 'A Comment on Taylor and Johnson', *British Journal of Social Psychology*, 25: 197–8.

Duncan, B. L. (1976) 'Differential Social Perception and Attribution of Intergroup Violence: Testing the Lower Limits of Stereotyping of Blacks', *Journal of Personality and Social Psychology*, 34: 590–8.

Edelman, M. (1977) *Political Language: Words that Succeed and Policies that Fail.* New York: Academic Press.

Eglin, P. (1979) 'Resolving Reality Junctures on Telegraph Avenue: A Study of Practical Reasoning', *Canadian Journal of Sociology*, 4: 359–75.

Elms, A. C. (1975) 'The Crisis of Confidence in Social Psychology', *American Psychologist*, 30: 967–76.

Eysenck, H. J. (1953) *The Structure of Human Personality.* New York: Wiley.

Eysenck, H. J. and S. B. Eysenck (1964) *Manual of the Eysenck Personality Inventory.* London: Hodder and Stoughton.

Farr, R. M. (1984) 'Social Representations: Their Role in the Design and Execution of Laboratory Experiments', in R. M. Farr and S. Moscovici (eds), *Social Representations.* Cambridge: Cambridge University Press.

Farr, R. and S. Moscovici, (eds) (1984) *Social Representations.* Cambridge: Cambridge University Press.

Festinger, L. (1954) 'A Theory of Social Comparison Processes', *Human Relations*, 7: 117–40.

Festinger, L (1957) *A Theory of Cognitive Dissonance.* Evanston, Illinois: Row, Peterson.

Feyerabend, P. (1975) *Against Method.* London: NLB.

Fishbein, M. and I. Azjen (1975) *Belief, Attitude, Intention and Behaviour: An Introduction to Theory and Research.* Reading, Mass: Addison-Wesley.

Fiske, J. and J. Hartley (1978) *Reading Television.* London: Methuen.

Forgas, J. (1979) *Social Episodes: The Study of Interaction Routines.* London: Academic Press.

Foucault, M. (1970) *The Order of Things.* London: Tavistock.

Foucault, M. (1971) 'Orders of Discourse', *Social Science Information*, 10: 7–30.

Foucault, M. (1972) *The Archaeology of Knowledge.* London: Tavistock.

Foucault, M. (1981) *The History of Sexuality, Vol. 1: An Introduction.* London: Penguin.

Frederickson, C. H. (1986) 'Cognitive Models and Discourse Analysis', in C. R. Cooper and S. Greenbaum (eds), *Studying Writing: Linguistic Approaches.* London and Beverly Hills, California: Sage.

Freedle, R. O. (ed.) (1977) *Advances in Discourse Processes*. Norwood, N. J.: Ablex.

Garfinkel, H. (1967) *Studies in Ethnomethodology*. Englewood Cliffs: Prentice Hall.

Garfinkel, H. (1974) 'On the Origins of the Term "Ethnomethodology"' ', in R. Turner (ed.), *Ethnomethodology*. Harmondsworth: Penguin.

Garvey, C. (1984) *Children's Talk*. London: Fontana.

Gergen, K. J. (1973) 'Social Psychology as History', *Journal of Personality and Social Psychology*, 26: 309–20.

Gergen, K. J. (1978) 'Experimentation in Social Psychology: A Reappraisal', *European Journal of Social Psychology*, 8: 507–27.

Gergen, K. J. (1982) *Toward Transformation in Social Knowledge*. New York: Springer-Verlag.

Gergen, K. J. (1985) 'Social Constructionist Inquiry: Context and Implications', in K. J. Gergen and K. E. Davis (eds), *The Social Construction of the Person*. New York: Springer-Verlag.

Gergen, K. J. (forthcoming) 'Warranting Voice and the Elaboration of the Self', in J. Shotter and K. J. Gergen (eds), *Texts of Identity*. London: Sage Publications.

Gergen, K. J. and K. E. Davis (eds) (1985) *The Social Construction of the Person*. New York: Springer-Verlag.

Di Giacomo, J.-P. (1980) 'Intergroup Alliance and Rejections Within a Protest Movement (Analysis of Social Representations)', *European Journal of Social Psychology*, 10: 329–44.

Gilbert, G. N. (1980) 'Being Interviewed: A Role Analysis', *Social Science Information*, 19: 227–36.

Gilbert, G. N. and M. Mulkay (1980) 'Contexts of Scientific Discourse: Social Accounting in Experimental Papers', in K. Knorr-Cetina, R. Krohn and R. Whitley (eds), *The Social Process of Investigation*. Dordrecht: Reidel.

Gilbert, G. N. and M. Mulkay (1982) 'Warranting Scientific Belief', *Social Studies of Science*, 12: 382–408.

Gilbert, G. N. and M. Mulkay (1984) *Opening Pandora's Box: A Sociological Analysis of Scientists' Discourse*. Cambridge: Cambridge University Press.

Giles, H. (ed.) (1977) *Language, Ethnicity and Intergroup Relations*. London: Academic Press.

Giles, H. and R. N. St. Clair (eds) (1979) *Language and Social Psychology*. Oxford: Blackwell.

Goffman, E. (1959) *The Presentation of Self in Everyday Life*. Harmondsworth: Penguin.

Goffman, E. (1961) *Asylums*. Harmondsworth: Penguin.

Goffman, E. (1971) *Relations in Public: Micro-Studies of the Public Order*. Harmondsworth: Penguin.

Goffman, E. (1981) *Forms of Talk*. Oxford: Blackwell.

Gombrowicz, W. (1979) *Ferdydurke*. London: Boyars.

Grady, K. and J. Potter (1985) 'Speaking and Clapping: A Comparison of Foot and Thatcher's Oratory', *Language and Communication*, 5: 173–83.

Grice, M. P. (1975) 'Logic and Conversation', in P. Cole and J. L. L. Morgan (eds), *Syntax and Semantics 3: Speech Acts*. New York: Academic Press.

Gusfield, J. (1976) 'The Literary Rhetoric of Science: Comedy and Pathos in Drinking Driver Research', *American Sociological Review*, 41: 16–34.

Halliday, M. A. K. (1978) *Language as Social Semiotic*. London: Edward Arnold.

Halliday, Q. and J. Potter (1987) 'Community Leaders in Discourse: Lay Environmental Psychology in Accounts of a "Riot"' ', mimeo, University of St Andrews.

Hamilton, D. L. (1979) 'A Cognitive-Attributional Analysis of Stereotyping', in L. Berkowitz (ed.), *Advances in Experimental Social Psychology* Vol. 12. New York: Academic Press.

Hamlyn, D. W. (1974) 'Person Perception and our Understanding of Others', in T. Mischel (ed.), *Understanding Other Persons*. Oxford: Blackwell.

Hammersley, M. and P. Atkinson (1983) *Ethnography: Principles and Practice*. London: Tavistock.

Harari, J. V. (ed.) (1979) *Textual Strategies: Essays in Post-Structuralist Criticism*. London: Methuen.

Harré, R. (1974) 'Some Remarks on "Rule" as a Scientific Concept', in T. Mischel (ed.), *Understanding Other Persons*. Oxford: Blackwell.

Harré, R. (1977a) 'Rules in the Explanation of Social Behaviour,' in P. Collett (ed.), *Social Rules and Social Behaviour*. Oxford: Blackwell.

Harré, R. (1977b) 'The Ethogenic Approach: Theory and Practice', in L. Berkowitz (ed.), *Advances in Experimental Social Psychology* Vol. 10. London: Academic Press.

Harré, R. (1977c) 'The Self in Monodrama', in T. Mischel (ed.), *The Self: Psychological and Philosophical Issues*. Oxford: Blackwell.

Harré, R. (1979) *Social Being: A Theory for Social Psychology*. Oxford: Blackwell.

Harré, R. (1983) *Personal Being: A Theory for Individual Psychology*. Oxford: Blackwell.

Harré, R. (1985a) 'Situational Rhetoric and Self-presentation', in J. Forgas (ed.), *Language and Social Situations*. New York: Springer-Verlag.

Harré, R. (1985b) 'The Language Game of Self-Ascription: A Note', in K. J. Gergen and K. E. Davis (eds), *The Social Construction of the Person*. New York: Springer-Verlag.

Harré, R. (1986a) 'Selves in Talk', *British Journal of Social Psychology*, 25: 271–3.

Harré, R. (1986b) *Varieties of Realism*. Oxford: Blackwell.

Harré, R. (forthcoming) 'Problems of Self-reference and the Expression of Selfhood', in J. Shotter and K. J. Gergen (eds), *Texts of Identity*. Greenwich, Conn.: JAI Press.

Harré, R. and P. F. Secord (1972) *The Explanation of Social Behaviour*. Oxford: Blackwell.

Harré, R., D. Clarke and N. de Carlo (1985) *Motives and Mechanisms: An Introduction to the Psychology of Action*. London: Methuen.

Harris, R. (1980) *The Language Makers*. London: Methuen.

Hartley, J. (1982) *Understanding News*. London: Methuen.

Heath, S. (1982) *The Sexual Fix*. London: Macmillan.

Hebdidge, D. (1979) *Subculture: The Meaning of Style*. London: Methuen.

Heelas, P. and A. Lock (eds) (1981) *Indigenous Psychologies*. London: Academic Press.

Heider, F. (1958) *The Psychology of Interpersonal Relations*. New York: Wiley.

Henriques, J., W. Hollway, C. Urwin, C. Venn and V. Walkerdine (1984) *Changing the Subject: Psychology, Social Regulation and Subjectivity*. London: Methuen.

Heritage, J. (1978) 'Aspects of the Flexibilities of Natural Language Use', *Sociology*, 12: 79–105.

Heritage, J. (1984) *Garfinkel and Ethnomethodology*. Cambridge: Polity Press.

Heritage, J. and D. Greatbatch (1986) 'Generating Applause: A Study of Rhetoric and Response at Party Political Conferences, *American Sociological Review*, 92: 110–57.

Herzlich, C. (1973) *Health and Illness: A Social Psychological Perspective*. London: Academic Press.

Hesse, M. (1974) *The Structure of Scientific Inference*. London: Macmillan.

Hewitt, J. P. and R. Stokes (1975) 'Disclaimers', *American Sociological Review*, 40: 1–11.

Hewstone, M., J. Jaspars and M. Lalljee (1982) 'Social Representations, Social Attribution and Social Identity: The Intergroup Images of "Public" and "Comprehensive" Schoolboys', *European Journal of Social Psychology*, 12: 241–71.

Hinde, R. A. (1975) 'The Concept of Function', in G. Baerends, C. Beer and A. Manning (eds), *Function and Evolution in Behaviour*. Oxford: Clarendon.

Hodge, R. and D. Tripp (1986) *Children and Television: A Semiotic Approach*. Cambridge: Polity.

Holsti, O. R. (1968) 'Content Analysis', in G. Lindzey and E. Aronson (eds), *Handbook of Social Psychology* Vol. 2. Reading, Mass: Addison-Wesley.

Husband, C. (1982) 'Introduction: "Race"', the Continuity of a Concept', in C. Husband (ed.), *'Race' in Britain: Continuity and Change*. London: Hutchinson.

Ickes, W., E. Robertson, W. Tooke and G. Teng (1986) 'Naturalistic Social Cognition: Methodology, Assessment and Validation', *Journal of Personality and Social Psychology*, 51: 66–82.

Israel, J. and H. Tajfel (eds) (1972) *The Context of Social Psychology*. London: Academic Press.

Jacobs, S. and S. Jackson (1983) 'Speech Act Structure in Conversation: Rational Aspects of Pragmatic Coherence', in R. T. Craig and K. Tracy (eds) *Conversational Coherence: Form, Structure and Strategy*. London and Beverly Hills, California: Sage.

James, W. (1968) 'The Self', in C. Gordon and K. J. Gergen (eds), *The Self in Social Interaction, Vol. 1: Classic and Contemporary Perspectives*. New York: Wiley.

Janis, I. (1972) *Victims of Groupthink*. Boston: Houghton Mifflin.

Jayyusi, L. (1984) *Categorization and the Moral Order*. London: Routledge and Kegan Paul.

Jefferson, G. (1985) An Exercise in the Transcription and Analysis of Laughter', in T. A. van Dijk (ed.), *Handbook of Discourse Analysis* Vol. 3. London: Academic Press.

Johnson-Laird, P. (1974) 'Experimental Psycholinguistics', in M. R. Rosenzweig and L. W. Portar (eds), *Annual Review of Psychology* Vol. 25. Palo Alto, California: Ann. Revs. Inc.

Jones, E. E. and K. E. Davis (1965) 'From Acts to Dispositions: The Attributional Process in Person Perception', in L. Berkowitz (ed.), *Advances in Experimental Social Psychology* Vol. 2. New York. Academic Press.

Kallen, D. B. P., G. B. Kosse, H. C. Wagenaar, J. J. J. Kloprogge and M. Vorbeck (eds) (1982) *Social Science Research and Public Policy-Making*. Windsor, Berks: NFER-Nelson.

Kelley, H. H. (1967) 'Attribution Theory and Social Psychology', *Nebraska Symposium on Motivation*, 15: 192–238.

Kinder, D. R. and D. O. Sears (1985) 'Public Opinion and Political Action', in G. Lindzey and E. Aronson (eds), *The Handbook of Social Psychology* (3rd Edition) Vol. 2. New York: Random House.

Krampen, M. (1983) 'Icons of the Road', *Semiotica*, 43: 1–204.

Kreckel, M. (1981) *Communicative Acts and Shared Knowledge in Natural Discourse*. London: Academic Press.

Kreckel, M. (1982) 'Communicative Acts and Extralinguistic Knowledge', in M. Von Cranach and R. Harré (eds), *The Analysis of Action*. Cambridge: Cambridge University Press.

Kress, G. (1983) 'Linguistic and Ideological Transformations in Newspaper Language', in H. Davis and P. Walton (eds), *Language, Image, Media*. Oxford: Blackwell.

Kress, G. (1985) 'Ideological Structures in Discourse', in T. A. van Dijk (ed.), *Handbook of Discourse Analysis* Vol. 4. London: Academic Press.

Kress, G. and R. Hodge (1979) *Language as Ideology*. London: Routledge and Kegan Paul.

Kress, G. and T. Trew (1978) 'Ideological Transformations of Discourse: Or How the *Sunday Times* Got its Message Across', *The Sociological Review*, 26: 755–76.

Kroger, R. O. (1982) 'Explorations in Ethogeny: With Special Reference to the Rules of Address', *American Psychologist*, 37: 810–20.

Kuhn, T. S. (1962) *The Structure of Scientific Revolutions*. Chicago: University of Chicago Press.

Kuhn, T. S. (1977) *The Essential Tension: Selected Studies in Scientific Tradition and Change*. London: University of Chicago Press.

Kulka, R. A. and J. B. Kessler (1978) 'Is Justice Really Blind? The Influence of Litigant Physical Attractiveness on Juridicial Judgment', *Journal of Applied Social Psychology*, 8: 366–81.

Labov, W. (1972a) *Language of the Inner City*. Philadelphia: Philadelphia University Press.

Labov, W. (1972b) 'Some Principles of Linguistic Methodology', *Language in Society*, 1: 97–120.

Labov, W. and D. Fanshell (1977) *Therapeutic Discourse: Psychotherapy as Conversation*. Academic Press: London.

Lakatos, I. (1970) 'Falsification and the Methodology of Scientific Research Programmes', in I. Lakatos and A. Musgrave (eds), *Criticism and the Growth of Knowledge*. Cambridge: Cambridge University Press.

Lakoff, G. and M. Johnson (1980) *Metaphors We Live By*. Chicago: University of Chicago Press.

Lalljee, M., L. B. Brown and G. P. Ginsberg (1984) 'Attitudes: Disposition, Behaviour or Evaluation', *British Journal of Social Psychology*, 23: 233–44.

Latour, B. and S. Woolgar (1979) *Laboratory Life: The Social Construction of Scientific Facts*. London and Beverly Hills, California: Sage.

Law, J. and P. Lodge (1984) *Science For Social Scientists*. London: Macmillan.

Layton, E. (1977) 'Conditions for Technological Development', in I. Spiegel-Rosing and D. J. de Solla Price (eds), *Science, Technology and Society*. London and Beverly Hills: Sage.

Lee, J. (1984) 'Innocent Victims and Evil-Doers', *Women's Studies International Forum*, 7: 69–73.

Levinson, S. (1983) *Pragmatics*. Cambridge: Cambridge University Press.

Litton, I. and J. Potter (1985) 'Social Representations in the Ordinary Explanation of a "Riot"', *European Journal of Social Psychology*, 15: 371–88.

Lock, A. (1981) 'Universals in Human Conception', in P. Heelas and A. Lock (eds), *Indigenous Psychologies*. London: Academic Press.

Lodge, D. (1978) *Changing Places*. Harmondsworth: Penguin.

Lyons, J. (1967) *Introduction to Theoretical Linguistics*. Cambridge: Cambridge University Press.

Lyons, J. (1978) *The Invention of the Self*. Carbondale, Illinois: Southern Illinois University Press.

McCabe, C. (1974) 'Realism and the Cinema: Notes on Some Brechtian Theses', *Screen*, 15: 7–27.

McConahay, J. B. (1985) 'Modern Racism, Ambivalence and the Modern Racism Scale', in S. L. Gaertner (ed.), *Prejudice, Discrimination and Racism: Theory and Research*. New York: Academic Press.

MacDonell, D. (1986) *Theories of Discourse: An Introduction*. Oxford: Blackwell.

McGuire, W. J. (1973) 'The Yin and Yang of Progress in Social Psychology: Seven Koan', *Journal of Personality and Social Psychology*, 26: 446–57.

McGuire, W. J. (1985) 'Attitudes and Attitude Change', in G. Lindzey and E. Aronson (eds), Handbook of Social Psychology (3rd Edition) Vol. 2. New York: Random House.

McHoul, A. W. (1982) *Telling How Texts Talk: Essays on Reading and Ethnomethodology*. London: Routledge and Kegan Paul.

McKinlay, A. and J. Potter (1987) 'Model Discourse: Interpretative Repertoires in Scientists' Conference Talk', *Social Studies of Science*.

McKinlay, A. and J. Potter (forthcoming) 'Social Representations: A Conceptual Critique', *Journal for the Theory of Social Behaviour*.

McLelland, D. C. (1961) *The Achieving Society*. Princeton: Van Nostrand.

Marsh, A. (1976) 'Who Hates the Blacks?', *New Society*, 23 September, 649–52.

Marsh, P. (1982) 'Rules in the Organization of Action: Empirical Studies', in M. von Cranach and R. Harré (eds), *The Analysis of Action*. Cambridge: Cambridge University Press.

Marsh, P., E. Rosser and R. Harré (1978) *The Rules of Disorder*. London: Routledge and Kegan Paul.

Maslow, A. H. (1968) *Toward a Psychology of Being* (2nd Edition). Princeton: Van Nostrand.

Matson, F. W. (1973) *Without/Within: Behaviourism and Humanism*. Monterey, California: Brooks/Cole.

Mead, G. H. (1934) *Mind, Self and Society*. Chicago: University of Chicago Press.

Mehan, M. (1979) *Learning Lessons: Social Organization in the Classroom*. Cambridge, Mass.: Harvard University Press.

Merritt, M. (1976) 'On Questions Following Answers (in Service Encounters)', *Language in Society*, 5: 315–57.

Merton, R. (1973) *The Sociology of Science*. Chicago: University of Chicago Press.

Milgram, S. (1963) 'Behavioural Study of Obedience', *Journal of Abnormal and Social Psychology*, 67: 371–78.

Miller, G. A. (1980) 'Giving Away Psychology in the 1980's', *Psychology Today*, 13: 38–50, 97–98.

Mills, C. W. (1940) 'Situated Actions and Vocabularies of Motive', *American Sociological Review*, 5: 904–13.

Milroy, L. (1980) *Language and Social Networks*. Oxford: Blackwell.

Mischel, W. (1968) *Personality and Assessment*. New York: Wiley.

Mixon, D. (1972) 'Instead of Deception', *Journal for the Theory of Social Behaviour*, 2: 145–77.

Moscovici, S. (1976) *La psychoanalyse: son image et son public*. (Revised Edition). Paris: Presses Universitaires de France.

Moscovici, S. (1981) 'On Social Representation', in J. Forgas, (ed.), *Social Cognition: Perspectives on Everyday Understanding*. London: Academic Press.

Moscovici, S. (1982) 'The Coming Era of Representations', in J. P. Codol and J. P. Lyons (eds), *Cognitive Analysis of Social Behaviour*. The Hague: Nijhoff.

Moscovici, S. (1984a) 'The Phenomenon of Social Representations', in R. Farr and S. Moscovici (eds), *Social Representations*. Cambridge: Cambridge University Press.

Moscovici, S. (1984b) 'The Myth of the Lonely Paradigm: A Rejoinder', *Social Research*, 51: 939–67.

Moscovici, S. (1985) 'Comment on Potter and Litton', *British Journal of Social Psychology*, 24: 91–3.

Moscovici, S. and M. Hewstone (1983) 'Social Representations and Social Explanations: From the "Naive" to the "Amateur" Scientist', in M. Hewstone (ed.), *Attribution Theory: Social and Functional Extensions*. Oxford: Blackwell.

Mostyn, B. (1985) 'The Content Analysis of Qualitative Research Data: A Dynamic Approach', in M. Brenner, J. Brown and D. Canter (eds), *The Research Interview: Uses and Approaches*. London: Academic Press.

Mulkay, M. (1974) 'Methodology in the Sociology of Science', *Social Science Information*, 13: 107–19.

Mulkay, M. (1979a) 'Interpretation and the Use of Rules: The Case of Norms in Science', in T. F. Gieryn (ed.), *Science and Social Structure*. Transactions of the New York Academy of Sciences, Series III, 39: 111–25.

Mulkay, M. (1979b) 'Knowledge and Utility: Implications for the Sociology of Knowledge', *Social Studies of Science*, 9: 63–80.

Mulkay, M. (1981) 'Action, Belief or Scientific Discourse?', *Philosophy of the Social Sciences*, 11: 163–71.

Mulkay, M. (1984a) 'The Ultimate Compliment: A Sociological Analysis of Ceremonial Discourse', *Sociology*, 18: 531–49.

Mulkay, M. (1984b) 'The Scientist Talks Back: A One Act Play, with a Moral, about Replication in Science and Reflexivity in Sociology', *Social Studies of Science*, 14: 265–82.

Mulkay, M. (1985) *The Word and the World: Explorations in the Form of Sociological Analysis*. London: Allen Unwin.

Mulkay, M. and G. N. Gilbert (1981) 'Putting Philosophy to Work: Karl Popper's Influence on Scientific Practice', *Philosophy of the Social Sciences*, 11: 389–407.

Mulkay, M. and G. N. Gilbert (1982a) 'Joking Apart: Some Recommendations Concerning the Analysis of Scientific Culture', *Social Studies of Science*, 12: 585–615.

Mulkay, M. and G. N. Gilbert (1982b) 'Accounting for Error: How Scientists Construct Their Social World When They Account for Correct and Incorrect Belief', *Sociology*, 16: 165–83.

Mulkay, M. and G. N. Gilbert (1983) 'Scientists' Theory Talk', *Canadian Journal of Sociology*, 8: 179–97.

Mulkay, M. and G. N. Gilbert (1985) 'Opening Pandora's Box: A New Approach to the Sociological Analysis of Theory Choice', *Knowledge and Society*, 5: 113–39.

Mulkay M., J. Potter and S. Yearley (1982) 'Why an Analysis of Scientific Discourse is Needed', in K. D. Knorr-Cetina and M. Mulkay (eds), *Science Observed: Perspectives on the Social Study of Science*. London and Beverly Hills, California: Sage.

Myers, G. (1985) 'Texts as Knowledge Claims', *Social Studies of Science*, 15: 593–630.

Nisbett, R. E. and T. D. Wilson (1977) 'Telling More Than We Can Know: Verbal Reports on Mental Processes', *Psychological Review*, 84: 231–59.

Orne, M. T. (1969) 'Demand Characteristics and the Concept of Quasi-Controls', in R. Rosenthal and R. L. Rosnow (eds), *Artifact in Behavioural Research*. New York: Academic Press.

Parker, I. (forthcoming a) 'Discourse and Power', in J. Shotter and K. Gergen (eds), *Texts of Identity*. London: Sage Publications.

Parker, I. (forthcoming b) 'Social Representations: Social Psychology's (Mis)Use of Sociology', *Journal for the Theory of Social Behaviour*.

Pecheux, M. (1982) *Language, Semantics and Ideology: Stating the Obvious*. London: Macmillan.

Perls, F. (1971) *Gestalt Therapy Verbatim*. New York: Bantam.

Peters, R. S. (1959) *The Concept of Motivation*. London: Routledge and Kegan Paul.

Pettigrew, T. F., G. W. Allport and E. V. Barnett (1958) 'Binocular Resolution and Perception of Race in South Africa', *British Journal of Psychology*, 49: 265–78.

Plummer, K. (1983) *Documents of Life*. London: Allen Unwin.

Polyani, M. (1958) *Personal Knowledge*. London: Routledge and Kegan Paul.

Pollner, M. (1974) 'Mundane Reasoning', *Philosophy of the Social Sciences*, 4: 35–54.

Pollner, M. (1975) 'The Very Coinage of Your Brain: The Anatomy of Reality Disjunctures', *Philosophy of the Social Sciences*, 5: 411–30.

Pomerantz, A. (1978) 'Compliment Responses: Notes on the Operation of Multiple Constraints', in J. Schenkein (ed.), *Studies in the Organization of Conversational Interaction*. London: Academic Press.

Pomerantz, A. (1984) 'Agreeing and Disagreeing with Assessments: Some Features of Preferred/Dispreferred Turn Shapes', in J. M. Atkinson and J. Heritage (eds), *Structures of Social Action: Studies in Conversation Analysis*. Cambridge: Cambridge University Press.

Pomerantz, A. (1986) 'Extreme Case Formulations: A New Way of Legitimating Claims', in G. Button, P. Drew and J. Heritage (eds) *Human Studies* (Interaction and Language Use Special Issue), 9: 219–30.

Popper, K. (1959) *The Logic of Scientific Discovery*. London: Hutchinson.

Popper, K. (1963) *Conjectures and Refutations*. London: Routledge and Kegan Paul.

Potter, J. (1982) '"Nothing so Practical as a Good Theory"': The Problematic Application of Social Psychology', in P. Stringer (ed.), *Confronting Social Issues*. London: Academic Press.

Potter, J. (1984) 'Testability, Flexibility: Kuhnian Values in Scientists' Discourse Concerning Theory Choice', *Philosophy of the Social Sciences*, 14: 303–30.

Potter, J. (1986) 'Reading Repertoires: A Preliminary Study of Some Procedures Scientists Use to Construct Readings', mimeo under submission, University of St. Andrews.

Potter, J. (1987) 'What is Reflexive about Discourse Analysis? The Case of Reading Readings', in S. Woolgar (ed.), *Knowledge and Reflexivity: New Frontiers in the Sociology of Knowledge*. London: Sage Publications.

Potter, J. and I. Litton (1985) 'Some Problems Underlying the Theory of Social Representations', *British Journal of Social Psychology*, 24: 81–90.

Potter, J. and M. Mulkay (1982) 'Making Theory Useful: Utility Accounting In Social Psychologists' Discourse', *Fundamenta Scientiae*, 34: 259–78.

Potter, J. and M. Mulkay (1985) 'Scientists' Interview Talk: Interviews as a Technique for Revealing Participants' Interpretative Practices', in M. Brenner, J. Brown and D. Canter (eds), *The Research Interview: Uses and Approaches*. New York: Academic Press.

Potter, J. and S. Reicher (1987) 'Discourses of Community and Conflict: The Organization of Social Categories in Accounts of a "Riot"', *British Journal of Social Psychology*, 26.

Potter, J., P. Stringer and M. Wetherell (1984) *Social Texts and Context: Literature and Social Psychology*. London: Routledge and Kegan Paul.

Quine, W. V. O. and Ullian (1970) *The Web of Belief*. New York: Random House.

Ravetz, J. R. (1971) *Scientific Knowledge and its Social Problems*. Harmondsworth: Penguin.

Reeves, W. (1983) *British Racial Discourse: A Study of British Political Discourse about Race and Race-Related Matters*. Cambridge: Cambridge University Press.

Reicher, S. and J. Potter (1985) 'Psychological Theory as Intergroup Perspective: A Comparative Analysis of "Scientific" and "Lay" Accounts of Crowd Events', *Human Relations*, 38: 167–89.

Rogers, C. (1961) *On Becoming a Person*. Boston: Houghton Mifflin.

Rorty, A. O. (1976) 'A Literary Postscript: Characters, Persons, Selves, Individuals', in A. O. Rorty (ed.), *The Identities of Persons*. Berkeley: University of California Press.

Rorty, R. (1978) 'Philosophy as a Kind of Writing', *New Literary History*, 10: 141–60.

Rosch, E., C. B. Mervis, W. D. Gray, D. M. Johnson and P. Boyes-Braem (1976) 'Basic Objects and Natural Categories', *Cognitive Psychology*, 8: 382–439.

Rosenthal, R. and R. L. Rosnow (eds) (1969) *Artifact in Behavioural Research*. New York: Academic Press.

Rosier M. (1974) 'Asking Silly Questions', in N. Armistead (ed.), *Reconstructing Social Psychology*. Harmondsworth: Penguin.

Rothbart, M. (1981) 'Memory Processes and Social Beliefs', in D. L. Hamilton (ed.), *Cognitive Processes in Stereotyping and Intergroup Behaviour*. Hillsdale, N. J.: Erlbaum.

Ryle, G. (1949) *The Concept of Mind*. London: Hutchinson.

Sabini, J. and M. Silver (1981) 'Introspection and Causal Accounts', *Journal of Personality and Social Psychology*, 40: 171–9.

Sabini, J. and M. Silver (1982) *Moralities of Everyday Life*. Oxford: Oxford University Press.

Sacks, H. (1972) 'An Initial Investigation of the Usability of Conversational Data for Doing Sociology', in D. Sudnow (ed.), *Studies in Social Interaction*. New York: Free Press.

Sacks, H. (1974) 'On the Analyzability of Stories by Children', in R. Turner (ed.), *Ethnomethodology*. Harmondsworth: Penguin.

Sacks, H. (1979) 'Hotrodder: A Revolutionary Category', in G. Psathas (ed.), *Everyday Language: Studies in Ethnomethodology*. New York: Irvington.

Sacks, H. (1984) 'Notes on Methodology', in J. Atkinson and J. Heritage (eds), *Structures of Social Action: Studies in Conversation Analysis*. Cambridge: Cambridge University Press.

Sacks, H., E. A. Schegloff and G. A. Jefferson (1974) 'The Simplest Systematics for the Organization of Turn-Taking in Conversation', *Language*, 50: 697–735.

Said, E. W. (1978) *Orientalism*. New York: Pantheon Books.

Said, E. W. (1981) *Covering Islam: How the Media and Experts Determine How We See the Rest of the World*. London: Routledge and Kegan Paul.

Sampson, E. E. (1983) 'Deconstructing Psychology's Subject', *Journal of Mind and Behaviour*, 4: 135–64.

De Saussure, F. (1974) *Course in General Linguistics*. London: Fontana.

Schegloff, E. A. (1968) 'Sequencing in Conversational Openings', *American Anthropologist*, 70: 1075–95.

Schegloff, E. A. and H. Sacks (1973) 'Opening Up Closings', *Semiotica*, 7: 289–327.

Schlenker, B. R. (1980) *Impression Management: The Self-Concept, Social Identity and Interpersonal Relations*. Monterey, California: Brooks/Cole.

Schlenker, B. R. and B. W. Darby (1981) 'Use of Apologies in Social Predicaments', *Social Psychology Quarterly*, 44: 271–8.

Schlesinger, A. M. Jr (1965) *A Thousand Days: John F. Kennedy in the White House*. London: Deutsch.

Schuman, H., G. Kalton and J. Ludwig (1983) 'Context and Contiguity in Survey Question-naires', *Public Opinion Quarterly*, 47: 112–5.

Schutz, A. (1972) *The Phenomenology of the Social World*. London: Heinemann.

Scott, M. B. and S. Lyman (1968) 'Accounts', *American Sociological Review*, 33: 46–62.

Searle, J. R., F. Kiefer and M. Bierwisch (eds) (1979) *Studies in Semantics and Pragmatics*. Dordrecht: Reidel.

Semin, G. R. and A. S. R. Manstead (1983) *The Accountability of Conduct: A Social Psychological Analysis*. London: Academic Press.

Shapiro, M. J. (1981) *Language and Political Understanding*. New Haven: Yale University Press.

Shapiro, M. (1983) 'Literary Production as a Politicizing Practice'. Paper presented at the American Political Science Association Conference, Palmer House, Chicago, September.

Shapiro, M. J. and M. G. Banham (1983) 'The Manipulation of Concepts in Reporting International Conflicts'. Paper presented at the International Society of Political Psychology Conference, Oxford University, July.

Sharrock, W. and R. Watson (1984) 'What's the Point of "Rescuing Motives"?' *British Journal of Sociology*, 35: 435–51.

Shears, R. and I. Gidley (1982) *Storm out of Africa!* Auckland, New Zealand: Macmillan.

Sherwin, C. W. and R. S. Isenson, (1967) 'Project Hindsight', *Science*, 156: 1571–7.

Shotter, J. (1981) 'Telling and Reporting: Prospective and Retrospective Uses of Self-Ascription', in C. Antaki (ed.), *The Psychology of Ordinary Explanations of Social Behaviour*. London: Academic Press.

Shotter, J. (1984) *Social Accountability and Selfhood*. Oxford: Blackwell.

Shotter, J. (1985) 'Social Accountability and Self-Specification', in K. J. Gergen and K. E. Davis (eds), *The Social Construction of the Person*. New York: Springer-Verlag.

Sigall, H. and N. Ostrove (1975) 'Beautiful but Dangerous: Effects of Offender Physical Attractiveness and the Nature of the Crime on Juridic Judgment', *Journal of Personality and Social Psychology*, 31: 410–14.

Sinclair, J. McH. and M. Coulthard (1975) *Towards an Analysis of Discourse*. London: Oxford University Press.

Sloman, A. (1976) 'What are the Aims of Science?', *Radical Philosophy*, 13: 7–17.

Smith, D. (1974) 'The Social Construction of Documentary Reality', *Sociological Inquiry*, 44: 257–68.

Smith, D. (1978) 'K is Mentally Ill: The Anatomy of a Factual Account', *Sociology*, 12: 23–53.

Smith, D. (1982) 'The Active Text'. Paper presented at the Tenth World Congress in Sociology, Mexico City.

Smith, D. (1984) 'Textually Mediated Social Organization', *International Social Science Journal*, 36: 59–75.

Smith, J. (1981) 'Self and Experience in Maori Culture', in P. Heelas and A. Lock (eds), *Indigenous Psychologies*. London: Academic Press.

Snyder, M. (1981) 'On the Self-Perpetuating Nature of Social Stereotypes', in D. L. Hamilton (ed.), *Cognitive Processes in Stereotyping and Intergroup Behaviour*. Hillsdale, N. J: Erlbaum.

Snyder, C. R., R. L. Higgins and R. J. Stucky (1983) *Excuses: Masquerades in Search of Grace*. New York: Wiley.

Stringer, P. (ed.) (1982) *Confronting Social Issues* Vols 1–2. London: Academic Press.

Stringer, P. (1985) 'You Decide What Your Title is To Be and [Read] Write to that Title', in D. Bannister (ed.), *Issues and Approaches in Personal Construct Theory*. London: Academic Press.

Stubbs, M. (1983) *Discourse Analysis*. Oxford: Blackwell.

Sturrock, J. (1986) *Structuralism*. London: Paladin.

Suleiman, S. R. and I. Crosman (eds) (1980) *The Reader in the Text: Essays on Audience and Interpretation*. Princeton: Princeton University Press.

Swartz, S. and L. Swartz (1982) 'Harré's *Social Being* and the Connection with Structuralism', *Journal for the Theory of Social Behaviour*, 12: 201–12.

Sykes, G. M. and D. Matza (1957) 'Techniques of Neutralization: A Theory of Delinquency', *American Sociological Review*, 22: 664–70.

Sykes, M. (1985) 'Discrimination in Discourse', in T. A. van Dijk (ed.), *Handbook of Discourse Analysis* Vol. 4. London: Academic Press.

Tajfel, H. (1969) 'Cognitive Aspects of Prejudice', *Journal of Biosocial Sciences*, 1, Supplement Mon. No. 1, *Biosocial Aspects of Race*, 173–91.

Tajfel, H. (1972) 'Experiments in a Vacuum', in J. A. Israel and H. Tajfel (eds), *The Context of Social Psychology*. London: Academic Press.

Tajfel, H. (1981) 'Social Stereotypes and Social Groups', in J. Turner and H. Giles (eds), *Intergroup Behaviour*. Oxford: Blackwell.

Tajfel, H. (1982) *Human Groups and Social Categories*. Cambridge: Cambridge University Press.

Tajfel, H. and J. Forgas (1981) 'Social Categorization: Cognitions, Values and Groups', in J. Forgas (ed.), *Social Cognition*. London: Academic Press.

Tajfel, H. and A. Wilkes (1963) 'Classification and Quantitative Judgement', *British Journal of Psychology*, 54: 101–14.

Tannen, D. (1984) *Coherence in Spoken and Written Discourse*. Norwood, N. J: Ablex.

Taylor, S. E. (1981) 'A Categorization Approach to Stereotyping', in D. L. Hamilton (ed.), *Cognitive Processes in Stereotyping and Intergroup Behaviour*. Hillsdale, N. J.: Erlbaum.

Tedeschi, J. T. and M. Riess (1981) 'Verbal Strategies in Impression Management', in C. Antaki (ed.), *The Psychology of Ordinary Explanations of Social Behaviour*. London: Academic Press.

Tetlock, P. E. (1984) 'Cognitive Style and Political Belief Systems in the British House of Commons', *Journal of Personality and Social Psychology*, 46: 365–75.

Tetlock, P. E. and A. S. R. Manstead (1985) 'Impression Management Versus Intra-Psychic Explanations in Social Psychology: A Useful Dichotomy?', *Psychological Review*, 92: 59–77.

Thompson, J. B. (1984) *Studies in the Theory of Ideology*. Cambridge: Polity.

Totman, R. (1980) 'The Incompleteness of Ethogenics', *European Journal of Social Psychology*, 10: 17–41.

Trew, T. (1979) 'Theory and Ideology at Work', in R. Fowler, B. Hodge, G. Kress and T. Trew (eds), *Language and Control*. London: Routledge and Kegan Paul.

Trilling, L. (1974) *Sincerity and Authenticity*. London: Oxford University Press.

Turner, C. F. and E. Krauss (1978) 'Fallible Indicators of the Subjective State of the Nation', *American Psychologist*, 33: 456–70.

Turner, J. C. (1981) 'Some Considerations in Generalizing Experimental Social Psychology', in G. M. Stephenson and J. H. Davis (eds), *Progress in Applied Social Psychology* Vol. 1. London: Wiley.

Ungar, S. (1981) 'The Effects of Status and Excuse on Interpersonal Reactions to Deviant Behaviour', *Social Psychology Quarterly*, 260–3.

Van der Vlist, R. (1982) 'Social Psychological Theory and Empirical Studies of Practical Problems', in P. Stringer (ed.), *Confronting Social Issues: Applications of Social Psychology* Vol. 1. London: Academic Press.

Wann, T. W. (1964) *Behaviourism and Phenomenology*. Chicago: University of Chicago Press.

Watson, R. (1978) 'Categorization, Authorization and Blame-Negotiation in Conversation', *Sociology* 12: 105–13.

Watson, R. (1983) 'The Presentation of Victim and Motive in Discourse: The Case of Police Interrogations and Interviews', *Victimology*, 8: 31–52.

Watson, R. and T. Weinberg (1982) 'Interviews and the Interactional Construction of Accounts of Homosexual Identity', *Social Analysis*, 11: 56–78.

Webb, E. J., D. T. Campbell, R. D. Schwartz and L. Sechrest (1966) *Unobtrusive Measures: Non-Reactive Research in the Social Sciences*. Chicago: Rand McNally.

Webley, I. A. (1986) 'Professional Wrestling: The World of Roland Barthes Revisited', *Semiotica*, 58: 59–81.

Weiss, C. H. and M. J. Bucuvalas (1980) *Social Science Research and Decision Making*. New York: Columbia University Press.

Wetherell, M. S. (1983) 'Socio-Psychological and Literary Accounts of Femininity', in P. Stringer (ed.), *Confronting Social Issues* Vol. 2. London: Academic Press.

Wetherell, M. S. (1986) 'Linguistic Repertoires and Literary Criticism: New Directions for a Social Psychology of Gender', in S. Wilkinson (ed.), *Feminist Social Psychology*. Milton Keynes: Open University Press.

Wetherell, M. S., R. McFadyen, J. Potter and B. Rothwell (1986) 'Categories in Discourse', mimeo, University of St. Andrews.

Wetherell, M. S. and J. Potter (1986) 'Majority Group Representatons of "Race Relations" in New Zealand'. Paper presented at the British Psychological Society, Social Psychology Section Annual Conference, University of Sussex, September.

Wetherell, M. S. and J. Potter, (forthcoming a) *Mapping the Language of Racism*.

Wetherell, M. S. and J. Potter (forthcoming b) 'Narrative Characters and Accounting for Violence', in J. Shotter and K. E. Gergen (eds), *Texts of Identity*. London: Sage Publications.

Wetherell, M. S., H. Stiven and J. Potter (1987) 'Unequal Egalitarianism: A Preliminary Study of Discourses Concerning Gender and Employment Opportunities', *British Journal of Social Psychology*, 26: 59–71.

Wicker, A. W. (1969) 'Attitudes Versus Actions: The Relationship of Overt and Behavioural Responses to Attitude Objects', *Journal of Social Issues*, 25: 41–78.

Wicker, A. W. (1979) *An Introduction to Ecological Psychology*. Monterey, California: Brooks/Cole.

Wieder, L. (1974a) 'Telling the Code', in R. Turner (ed.), *Ethnomethodology*. Harmondsworth: Penguin.

Wieder, L. (1974b) *Language and Social Reality*. The Hague: Mouton.

Wilder, D. (1978) 'Perceiving Persons as a Group: Effects on Attributions of Causality and Beliefs', *Social Psychology*, 1: 13–23.

Wilder, D. A. (1986) 'Social Categorization: Implications for Creation and Reduction of Intergroup Bias', in L. Berkowitz (ed.), *Advances in Experimental Social Psychology* Vol. 19; New York: Academic Press.

Williamson, J. (1978) *Decoding Advertisements*. London: Boyars.

Wittgenstein, L. (1953) *Philosophical Investigations*. Oxford: Blackwell.

Wittgenstein, L. (1980) *Remarks on the Philosophy of Psychology* Vols 1–2. Oxford: Blackwell.

Woolgar, S. (1980) 'Discovery: Logic and Sequence in a Scientific Text', in K. Knorr-Cetina, R. Krohn and R. Whitley (eds), *The Social Process of Scientific Investigation*. Dordrecht: Reidel.

Woolgar, S. (1982) 'Irony in the Social Studies of Science', in K. D. Knorr-Cetina and M. Mulkay (eds), *Science Observed: Perspectives on the Social Study of Science*. London and Beverly Hills, California: Sage.

Woolgar, S. (ed.) (1987) *Knowledge and Reflexivity: New Frontiers in the Sociology of Knowledge*. London: Sage Publications.

Wootton, A. (1977) *Dilemmas of Discourse*. London: Allen Unwin.

Wowk, M. T. (1984) 'Blame Allocation, Sex and Gender in a Murder Interrogation', *Women's Studies International Forum*, 7: 75–82.

Wynne, A. (1987) 'Accounting for Accounts of Multiple Sclerosis', in S. Woolgar (ed.) *Turning the Pages of Science: Knowledge and Reflexivity*. London and Beverly Hills, California: Sage.

Yearley, S. (1981) 'Textual Persuasion: The Role of Social Accounting in the Construction of Scientific Arguments', *Philosophy of the Social Sciences*, 11: 409–35.

Yearley, S. (1984a) *Science and Sociological Practice*. Milton Keynes: Open University Press.

Yearley, S. (1984b) 'Proofs and Reputations: Sir James Hall and the Use of Classification Devices in Scientific Argument', *Earth Sciences History*, 3: 25–43.

Yearley, S. (1985) 'Vocabularies of Freedom and Resentment: A Strawsonian Perspective on the Nature of Argumentation in Science and the Law', *Social Studies of Science*, 15: 99–126.

Zimmerman, D. H. (1971) 'The Practicalities of Rule Use', in J. Douglas (ed.), *Understanding Everyday Life*. London: Routledge and Kegan Paul.

Zimmerman, D. and M. Pollner (1971) 'The Everyday World as a Phenomenon', in J. Douglas (ed.), *Understanding Everyday Life*. London: Routledge and Kegan Paul.

Zuckerman, H. A. (1977) 'Deviant Behaviour and Social Control in Science', in E. Sagarin (ed.), *Deviance and Social Change*. London and Beverly Hills, California: Sage.

Index

Ability, 86
Abraham, C., 41, 173
Absence, 28, 31
Accent, 38
Acceptances, 82–3, 86
Accountability, 106
Accounts, 1, 74–81, 84–94, 122, 177–8
    (*see also* discourse)
    of accounts, 4, 182–4
    as accurate/inaccurate descriptions of
        mental states, 178–80
    conventional character, 85
    effectiveness, 77–9
    factual, 181–2, 183
    of self, 111–5
Accounting
    device/strategy, 107, 113–4
    for error, 149–53, 155, 161, 169
    for freedom and constraint, 75, 91–2
Accusations, 87–93, 130, 170
Achievement motivation, 41
Acknowledgements, 77
Actions, 57–8, 61–2
    expressive versus practical, 60
    versus movements, 57
    semiological character, 58, 63, 103–4
    unitary meaning, 63
Adams, J., 186
Adenosine triphosphate, 146–7
Adjacency pairs, 81–6, 88, 92–4, 138
    central organization of conversation, 83
    typed, 82
Aesthetics, 184
African National Congress, 6
Aggression, 36, 59–62, 112, 113, 136
Agnes, 126
Agreements, 84
Allen, V. L., 118
Allport, G., 43
Althusser, L., 109
Anchoring, 123, 132, 141–2, 145–6 (*see
    also* social representations)
Anger, 180
Animal behaviour, 63
Anonymity, 79

Anscombe, E., 180
Answers, 82–5, 87, 89
Anthropology, 6, 57
Anti-Apartheid, 111
Anything goes, 159
Apologies, 76–7
Appeal to
    accident, 76
    facework, 78
    higher authority, 78
    loyalties, 76
    mental elements, 76
    mitigating circumstances, 78
    natural drives, 76
    retribution, 78
    utilitarianism, 78
    values, 78
Applause, 47, 87, 175
Application
    of discourse analysis, 174–5
    of knowledge, 186
Arbitrariness of the sign, 25
Architecture of conversation, 81
Argyris, C., 40
Ashmore, M., 30, 168, 183, 184
Assessments, 82
Atkinson, M., 30, 47, 83, 87–92, 153,
    162, 166, 170, 175, 187
Atkinson, P., 30, 40
Attitudes, 1, 32, 25, 37, 43–55, 122,
    142–6, 157, 160, 178, 179, 184
    definitions, 43–4
    predicting behaviour, 53–4
    traditional approaches, 43–6
    as underlying entities, 46, 49–50,
        53–4, 164
Attributions, 91, 140, 142, 146
Austin, J., 14–18, 28, 74–6, 81
Authenticity, 97
Azjen, I., 53–4, 178

Bainbridge, L., 178
Balzac, H. de 187
Banham, M. G., 187
Bar-Hillel, Y., 23

Barjonet, P. E., 139
Barnes, B., 23, 79, 159
Barthes, R., 26–8, 31, 187
Baumeister, R. F., 37
Bay of Pigs, 183
Bazerman, C., 64, 183
Beattie, G., 81
Becker, H., 19
Behaviourism, 12, 14, 95
Beliefs, 17, 179–80
Berelson, B., 167
Berger, P. L., 142
Best, E., 104
Billig, M., 53, 121–2, 137, 144, 187
Biochemistry, 146–56, 160, 169–70, 175
Biology, 181
Blamings, 37, 48, 54, 79–80, 89–91,
        116, 128–30, 132, 136–7
    no blame accounts, 86
Bogdan, R., 42, 63
Bourhis, R. Y., 38
Bower, G. H., 7
Boxing, 27–8
Brannigan, A., 64
Brazil, D., 166
Breakdowns in normal conduct, 74
Brenner, M., 34, 163
Brewer, M., 119, 125
Broadbent, G., 26
Brown, D., 33, 80
Brown, G., 6
Brunswik, E., 79
Bucuvalas, M. J., 174
Buildings, 26
Bureaucratic model of thought, 121–2
Button, G., 13

Cannell, C. F., 163
Cantor, N., 119–20, 122, 132
Casey, N., 13
Categories, 1, 2, 5, 6, 19, 20, 52,
        116–37, 141, 143, 179 (*see also*
        membership)
    base for inferences, 126, 129–32
    bound activities, 129, 132, 136
    duplicative organization, 129, 131
    exemplify world views, 127–8
    fixed structure, 120, 136
    hierarchical organization, 119–20,
        125, 136

inductive errors, 129
occasioned use, 133
over-inclusion, 132
preformed entities, 120–1, 136
process of assignment, 119
puzzle, 131–2
Categorization, 116–37, 138, 143
    analytic, 29, 33, 41, 44–6
    consequences of, 116
    flexibility, 116
    mechanical process, 118–21, 137
    perceptual effects, 116–7, 119–21,
        133, 136–7
    of physical world, 117
    suppressing variability, 35, 39, 40–2,
        123–4, 144, 164
    simplifying, 117
    as social accomplishment, 53, 77,
        116, 120–1, 126, 156
    of social world, 118
Cattell, R., 96
Causal
    constraints on behaviour, 40
    laws, 56, 159
Causes of action, 75
Ceremony, 29
Challenges, *see* accusations
Chalmers, A., 79
Character types, 96–7, 102, 111–5
Chemiosmosis, 146–7
Chomsky, N., 9–14, 28, 57, 58
Chua, B. H., 186
Cicourel, A. V., 40
Cirilo, R. R., 7
Clarke, D., 56, 138
Classrooms, 87
Closings, 138, 171
Code, 9
Coding, 41, 66, 161, 167, 173–4
    cyclical process, 167
Cognition, 7, 9, 10, 146
Cognitive
    consistency, 37
    dissonance, 36–8
    psychology, 119, 140, 145
    processes, 116, 120, 137, 157,
        178–80, 185–6
    reductionism, 56, 121, 142, 157
Collett, P., 58
Collins, H., 79, 159, 173, 175, 181

Commonsense assumptions, 30, 42
Communication, 9
Community, 132–7, 138, 167
    attributes, 134–6
    policing, 135–6
    relations, 134–5
    repertoire, 138, 149, 160
    variable application, 134
Competence,
    linguistic, 10–12, 56–8
    social, 56–60, 73, 177
Concepts, 25
    see also signifieds
Conditional relevance, 82–3
Confirmation through exception, 69–71, 170
Conflict,
    linguistic, 6,
    political, 6
Connotation, 5
Conservative Party, 139–42
Consistency/inconsistency, 34, 37–8, 54, 122, 126, 156, 163–5, 168–70
    as indicator of validity, 34, 163
    as variable states, 38
    of behaviour, 40
Constative utterances, 15–17
Constitution, 50–2
Content analysis, 41, 167, 173, 175
Context, 10, 14, 18, 23, 29, 33–5, 37–8, 41, 45–50, 54, 58, 72–3, 79–81, 126, 133, 156, 164, 169
    of discourse, 147–9, 157
    formal versus informal, 147–9
Contingent repertoire, 149–55, 160, 169
    basic principle, 149–50
Contrast structures, 47
Conversation, 20, 23, 29, 38, 59, 116, 166, 174
Conversation analysis, 7, 30, 74, 80–94, 102, 103, 138, 160, 161, 170–1, 184, 187
The Convict Code, 19–23, 30, 72–3
    as persuasive device, 22, 72
    open flexible texture, 22
    as explanation, 19–20, 22
Cooley, C. H., 98
Coulter, J., 178, 179, 180
Coulthard, M., 6, 29
Counsel, 87–92

Course in General Linguistics, 24
Courtroom discourse, 87–93, 156, 170, 182
Coward, R., 104, 109–10
Craft skills, 148
von Cranach, M., 138
Crane, D., 65
Crisis in social psychology, 2–3, 40
Criteria for understanding, 179–80
Criticism, 68
Crosman, I., 187
Cross-cultural comparison, 104–6
Cuff, E. C., 128, 182
Culler, J., 26, 30, 184, 187
Cultural
    conventions, 27
    universals, 104
Culture, 9, 25, 27

Dahrendorf, R., 98–9
Darby, B. W., 77, 79, 85
Davidson, J., 85
Davis, K. E., 92, 95
De Carlo, N., 56
Delay, 80, 82, 84–6, 93, 166
    inferentially rich, 85
Delivery, 84–6
Denial of
    injury, 76
    intent, 78
    victim, 76
    volition, 78, 91
Denzin, N. K., 63
Derrida, J., 31
Descriptions, 2–4, 6, 15–17, 21, 23, 28, 30, 33–4, 36, 44–5, 48, 51–2, 58, 61, 64–5, 69, 72, 90, 92, 116, 123–4, 126–7, 130, 137, 140, 143, 158, 160
Deviance, 20
van Dijk, T., 6–7, 121
Dialect, 38
Dickens, C., 96–7
Dimensions of judgement, 43, 46, 52
Disagreements, 84
Disclaimers, 48, 54, 76–8, 180
Discourse, 6–7, 46, 116
    action orientation, 28–9, 48, 54, 93, 126, 134, 160
    as social behaviour, 14

consequences of, 18, 21, 28, 34–6, 43, 46, 55, 64, 91, 137, 146, 164, 168, 170
constructive, 2–3, 6, 23, 32–6, 41, 43, 51, 52, 55, 64, 67, 72, 128, 146, 152, 157, 160–1, 162, 164, 169, 175, 178, 180, 181, 182–4, (*see also* constitution)
as dependent variable, 173
as function, 14–8, 23, 28, 32–6, 38, 41, 45, 49, 54, 57, 61, 67, 72, 74, 79, 93, 110, 114–5, 122, 126, 136, 145, 157, 160–1, 164, 168–70, 174, 176, 178, 180, 185
specific versus global, 33
conscious versus unconscious, 34, 153
direct versus indirect, 33
intentional versus unintentional, 34
literal, 61–2, 64, 67, 160 (*see also* truth)
and mental states, 177–80
organization, 46–7, 54, 64, 67, 69, 71–2, 80, 137, 164, 174, 178, 179, 185, 186
pathway to actions, beliefs, events, 34–5, 41, 49, 57–62, 160, 179–80
persuasive, 33, 41, 47, 61, 92, 122, 187
primary psychological reality, 81
and the 'real' world, 177, 180–2, 184
as topic, 34–5 (*see also* topic/resource distinction)
Discourse analysis, 11, 14, 23, 30, 32–8, 42–5, 93, 53–7, 61, 64–5, 67, 69, 71–3, 116–7, 122, 124, 126, 136, 138, 145, 146, 157, 178–87
application of, 186–7
definitions, 6–7
major components, 32–5
principal tenet, 33
process of, 46, 65–7, 111, 123, 133, 146–7, 153, 155, 168–9
self-referential, 183–4
and social psychology, 185–6
Discrediting, 114–5
Dispreferred seconds, 84–6, 93
organization of, 84–6
Documents, 11, 40, 42, 64–5, 133, 147–8, 161–3, 166, 168, 172–4

Drew, P., 30, 33, 83, 86, 87–92, 130, 133, 170
Duncan, B. L., 36

Ecological
psychology, 63
validity, 79
Edelman, M., 187
Eglin, P., 161, 186
Ellis, J., 109
Elms, A. C., 2
Empiricist repertoire, 149–51, 153–5, 169
basic principle, 149–50
Envy, 180
Etcetera clause, 22–3, 72
Ethnography, 30, 40
Ethnomethodology, 1, 18–23, 28–30, 32, 41, 75, 81, 102, 116, 126, 128–9, 143, 153, 168, 173, 179–80
Ethogenics, 42, 56–64, 173, 177
central hypothesis, 57
Ethology, 63
Evaluation, 3, 5, 30, 51, 54, 116, 134, 138–9, 149, 175
Evolutionary theory, 70
Examination, 87–92
Excuses, 74–80, 85, 91–2, 113
Experimenter effect, 185
Experiments, 2, 36–40, 56, 65, 74, 77, 79–80, 85–6, 93, 116–8, 158, 159, 168, 172, 275–6, 185–6
field, 77, 79–80
generalizability of findings, 40, naturalism, 79–80
as social accomplishments, 175
Extraversion, 96–7
Extreme case formulations, 47–8, 91
Eysenck, H. J., 96–7
Eysenck, S. G., 96–7

Facts, 18, 52, 63, 72, 92, 143, 154, 161
as construction, 92
Falsifiability, *see* testability
Fanshell, D., 29
Farr, R., 139
Fashion, 26
Feature matching, 119, 133
Felicity conditions, 16–7, 29
Femininity, 109–10

Festinger, L., 37, 98
Feyerabend, P., 158, 159
Fishbein, M., 53–4, 178
Fiske, J., 26, 184
Football fans, *see* soccer fans
Forgas, J., 117, 138
Foucault, M., 6–7, 31, 109
Fractures in social order, 75
Frankfurt School, 109
Frederickson, C. H., 7
Freedom fighters, 5
Free will, 75
Functions of discourse, *see* discourse
Fuzzy sets, 119–20, 136

Garfinkel, H., 18–19, 22–3, 75, 126,
    156, 168, 179
Garvey, C., 81
Gender, 126, 128, 130, 156
Generalizability of findings, 40
Generative
    grammar, 10, 13, 14
    mechanisms, 56
Gergen, K., 2, 40, 63, 95, 101–3, 106,
    108–9, 178
Di Giacomo, J. P., 139, 144
Gidley, I., 111
Gilbert, N., 6–7, 35, 64, 65, 68, 136,
    138, 146–55, 156, 160, 162, 169,
    170–1, 172
Giles, H., 7, 38
Goffman, E., 19, 76, 82, 98
Gombrowicz, W., 98
Grady, K., 187
Grammar, 11, 13, 14, 24, 57
Greatbatch, D., 47, 187
Greetings, 57–8, 80, 82
Grice, M. P., 30
Gross categorization, *see* categorization
Group dynamics, 183
Gusfield, J., 161, 183

Halliday, M. A. K., 7
Halliday, Q., 133
Hamilton, D., 118, 121
Hamlyn, D. W., 99
Hammersley, M., 30, 40
Hansard, 163
Harari, J. V., 187

Harré, R., 2, 29, 40, 42, 56–61, 63, 73,
    79, 95, 102, 103, 104–5, 106–7,
    138, 159, 173, 177, 179, 180
Harris, R., 11
Hartley, J., 26, 184
Heath, S., 109
Hebdidge, D., 26
Heelas, P., 103
Heider, F., 92
Henriques, J., 95, 101, 103, 104, 109
Heritage, J., 18, 28, 47, 73, 81, 82, 86,
    87, 153, 162, 166, 187
Herzlich, C., 139, 144
Hesse, M., 158
Hewitt, J. P., 48, 76–7
Hewstone, M., 142, 144
High-energy physics, 75
Hijack, 5
Hinde, R., 63
History of science, 70–1, 158–9
Hodge, R., 184, 186
Hollway, W., 109
Holsti, O. R., 41, 167, 173
Honour, 60
Hotrodders, 127–8
How To Do Things With Words, 16
Humanist, 95, 108
    theories of self, 99–100, 101, 102,
        107
Human nature, 111–2, 114
Humour, 68, 155, 172
Husband, C., 44
Hustler, D. E., 128
Hypothesis testing, 41

Ickes, W., 178
Idealization, 10, 11, 13, 18, 29,
    decontextualization 10, 18, 28
    regularization, 10
    standardization, 10
Identity crisis, 97
Ideology, 118, 140, 163, 187
Immigrants, 45–54
    coloured, 43–5
    Polynesian, 46, 49–53
Impression management, *see* self-
    presentation
Indexicality, 23, 41, 104, 145, 168
Indigenous psychologies, 103, 104–6
Infinite regress, 182

Insertion sequences, 82
Insults, 58
Integrative complexity, 173
Intentions, 180
Intergroup
    distinctiveness, 38
    psychology, 7
Intermission, 166
Interpretative
    procedures, 128, 146, 153–5, 173
        generate problems, 153, 155
    sociology, 173
    repertoires, 137–9, 146–57, 164,
        169–71
        definition, 149
        uses and functions, 149
    research, 31
Inter-rater reliability, 173
Interviews, 1, 40, 46, 49, 59, 123, 133,
        145, 147–8, 153–5, 162–5
    confrontational arena, 164
    comparability of responses, 163
    craft skill, 165
    schedule, 165
Intonation, 10, 38–9, 166
Introversion, 96–7
Invitations, 83, 85–6, 88, 122
Ironization, 42, 181
Isenson, I. S., 174
Israel, J., 2

Jackson, S., 29
Jacobs, S., 29
James, W., 108
Janis, I., 183
Jayyusi, L., 129, 130, 133
Jefferson, G., 80, 166
Johnson, M., 107
Johnson-Laird, P., 10
Jones, E., 92
Jurors, 18–9
Justification, 3, 52, 61, 65, 69–72,
        75–80, 84–5, 90, 116, 108–9,
        130, 150

Kahn, R. L., 163
Kallen, D. B. P., 174
Kelley, H. H., 92
Kennedy, President, 183
Kessler, J. B., 92

Kinder, D. R., 40
Kintch, W., 6–7
Kiss ass, 19
Knowledge application, 155
Krampen, M., 26
Krauss, E., 40
Kreckel, M., 166
Kress, G., 186
Kroger, R. O., 56
Kuhn, T. S., 65, 158, 159
Kulka, R. A., 92

Laboratory research, 79
Labov, W., 7, 29, 163
Lakatos, I., 159
Lakoff, G., 107
Lalljee, M., 55
Language, (*see also* discourse)
    abstract system, 14, 18, 28
    acquisition, 12, 81
        device, 12
    historical origins, 81
    medium for action, 9, 173
    as naming process, 25
    social nature of, 18, 28
    subject/object property, 107
La langue, *see* underlying system
Latour, B., 159
Law, J., 23, 159
Lay explanations, 2, 20–1, 34, 51–2, 79,
        140, 144–5
Layton, E., 174
Lee, J., 130
Legal discourse, 156
Levinson, S. C., 7, 28, 29, 30, 33, 80,
        81, 83, 85, 86, 153, 155, 162,
        171, 172
Linguistic
    philosophy, 1, 14, 74–5, 179–80
    repertoires, *see* interpretative
        repertoires
Linguistics, 6, 7, 138
Literary studies, 6, 8, 31, 187
Literature 26, 103
Litton, I., 42, 52, 138, 142, 144
Lock, A., 103, 104
Lodge, D., 99
Lodge, P., 159
Luckmann, T., 142
Lyons, J., 10, 103

Lyman, S., 74, 76, 130
Lyttleton, H., 186

McCabe, C., 101
McClelland, D. C., 41
McConahay, J. B., 53
MacDonell, D., 6
McFadyen, R., 123
McGuire, W. J., 2, 43
McHoul, A. W., 187
McKinlay, A., 68, 138, 139, 145, 152, 155
Manstead, A., 37, 74, 76–8, 90–1
Maoris, 58, 104–6, 123–6, 128
    cosmology, 105
Marsh, A., 43–7, 53
Marsh, P., 40, 56, 59–62, 64, 65, 66–7, 72
Marxist analyses, 109
Masculinity, 109
Maslow, A. H., 100
Material reality, 180–2
Matson, F., 95
Matza, D., 76
Mead, G. H., 81, 98
Meals, 24
Meaning, 25–7, 31
    of actions, 27–8, 57–8, 63
    contextual, *see* indexicality
    equivalence, 45
    versus force, 17
    of utterances, 23
    as accomplishment, 23
    taken-for-granted, 27
Mehan, M., 87
Membership
    categories, 44, 116, 122, 128, 130
    categorization devices, 128, 131
    consistency rule, 128, 130–1
Memory, 179–80
Mental
    illness, 3–5
    states, 45, 177–80
Mentalistic terms, 179–80
Merritt, M., 86, 172
Merton, R., 65
Metaphors, 91, 107–8, 112, 134, 138, 145, 149
Micro-sociology, *see* sociology
Milgram, S., 39

Miller, G. A., 175
Mills, C. W., 76, 130, 180
Milroy, L., 7
Mind, 107–8, 113, 178
Mischel, W., 97, 119–20, 122
Mitigations, 128, 130, 132
Mixon, D., 39
Molecular theory of gases, 70
Moscovici, S., 81, 138–146, 157
Mostyn, B., 41, 167
Motives, 5, 19, 21–2, 37, 48, 71, 113–4, 126, 130–1, 177, 180
Mulkay, M., 6–7, 22, 30, 35, 42, 64, 65, 68, 87, 136, 138, 146–55, 156, 159, 160, 162, 163, 164, 169, 170–1, 172, 175, 183, 184
Multiple partial indicators, *see* triangulation
Multiple sclerosis, 184
Murder confession, 130–2
Myers, G., 64
Myth, 26–7, 31

Narrative, 3, 5, 52, 60–1, 71, 135–6
National Health Service, 174–5
Natural science, 56, 70, 147, 174
    idealized view of, 159
    social science as copy of, 56
Naturalistic research, 79, 162, 176
New literary forms, 183–4
Newspapers, 5, 59–60, 62, 64, 116, 133, 163, 174, 187
Newton, I., 11
New Zealand/New Zealanders, 46, 48–52, 58, 104, 111, 113, 114, 123, 164
Nisbett, R. E., 177–8
The Normal, 7
Normative expectations, 82
Northern Ireland, 88

Objectification, 141–2, 145 (*see also* social representations)
Objects of thought, 43, 46, 50–4
Observation, 57–8, 62–4,
    conventions for interpreting, 66
    theory laden, 158
Occasion, *see* context
Offers, 82, 86, 93
Open-ended interviews, *see* interviews
Open souls doctrine, 177–8

212 Discourse and social psychology

Operationalization of variables, 79
Opinion polls, 40, 43–4, 48, 139–40,
    158, 168, 176
  variations in wording, 40
  contradictory responses, 40
  limitations on responses, 40
  interpretation of responses, 40
Opinions
  as discursive acts, 48
  flexible, 40
  tailored to context, 40
Ordinary
  reasoning, 126, 128–32
  talk, 11–3, 18–9, 29, 64, 80–8, 140,
    162 (see also discourse)
  as joint achievement, 13
  constitutive part of action, 21
  as explanatory resource, 20
  multiconsequential, 21, 28, 30
  multiformative, 21, 28, 30
  conventional representation, 13
The Orient, 187
Orne, M. T., 37
Ostrove, N., 92
Overlap, 82, 84, 166

Pain, 27, 58
Parliament, 133
Parker, I., 104, 109, 139
Parole, 31
Participant
  observation, 19, 173
  orientation, 153
Particularization, 121–2
Pauses, see delay
Pecheux, M., 6
Performance, 56–7, 73
  linguistic, 10–14, 57
Performative
  utterances, 15–7
  verbs, 17, 28
Perls, F., 100
Personality inventories, 96–7
Peters, R., 180
Pettigrew, T. F., 132
Philosophy, 6, 14, 18, 23, 29, 180, 181,
    182
  of language, see linguistic philosophy
  of mind, 109
  of science, 65, 72, 158–9, 172

Play dialogue, 13
A Plea for Excuses, 74
Plummer, K., 40, 42, 163
Polanyi, M., 175
Police, 111–2, 113, 115
Politeness, 32–3, 80
Political science, 187
Pollner, M., 20, 143, 182
Pomerantz, A., 47, 68, 91
Popper, K., 65, 158, 159
Positivism, 2, 3, 14, 158, 172
Post-structuralism, 31, 102
Potter, J., 35, 42, 52, 53, 65, 68, 72, 96,
    102–3, 111, 112, 114, 133, 138, 139,
    142, 144, 145, 146, 150, 152, 155,
    156, 161, 162, 164, 167, 168, 174,
    183, 184, 187
Power, 108–10
Pragmatics, 7
Preference structure, 81, 83–92
  as normative ranking, 83
Prejudice, see racism
Pronunciation, see intonation
Protestors, 111, 112–5
Prototypes, 119–26, 128, 132–3, 136, 141
Psycholinguistics, 9, 11, 13, 18, 28–9
Public speaking, 47, 160, 173, 175

Qualitative research, 42
Quantification, 39
Questionnaires, 40, 47, 116, 145
  contradictory responses, 40
Question wording, 40
Questions, 82–4, 87–9, 165, 170
Quine, W. V. O., 65

Race theories, 44
Racism, 36, 43, 48, 52, 118, 121–3,
    130, 139–40, 187
Railway timetable, 25–6
Rating scale, 43–5, 48, 50, 52, 145
  one versus multi-dimensional, 53
Rationality, 113
Ravetz, J. R., 175
Reading for gist, 168
Readings, 5
Realist
  model of language, 34–6, 42, 72,
    134, 169, 182
  principle, 101, 103

Rebuttals, 87–92
Records, *see* documents
Reeves, W., 45, 53, 121, 163
Reference, 2
Reflexivity, 2, 21–3, 28, 72–3, 177, 182–4
  as topic/strategy, 183–4
Refusals, 85, 87
  conventional format, 87
Refutability, *see* testability
Reicher, S., 114, 133, 138, 184
Reification, 42, 106, 113, 181, 187
Repair, 75
Replication, 159, 172, 183
Requests, 32–3, 76
  indirect, 33
Research
  programmes, 159
  questions, 160–1
  report, 172–4
Resource, *see* topic/resource distinction
Response, 30
Responsibility, 77
Restriction, 35, 39–40, 42
Revolution in conception of science, 158–9
Rhetoric, 38, 52, 70, 73, 91, 121, 144, 155, 173, 182, 187
  functional, 61–3, 72
Riess, M., 76
Riots, 63, 88–90, 111, 133–6, 138, 162
  versus disturbance, 63, 135, 184
Ritual chase, 60
Rock music, 26
Rogers, C., 100
Roles/Role theory, 21, 97–9, 100, 101, 102, 107
Rorty, A., 97
Rorty, R., 187
Rosch, E., 119, 136
Rosenthal, R., 37
Rosier, M., 40
Rosnow, R. L., 37
Rothbart, M., 121
Royal Ulster Constabulary, 88–90, 92
Rules, 10, 56, 62, 64, 103, 122, 179
  breaking, 20
  as cognitive resources, 57–8
  as representations, 10, 23
  derived from talk, 56

explanatory, 21, 59, 72–3
generative, 11–2
identification of, 56, 58
indeterminacy of application, 22–3
informal, 19
interpretative, 58–9
official, 20
paradigmatic, 24
prescriptive, 24
procedural, 150
regulative, 58–60, 68, 72
sequencing, 29
strategic use, 68–9
as symbolic resources, 73
syntagmatic, 24
as template, 19, 22–3, 69, 73
transformational, 12
The Rules of Disorder, 56
Ryle, G., 179

Sabini, J., 178, 179, 180
Sacks, H., 13, 80–2, 126–9, 162, 171
Said, E., 187
St Clair, R., 7, 38
St Paul's riot, 133, 144–5
Sample
  selection, 161–2
  single texts, 161
  size, 161
Sampson, E. E., 95, 101, 109
Saussure, F. de, 24–7, 81
Scapegoating, 76
Scarman Tribunal, 88–9
Schegloff, E. A., 80, 82, 171
Schemata, 7
Schlenker, B., 76, 77, 79, 85
Schlesinger, J., 183
Schuman, H., 40
Schutz, A., 63
Scientists'
  conferences, 65–71, 163
  discourse, 3, 64–73, 146–57, 160, 169–72, 175, 182
    basic principle, 150, 155
    as hard case, 64
    readings, 155
    model talk, 155
    letters, 155
    Nobel Prize speeches, 87, 162
  rule use, 56, 64–71

Scott, M., 74, 76, 130
Scripts, 7
Searle, J., 18
Sears, D. O., 40
Secord, P. F., 2, 40, 56, 79, 177
Selective reading, 35, 40, 42
Self, 1, 5, 9, 31, 95–115, 122, 181
    alienated, 100
    authentic, 100, 107
    as centre of experience, 101, 102, 105
    in conflict, 97, 98, 107
    as culturally/historically relative,
        102–3
    definitive descriptions of, 95–6, 102
    and discourse, 102–115, 178, 179,
        180
    grammatical and metaphorical, 106–8
    as honest soul, 96–7, 114
    and ideology, 108–10, 113–4
    and intergroup conflict, 111–5
    looking glass self, 98
    Maori image of, 104–6
    phenomenological significance, 107
    and political practice, 104
    public and private, 99–100
    romantic image, 99–100
    scientific study of, 95
    and sincerity, 98–9
    as socially determined, 97–9
    theatrical image, 97–9
    traditional models, 95–101, 115
    violent, 111–5
    Western models of, 105–6
    in women, 110
Self-actualization, 100
Self-blaming, 77
Self-control, 112, 115
Self-fulfilment, 78, 100
Self-praise, 68
Self-presentation, 33, 37–8, 60, 97,
        108–9, 115
    variation in, 37
Semantics, 184
Semantics of trivia, 26
Semin, G., 74, 76–8, 90–1
Semiology, 1, 9, 23–31, 32, 58, 102,
        103, 184
Semiotics, *see* semiology
Sequential discourse, 6, 13, 46, 80–1,
        83, 88, 92–4, 161, 171, 184

Sex roles, 98
Sexual relations, 110
Shapiro, M., 187
Sharrock, W., 180
Shears, R., 111
Sherwin, C. W., 174
Shotter, J., 81, 95, 103, 106, 107,
        178
Sigall, H., 92
Sign, 25
Signification, 26
    second level, 26–8
Signifieds, 25–6
Signifiers, 25–6
Silver, M., 178, 179, 180
Sinclair, J. McH., 6, 29
Skinner, B. F., 14
Sloman, A., 159
Smith, D., 161, 182, 187
Smith, J., 104–5
Snitch, 19
Sniveler, 19
Snyder, C. R., 74
Snyder, M., 121
Soccer
    fans, 56, 58–61, 64–7, 160
    violence, 59–61, 63, 71–2
Social
    cognition, 121–2, 128, 132–3
    comparison, 78, 98
    competence, *see* competence
    constructivism, 95, 101–2
    desirability, 185
    differentiation, 185
    influence, 92–3
    knowledge, 57
        underlying action and accounts,
        57–9
    perception, 36, 52, 178
    psychology, 2, 3, 6, 7, 9, 18, 29, 31,
        32, 34–9, 41–3, 53, 56, 63–5,
        74–6, 79, 92–3, 116–7, 119–20,
        123, 127, 129, 132, 138, 142–3,
        146, 157, 169, 173, 175, 178,
        179, 183, 185–6
    of discourse, 14
    European, 138
    of persuasion, 187
    laboratory, 39, 185
    non-cognitive, 178–80

representations, 1, 138–46, 155–7,
178, 179
coherence, 138, 145–6
code for communication, 138, 140–3
cognitive versus linguistic, 145
consensual, 142–5, 156
constructive, 141–2
distinguishing groups, 138, 141–3,
146, 156
elements, 139–40, 145
figurative nucleus, 139
homogenizing force, 141
organizing beliefs and attributions,
138
originate in interaction, 140
operationalization, 144
problems with, 142–6
irreducibly social, 140, 146
structure, 126
texts, 1–6, 8, 32, 42, 182–3, 187
complex, 186
self-referential, 183–4
Socialization, 98
Socialist Challenge, 135
Sociolinguistics, 7
Sociology, 6, 8, 40, 42, 63, 76
of science, 65, 72, 159, 172, 174
South Africa, 111
Speaker changeover, 81, 87
Speaker's
creativity, 10, 11–4
intuitions, 10–11, 13–4
Speech
accommodation, 7, 36, 38
acts, 14–8, 23, 28–30, 32, 61, 102
indirect, 29, 61, 172
errors, 10
sounds, *see* signifiers
Springbok rugby tour, 111–5, 164
Status, 77, 79, 81, 92–3
Stereotypes, 36, 52–3, 118
consequences of categorization,
118–23, 132
Stirrer, 113–4
Stokes, R., 48, 76–7
Strangers, 80
Stream of consciousness, 108
Stringer, P., 35, 174, 183
Structuralism, 6
Stubbs, M., 6, 163, 165

Sturrock, J., 28
Subject/object dichotomy, 181
Subjectivity, 109
Submissive display, 60
Suleiman, S. R., 187
Swartz, L., 58
Swartz, S., 58
Sykes, M., 45, 76

Tajfel, H., 2, 117–8, 120, 129, 132, 186
Tannen, D., 6
Taperecording, 163, 166
Taylor, S. E., 118
Taylor, S. J., 42, 63
Tedeschi, J. T., 76
Teenage drivers, 127
Television, 26, 174, 187
news, 87, 133, 162
Territory, 59
Terrorists, 5, 30–1
Testability, 65–73, 159, 172
versions of, 66–71
Tetlock, P., 37, 173
Text,
comprehension, 7
mental organization, 7
memory for, 7
That's how it is response, 152
Theory
choice, 56, 65–72, 155, 167, 183
contingent and empiricist accounts
of, 152
rules of, 65–71, 152
versus practice, 144–5
Thompson, J. B., 187
Topic, 87
Topic/resource distinction, 20, 30, 143,
173
Total institutions, 19
Totman, R., 58
Traditional social science, 19–20, 23, 32,
54–6, 136, 158
Traits/Trait theory, 96–7, 98, 99, 100,
101, 102, 114
Transcript, 11, 12, 13, 30, 49, 65, 67, 81,
133, 147, 161–6, 168, 172, 174
as constructive activity, 165
readability, 166
speed, 166
word processed, 166

Transformation of responses, 45–6, 53
Transsexual, 126
Trew, T., 136, 187
Triangulation, 62–4
Trilling, L., 96–7, 103
Tripp, D., 184
Truth
    and falsity, 14–7, 62–4, 92–3,
        149–55
    will out device, 153–5, 171
Turn organization, 82, 184
Turner, C. F., 40
Turner, J. T., 79
Typologies
    of accounts, 76–8, 90, 93
    of cars, 127–8

Ullian, J., 65
Underlying system, 24–31
Ungar, S., 77–80, 86
Use versus mention, 144–5

Validity, 1, 34, 169–72
    coherence, 169–70
    fruitfulness, 169, 171–2
    new problems, 169, 171
    participants' orientation, 169–71
Variation in discourse, 5, 32–43, 45,
        49–50, 53–4, 63–4, 67, 67–9,
        109, 123–6, 136, 144, 147–8,
        156, 164–5, 168–70, 181, 185
    between and within accounts, 67, 152
    suppression of, 35, 39–43
    organization of 67–9
Verification, 14
Versions, 4, 6, 33–4, 51, 63, 66, 73, 92,
        122, 130, 137, 175, 182–3, 186
    conflict between, 49–50, 68, 127, 135

Video, 59, 118
Vignettes, 77, 79, 85, 93
Violence, *see* aggression, soccer violence
Van der Vlist, R., 186
Vocabularies of motive, 76

Wann, T. W., 95
Warranting, *see* justification
Watson, R., 127, 129, 130–1, 180
Webb, E. J., 162
Webley, I. A., 28
Weinberg, T., 127, 130
Weiss, C. H., 174
Well, 84–5
Wetherell, M. S., 35, 53, 103, 111, 112,
        123, 126, 138, 156, 162, 167,
        187
Whitelaw, Lord, 135
Wicker, A. W., 53, 63
Wieder, L., 19–23, 28, 30, 72–3, 182
Wilder, D., 118, 120, 132
Wilkes, A., 117–8
Williamson, J., 104
Wilson, T. D., 177–8
Witness, 87–92
Wittgenstein, L., 81, 179
Wooden presentation, 80
Woolgar, S., 159, 161, 183, 187
Wootton, A., 22
Wowk, M., 130, 131–2
Wrestling, 27–8, 58
Wynne, A., 184

Yearley, S., 30, 136, 152, 156, 159, 187
Yule, G., 6

Zimmerman, D., 20, 22, 143
Zuckerman, H. A., 65